*Common Women,*
*Uncommon Practices*

D1188625

# Common Women, Uncommon Practices

*THE QUEER FEMINISMS OF GREENHAM*

**Sasha Roseneil**

CASSELL
London and New York

Cassell    323483
Wellington House, 125 Strand, London WC2R 0BB
370 Lexington Avenue, New York, NY 10017-6550

First published 2000

The author and publisher gratefully acknowledge permission to quote the following
material:
Judy Grahn, verse from 'Vera, from My Childhood', from *The Common Woman Poems*,
© Judy Grahn, 1969
Leon Rosselson, 'The World Turned Upside Down'

**British Library Cataloguing-in-Publication Data**
A catalogue record for this book is available from the British Library.

ISBN 0-304-33553-3 (hardback)
   0-304-33554-1 (paperback)

**Library of Congress Cataloging-in-Publication Data**
Roseneil, Sasha, 1966–
   Common women, uncommon practices : the queer feminisms of Greenham/
   Sasha Roseneil.
      p.   cm.
   Includes bibliographical references and index.
   ISBN 0-304-33553-3 (hb). – ISBN 0-304-33554-1 (pbk.)
   1. Lesbians–England–Berkshire–Political activity.   2. Women and
peace–England–Berkshire.   3. Feminism–England–Berkshire.
4. Greenham Common Women's Peace Camp.   I. Title.
HQ76.3.G72B477   2000
305.48′9664–dc21                                                99-29093
                                                                    CIP

Typeset by BookEns Ltd, Royston, Herts.
Printed and bound in Great Britain by TJ International Ltd, Padstow, Cornwall

# Contents

# Acknowledgements

**The Greenham Women**

My first and biggest thanks go to the women I interviewed. Their stories are the heart of this book:

| | |
|---|---|
| Ann Lukes | Lesley Brinkworth |
| Ann Armstrong | Linda |
| Ann Francis | Liz Galst |
| Barbara Rawson | Lynne Fortt |
| Barbara Schulman | Margery Lewis |
| Bridget Evans | Nell Logan |
| Carmel Cadden | Pat Paris |
| Carol Harwood | Penni Bestic |
| Carola Addington | Penny Gulliver |
| Christine King | Rowan Gwedhen |
| Clare Hudson | Sarah Benham |
| Helen Mary Jones | Sian Edwards |
| Helen John | Simone Wilkinson |
| Jenny Heron | Susan Lamb |
| Jinny List | Trina |
| Katrina Allen | Trisha |
| Kim Smith | Vee Wright |
| Leah Thalmann | |

Discussions with many other friends over the years have contributed to the gestation of my ideas, above all the women living at camp in 1983 and 1984 who were *my* Greenham, particularly the Green Gate 'old girls' and Nicky Edwards, Rebecca Johnson, Rebecca Long and Annie King.

This book is dedicated to the memory of two Greenham women of different generations, Annie King and Pat O'Connell.

I met Annie when we both arrived to live at Green Gate late in 1983. I shared many wonderful times with her, both at camp and afterwards. Her friends will always remember her disarming manner with policemen and soldiers (deployed while engaging in the most anarchic and wickedly disruptive actions) and her ability to make hours in police cells speed by in laughter and song. Many women at Greenham watched her dismantle engines and fix cars, and were inspired by her example to don overalls and pick up a socket set for the first time. And several million people heard Annie chain herself to Sue Lawley's chair during the lesbian 'invasion' of the BBC Six O'Clock News in protest against Section 28 of the Local Government Act 1988. Annie died with her lover Bel Rowe in an accident in northern Scotland in 1995, and is greatly missed.

Pat O'Connell was my grandmother, a life-long socialist and peace activist. Pat was a member of the Committee of 100 in the 1950s and 1960s, and inspired me as a child with her stories of the Holy Loch march, sit-downs in Berkeley Square and doing time in Holloway. When in 1983 I left school and went to live at Greenham she offered to go in my place, if I would stay at school to complete the education she had never had. I declined her offer, but she often came to Greenham anyway, and was with me the first time I cut the fence.

## The Others

I also wish to acknowledge the financial support of the Economic and Social Research Council, the London School of Economics and the University of London during the research on which the book is based. Later, support was provided by the Institute of Commonwealth Studies (the Robert Menzies Fellowship) and Macquarie University and the University of Melbourne, where I held visiting fellowships in 1996. The Department of Sociology and Social Policy and the Centre for Interdisciplinary Gender Studies at the University of Leeds have been a stimulating intellectual home while I wrote this book.

## The Greenham Women

| Name | Age[1] | Gate[2] | Level of involvement[3] |
|------|------|------|------|
| Ann Lukes | 52 | Orange | Visitor |
| Ann Armstrong | 44 | Violet | Stayer |
| Ann Francis | 41 | Orange | Camper |
| Barbara Rawson | 52 | Green | Camper |
| Barbara Schulman | 25 | Green | Stayer |
| Bridget Evans | 23 | Blue | Camper |
| Carmel Cadden | 30 | Violet | Camper |
| Carol Harwood | 36 | Yellow/Orange | Stayer |
| Carola Addington | 29 | Yellow/Orange/Violet | Camper |
| Christine King | 27 | Yellow/Orange | Stayer |
| Clare Hudson | 25 | Orange | Stayer |
| Helen Mary Jones | 23 | Orange | Visitor |
| Helen John | 34 | Yellow | Camper |
| Jenny Heron | 30 | Green | Camper |
| Jinny List | 20 | Blue | Camper |
| Katrina Allen | 31 | Green/Violet | Camper |
| Kim Smith | 25 | Yellow/Green | Camper |
| Leah Thalmann | 53 | Green | Camper |
| Lesley Brinkworth | 22 | Yellow/Orange | Stayer |
| Linda | 22 | Blue | Camper |
| Liz Galst | 20 | Red/Indigo/Orange | Camper |
| Lynne Fortt | 27 | Yellow/Orange | Stayer |
| Margery Lewis | 64 | Orange | Visitor |
| Nell Logan | 71 | Yellow | Stayer |
| Pat Paris | 33 | Blue | Camper |
| Penni Bestic | 31 | Orange | Camper |
| Penny Gulliver | 22 | Blue | Camper |
| Rowan Gwedhen | 24 | Yellow/Red/Violet | Camper |
| Sarah Benham | 17 | Yellow/Green | Stayer |
| Sian Edwards | 33 | Orange | Visitor |
| Simone Wilkinson | 36 | Yellow | Stayer |
| Susan Lamb | 28 | Yellow/Orange | Stayer |
| Trina | 19 | Blue | Camper |
| Trisha | 20 | Blue | Camper |
| Vee Wright | 25 | Green | Stayer |
| Sasha Roseneil | 16 | Green | Camper |

1. Age at first getting involved with Greenham.
2. This is the gate(s) at which the woman spent most time and to which she felt most attached.
3. **Camper**: a woman who made her home at Greenham for longer than 2 months (2 months was approximately the length of time taken to integrate into the community of the camp); **stayer**: a woman who stayed overnight at the camp either regularly or for a period of up to 2 months; **visitor**: a woman who made daytime visits to Greenham, and who may have stayed overnight on a few occasions.

   These distinctions are somewhat problematic, given the fluidity of forms and degrees of involvement in each woman's history; each woman is categorized by her highest level of involvement.

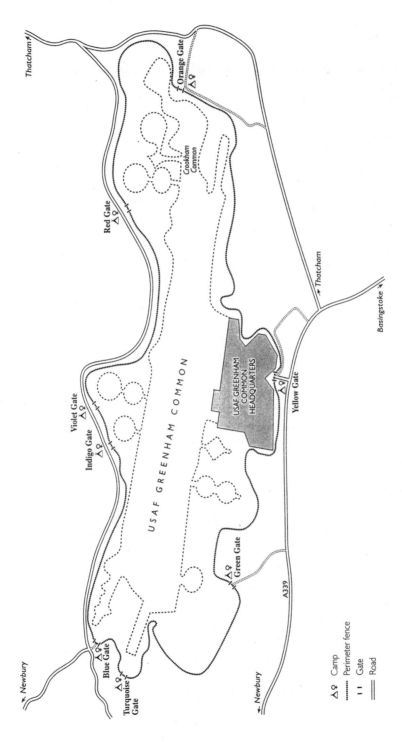

Map of USAF Greenham Common, and the Greenham Common Women's Peace Camp

For all the world we didn't know we held in common
all along
the common woman is as common as the best of bread
and will rise
and will become strong – I swear it to you
I swear it to you on my own head
I swear it to you on my common
woman's
head

*Judy Grahn, The Common Woman Poems*

It's difficult to explain. People say to me, what did you do for a
year? Sat in a puddle for a year. Why? I don't know really. I don't
know what we did. It didn't rain all the time, I say. I don't know
what to say. You can't explain it. It's something you have to do. No,
something *some of us* had to do. It's probably like National Service.
Those people who say, the good old days. They had a good time.
It's definitely something about being different. I sometimes wonder
what I'd have been like without it, but I can't imagine.

*Jinny List*

The things that were wrong with Greenham were also right as well
… because Greenham existed in a paradox. I don't really know
how to explain it, except that the thing that kept it going was this
immense anger against what was happening. But then the other
thing that kept it going was that we enjoyed ourselves so much.
Sometimes it was awful and unpleasant – wet and cold and
boring. It was also incredibly exciting, and you had the attention
of the world, and my god, what power … I thought it was
sometimes like we were living in an Enid Blyton novel. It was like
'Five Go Mad at Greenham'. How many tins of pineapple chunks
shall we eat today? Lashings of Christmas pudding. Cop-baiting.
And that was also what kept it going.

*Penni Bestic*

'We're here because we're here because we're here because we're here.'
*Sung by British soldiers during World War I, to the tune of 'Auld Lang Syne'*


'We're here because we're queer because we're here because we're queer.'
*Sung by Greenham women during the Cold War, to the tune of 'Auld Lang Syne'*

In memory of
Annie King (1959-1995)
and
Pat O'Connell (1920-1995)

# Chapter 1
# Common Women, Uncommon Practices

## 1983: Greenham Common, Berkshire, England

*A chaotic heap of women covers an old double mattress, limbs entwined, joyous in each other's company, singing, laughing, defiant in the face of eviction, resisting policemen and bailiffs who are struggling to seize the mattress from them. Somewhere in the background: lead-lined silos built to house 96 Cruise missiles, guarded by nine miles of fence and razor wire, floodlights, electronic sensors, and several thousand British and US military personnel.*

Sifting through hundreds of photographs of the Greenham Common Women's Peace Camp, I chose this one for the cover of the paperback edition because it captures something of the spirit and attitude of Greenham that I am trying to convey in this book. The photo speaks to me of the pleasure, passion, defiance, irreverence and humour of Greenham, of its untidiness, disorderliness and anarchic excess. It offers a visual taste of Greenham's 'queer feminisms'.

*Common Women, Uncommon Practices* is about a moment in history when ordinary women did some extraordinary things, when common women engaged in some decidedly uncommon practices. It is about the social movement and community built by a group of women – of a variety of ages, backgrounds, nationalities and sexualities – outside the United States Airforce Base at Greenham Common; and it is about their experimentations with values, politics and ways of living which took feminism in new, queer directions. It is about the actions these women took to resist the momentum towards nuclear war, and it is about the destabilizations, disruptions and transformations of gender, sexuality and political order they set in train through their actions.

The histories of women, radical dissenters, and all those who self-consciously challenge the gender and sexual order are too easily forgotten, passed over by mainstream historians and fading from the collective memory as new generations are swept up in the politics and cultures of their times. The 1980s tend now to be remembered as the decade of the Right, of greed, conspicuous consumption and rampant individualism. Certainly the New Right governments in Britain and the United States were driven by an ideological opposition to the political philosophies of the social movements of the 1960s and 1970s and the determination to install a new popular capitalism. But alongside and in opposition to this, the 1980s were also a time of mass protest and the flowering of alternative cultures. It was the decade when feminism really moved into popular consciousness and the existence of lesbians began to be widely acknowledged in the media. It was the period of mass anti-nuclear peace protests throughout Europe, North America and Australasia when millions rallied and took direct action against US and Soviet nuclear weapons. In Britain, the history of the 1980s can be written as one of a string of important moments of protest. Groups of people around the country came into conflict with the forces of the state: mining communities, New Age travellers, lesbian and gay activists, animal rights campaigners. And inspiring and influencing all of these, the women of Greenham Common.

Through its representation in the media, Greenham has entered the popular imagery of the late twentieth century  in two contrasting ways.[1] The 'sympathetic' portrayal of Greenham in the liberal press characterized Greenham as middle-class, middle-aged women who were sacrificing the comforts of home in order to save the world for the next generation.[2] Greenham women were worthy – they decorated the fence with nappies, babies' boots and photos of their children. They were at times brave – they laid their bodies in front of bulldozers and were then sent to prison. But they were also rather dull and dowdy in their duffel coats, not to be taken entirely seriously as political actors, their politics sentimental 'women's business', successful at raising the issue of nuclear weapons but little more. The 'hostile' portrayal of Greenham, the preserve of the tabloid newspapers, sought to evince not admiration but disgust. They wrote of Greenham as the gathering place of 'militant feminists and burly lesbians' who hung tampons on the fence whilst pursuing an agenda of 'man-hating' and sexual liaisons with each other.[3]

Few historians of feminism and analysts of women's politics have devoted much attention to Greenham, which is surprising given that the women's peace movement was the largest mobilization of women in Britain since the suffrage campaigns of the early twentieth century.[4] I sense, at times, amongst those who document and theorize feminism a certain embarrassment about the colourful exuberance of Greenham, its uncompromising rhetoric and stark symbolisms. And perhaps a certain discomfort with a phenomenon that is hard to summarize, categorize and re-present within the existing frameworks within which feminist theory and politics are discussed.[5] Those feminists who have written about Greenham have tended either to distance themselves from it, accepting its media representation as maternalist and veering towards a problematic anti-feminism,[6] or they have claimed Greenham as their own by attempting to fit it into a particular brand of feminism (socialist or anti-militarist for example) which they are more able to endorse.[7]

The space occupied by Greenham in the contemporary lesbian imagination often seems to be the repository of all that is unfashionable and passé - scruffy clothes and goddess worship.[8] Greenham is 'old hat', woolly hats at that, and not at all lesbian chic, queer and 'now'. Greenham was of the era of 'women-only', before the collective rapprochement between lesbians and gay men which began in the late 1980. It seems an irrelevance to the self-confident lesbian babe, baby butch or queer girl of the post-Cold War world who stays up all night dancing, not worrying about nuclear war.

Contrary to this, I believe that Greenham has much to say to contemporary feminists, lesbians, radicals and queers, not least because it played an important role in constructing some of the possibilities of identity, community and political action which are open to us today. The picture I paint of Greenham is rather different from those which have taken root in popular and academic histories. The Greenham in this book was at the cutting edge of political action and cultural change; it was witty, daring, confrontational, brave and erotically charged. It was a Greenham which was unwieldy and untidy, anarchic, spontaneous, constantly innovative and in flux, and impossible to pin down into pre-existing feminist categories. It was a Greenham which destabilized ideas about what women could do, which overturned notions about what women should do, and reinvented the category 'woman'. It was a Greenham where lesbians could live openly, where women could question their sexuality, where women could create themselves anew. This Greenham directly and effectively challenged the nuclear militarism of the most powerful nation on earth, but this Greenham was about far more than nuclear weapons.

I have not written this book to set the record *straight* about the histories of feminism, of Greenham and of the 1980s; rather my aim is to *queer* the records of these times, to tell a story of disruptions to the social order and to feminist orthodoxies. Writers on feminist politics have tended to smooth over the rough edges of activism, to close their eyes to its sexual and erotic dynamics, to focus their gaze on more respectable, 'straight' feminisms as they have engaged with government, the law, organizations and academia. Feminism's 'straight tendencies' (which invoke the category of 'woman' in order to gain rights for women) ask nicely, play within the rules of the existing game and present themselves as motivated by rational demands for equality. While I do not wish to deny the importance of the successes achieved in this way – they have had a radically transformative impact on the social world[9] – straight feminisms can take existing hierarchies and ways of ordering the world too seriously. Engaging with them on their own terms, they can actually reinforce the hold of the status quo, at times serving to reproduce women's sense of victimhood and lack of agency.

At the opposite end of the continuum of respectability and rationality, I want to introduce the notion of feminism's 'queer tendencies'.[10] Much less acknowledged and documented than feminism's straighter tendencies, these are feminism's anarchic, unruly elements, which seek not to enter the corridors of power but to re-locate power. They ridicule and laugh at patriarchal, military and state powers and those who wield them in order to undermine and disarm them. Feminism's queer tendencies are loud and rude. They embrace emotion, passion and erotics as the wellspring of their politics and revel in spontaneity and disorderliness. In contrast to straighter feminisms, they are less concerned with achieving rights for women, more concerned with the cultural politics of opening up and re-configuring what it means to be a woman, in expanding the possibilities of different ways of being in the world beyond the modes which are currently available. They queer gender, unstructuring, de-patterning, and disorganizing it.

It may seem strange, for a number of reasons, that I should use the concept of 'queer' to explore the politics of Greenham. In the academic practice of 'queer theory' (and in the self-proclaimed 'queer politics' of urban groups such as ACT-UP, Queer Nation, OutRage! and the Lesbian Avengers) it is only in the 1990s that it has gained widespread currency as anything other than a term of abuse. Greenham was queer *avant la lettre*.[11] Moreover 'queer' has been widely criticized by lesbian feminists for sidelining concerns with inequalities of power and differences between men and women, and for treating feminism as no longer relevant.[12] How can 'queer' refer to a movement and community of the 1980s which was fundamentally characterized by its commitment to 'women-only' action? Greenham was not the politics of a young, post-feminist, mixed-gender generation of activists living in the Aids-torn global gay cities of New York, San Francisco and London. It involved women, and only women, of all ages - no gay men or self-identified transgendered people. It had its geographical heart in the rural Home Counties of England, and was not even ostensibly 'about' sexuality.[13] Yet queer I believe it was.

As Steven Angelides suggests, the notion of queer operates at two levels: as a noun in the realm of sexuality it refers to those outside the boundaries of heterosexual normality; and, more widely, as an adjective, it denotes that which is strange, odd, eccentric, of questionable character, shady, suspect, and which differs from the normal or usual.[14] Much of the appeal of queer lies in its openness to these multiple meanings and in the resistance to definitive definitions of those who use it. It is a postmodern concept. It describes a postmodern attitude, sensibility and politics - against closure, fixity and dualisms, and for fluidity and change. A queer approach to social analysis sees unruly sexualities, desires and emotions as dynamic forces which disturb the heteronormative social order and produce their own important solidarities and communities.[15]

This book embraces the ambiguity and openness of the term, and further widens its meaning, bringing it more explicitly into dialogue with feminism and placing women firmly within its conceptual scope. It seeks to make those who engage in queer studies more fully aware that women and men are positioned differently in social and cultural terms, and that they have different histories and different political demands, dreams and ways of working. It also aims to challenge a tendency which I see in some queer theory to assert the radical transgressiveness of the contemporary by presenting an overly straight story about the past, particularly the feminist past.[16] As Biddy Martin puts it, in some queer theory feminism has become 'the anti-sexual, identificatory muck out of which any good queer must pull him- or herself'.[17] A feminism which is characterized as 'maternal, anachronistic and putatively puritanical' is seen as irrevocably tied to the 'stagnant and ensnaring' feminine,[18] and is therefore ripe for overthrow by queer. Against this, I draw attention to how queer feminist politics and communities can be and have been; how disrespectful of the social and cultural order; how concerned with pleasure and desire; how eroticized and sexually charged; how disruptive and transforming of sexual and gender identities.

Speaking of the queer feminisms of Greenham carries queer back in time, to before queer theory and queer studies, but recognizes that women at Greenham themselves deliberately appropriated the appellation which was regularly directed at them as an insult by local vigilantes and the tabloid press.[19] These ironic, self-mocking gestures - in songs, on banners, badges and leaflets, spray-painted on road signs and walls all over Berkshire and beyond - made a clear statement about where Greenham women were locating themselves in relation to 'regimes of the normal'.[20] But it should not be read straightforwardly as individual women identifying themselves as lesbians. This was the case for many, but the term meant far more than this, and was embraced by women irrespective of their sexual preferences and practice.

Similarly, in calling Greenham's feminisms queer, I am *not* saying that everyone involved with Greenham was a lesbian. Some were lesbians before Greenham and many more came to think of themselves as lesbians through being involved with Greenham, far more than Greenham's straight supporters often wished. But it is precisely the beauty of the notion of queer that it does not demand identifications on either side of a rigid lesbian/straight binary. Greenham was collectively queer, over and above the personal identifications of individual women. Living at Greenham destabilized gender and sexual identities, and provoked radical reworkings of ways of thinking about and being a 'woman'. Dominant heterosexual and heterorelational modes of existence were displaced in a social world in which relations with other women were central. Assumptions about men's and women's complementarity, and practices of female dependency, hesitancy and quiescence were challenged. Greenham was liminal space, a place for gender and sexual dissent, outside many of the conventions and routines of gender and sexuality as they are normally lived, a place where heteronormativity was, for a time, displaced and where lives were queered in a multiplicity of ways (Chapter 10).

The queerness of Greenham also refers more broadly to the strangeness and unusualness of its politics and practices, to how life there uncompromisingly challenged authority and convention. Living at Greenham was living outside, both literally outdoors, and metaphorically outside the patterns and structures of families, households and ordinary residential communities (Chapter 5). Women at Greenham created their own queer set of common values, a postmodern feminist ethics which offered a model of community, politics and self which ran against the grain, valuing life and pleasure, difference, diversity and conflict in ways uncommon within feminism (Chapters 6 and 7). Greenham's way of protesting against nuclear militarism also que(e)ried the norms of political action. Its strand of anarchism rejected the authority of the state and refused to obey its officers (Chapter 9).

## Telling Stories of Greenham

> I think that if twenty-seven different people wrote their history books of Greenham they'd be very different. For instance, very few people would put the visit of the South African Women's Theatre Troupe to Greenham down in their histories, but I really think that it was a really significant thing, for me.
>
> *Liz Galst*

This is a postmodern book, reflecting the postmodern character of its subject matter. It does not seek to tell *the* story of Greenham. There is no one story of Greenham to be told. To attempt to pin down the diverse experiences which constituted Greenham in order to construct a seamless chronological narrative would be to do grave injury to the constantly changing character of Greenham, and to the multiplicity of stories of Greenham, the many Greenhams which existed in the lives of the women who composed it and which live on in their memories. The stories women gave to me when I interviewed them between 1989 and 1991 would probably not be told in the same way today, and they had undoubtedly been reworked and reconstructed since their tellers were actively involved with Greenham several years before. Recognizing this, I have attempted to weave together the voices and experiences of the women I interviewed in a manner which does not claim the set-in-stone authority of a unilinear history. I have tried also to be respectful of the differences between women's stories, to allow the tensions and contradictions a rightful place, while at the same time reflecting too the commonalities. Through individual women's stories I have attempted to tell a story of the collectivity of Greenham, to give the reader a *feeling* of Greenham, and to develop an *analysis* of Greenham's queer feminisms, of Greenham's engagement with feminism and radical politics. In the process the book has become a hybrid work of history, ethnography, biography and theory.[21]

Whereas my earlier book *Disarming Partriarchy* offered a sociological analysis of Greenham as a social movement, this book focuses on exploring the particularities of the feminist politics of Greenham and on telling stories of Greenham through the accounts given to me by the women I interviewed. Both books draw on the same set of source materials – interviews, written documents, and my own personal experience – but use them to rather different ends:

1. I interviewed 35 Greenham women who ranged in age (at the time they first got involved with Greenham) from 17 to 71 and who were from a wide variety of social, political and educational backgrounds. These women came from all over the UK and beyond, and had been involved in a range of ways for differing lengths of time.[22] The interviews, which lasted between two and four hours and were tape-recorded, were loosely structured around a set of themes and questions drawn up in advance, and involved encouraging women to tell me about their lives before and after Greenham, as well as about their experiences of involvement. The interviews took a 'dialogic' form, with women almost always asking me about my experiences and opinions, and with me testing out my emerging ideas and generalizations on those I was interviewing. The interviews often involved intense exchanges of stories, lively debate and discussion, shared recollections and the consideration of points of political principle. The women I interviewed were all, in different ways, the 'theorizing informants' which mainstream social science has traditionally found problematic, and I was the 'insider'-turned-researcher.

2. Written documents – public archives and private collections of Greenham leaflets, newsletters, pamphlets, song-books, photographs, newspaper cuttings and diaries;[23]

3. My own personal experience of being a part of Greenham which began when I was 16 with my first visit in December 1982 and included the ten months I lived at the camp in late 1983 and 1984. During this time I had the whole range of 'Greenham experiences' – actions, arrests, court appearances, imprisonment, evictions, harassment from police, soldiers and vigilantes, and 'ordinary' daily life as part of the camp. These experiences are not just the backdrop to the research on which this book is based; rather they are woven into its very fabric.In *Disarming Patriarchy* and elsewhere[24] I discussed how my analysis and understanding of Greenham was fundamentally shaped by my own involvement and how this affected my selection of the interviewees; how it guided the direction, flavour and content of the interviews; and how I used it in the analysis of the interviews. I argued that my 'insider status' gave me access that an outsider, however sympathetic or skilled an interviewer, could not have achieved. I understood the social world of Greenham – the experience of living there, of being arrested, imprisoned – from inside, and as a result the women I interviewed trusted me and entrusted me with their stories.

Several years on, in writing this book, I have revisited in detail the transcripts of the interviews and have reanalysed them, asking new questions. These reflect the ways in which my thinking has shifted since *Disarming Patriarchy*, as I have engaged further with writing on postmodernity and the new body of queer theory, and as the social and cultural milieux in which I move have changed, indeed as I have changed. Developing an understanding of Greenham's feminisms as queer is the product. Working with the notion of 'queer' has allowed me to better express the peculiarities of Greenham's politics, which were, in many ways, outside the categories and typologies of its time, and were culturally ahead of the game. My analysis of Greenham in this book is therefore subtly, rather than fundamentally, different, but if the two books are read together a shift may be detected. I always emphasized Greenham's fluidity, reflexivity and openness to change, its encompassing of difference, diversity and conflict; but naming Greenham's queerness gives an even greater prominence to these elements of Greenham, and to the tensions and ambiguities which characterized it, particularly in the realm of sexuality. I always emphasized the humour, pleasure and enjoyment that was central to Greenham, but giving queerness centre-stage allows more attention to the sheer delightful naughtiness, the excitement, the communal erotic charge, the passion of 'coming together', which fuelled Greenham.

The process of returning to the interviews and finding they speak to me in slightly different tones, with different inflections and nuances, has underlined the inherent incompleteness of any historical or sociological writing project and its situatedness in a particular time and place. And I am aware that while I have had the opportunity to re-engage with the words of my interviewees, the women have remained frozen in time, recorded and fixed, subject to my shifting analyses, but unable to reconsider for themselves their experiences, stories and interpretations of this often life-changing, epiphanic period in their lives. Such is the unequal nature of the relationship between the writer and those she writes about.

I make no apology for the fact that this is a partisan and impassioned book. Eighteen years after I first went to Greenham at the age of sixteen, I am still energized by having been part of it. I have spent many years thinking about Greenham, talking about Greenham, trying to understand its social, political and cultural significance, as well as listening to and developing criticisms and critiques of its politics and practice. Greenham has lived with me, and I have lived with Greenham, long after I stopped living there. Greenham is in my history and in my blood. Whatever I do, whatever else I am, I am always, somehow, a Greenham woman. This is a book about part of my life, one of my spiritual homes, one of my postmodern family-communities, like any family or community, with its loyalties and ties of affection, its conflicts and problems, postmodern in its shifting forms across time and space, and in its queer ability to have melted into air, while living on indelibly in hearts and minds.

Like Jinny List,

I have a strong loyalty to Greenham and to the women of Greenham. And I probably always will have.

*Jinny List*

## Notes

1. Such was the impact of Greenham during the peak of the protest that 94 per cent of the British public had heard of it (Hastings and Hastings, 1984). During 1983 and 1984 it was rarely out of the newspapers, and the designation 'Greenham woman' came to be applied to any woman who was thought to be behaving inappropriately to her gender or expressing feminist views.

2. The *Guardian*, *Observer*, and to a lesser extent *The Sunday Times* carried stories in this mode.

3. Above all, the *Sun*, *Daily Mail*, and *Daily Express*. See, for example, the *Sun* (Monday, 7 November 1983) and the *Daily Express* (Tuesday, 10 April 1984).

4. Liddington's history of women's anti-militarism (1989) is the major exception to this. Other books about Greenham are: Nicky Edwards's novel *Mud* (1986); two collections of writings by Greenham women, Cook and Kirk (1983) and Harford and Hopkins (1984); Young's (1990) study of media representations of Greenham, and my (1995) sociological study of Greenham as a social movement. A number of articles have also been written about Greenham: Finch (1986), Jones (1983, 1987), Wallsgrove (1983), Snitow (1985a, b), McDonagh (1985), Kirk (1989a, b), Emberley and Landry (1990). See also Kitzinger (1984).

5. The most common of these is the liberal, radical, socialist/Marxist trilogy of types of feminism.

6. See, for example, the radical feminists in Onlywomen Press (1983) and the socialist feminists Segal (1987) and Williamson (1992). Even more problematically, humanist feminist Oldfield (1989) focuses less on the alleged maternalism of Greenham and more on its 'entrenched' 'female separatism', and argues that 'one fascism cannot be defeated by another' (1989: 218).

7. For instance, Liddington (1989).

8. See, for example, Ainsley (1995: 67, 77, 124–5).

9. Walby (1997).

10. For this notion I owe a particular debt to Sedgwick's (1994) book *Tendencies* in which she provides one of the first major discussions of the meaning of 'queer'.

11. Similarly Merck refers to the era of left sexual politics in London in the 1970s as one of Queer Studies *avant la lettre* (1993: 1). Other writers have argued that the roots of 'queer' are to be found in radical feminism (Richardson, 1997) and British sociology of sexuality (Plummer, 1998).

12. See Jeffreys (1994) and Wilkinson and Kitzinger (1994). For an extended discussion of the relationship between queer theory and feminism see contributions to Weed and Schor (1997).

13. Recently the term 'queer' has increasingly been extended in scope to include considerations of race, ethnicity and nationality; see *Social Text* (December 1997).

14. Angelides (1994).

15. There is a growing body of work exploring the meaning of a queer approach to a range of different disciplines. A queer sociology is being developed by, among others, Epstein (1996), Seidman (1996, 1997), Stein and Plummer (1996), and myself Roseneil (1998). Important contributions to a queer history have been

made by Braverman (1996), to queer political theory by contributors to Phelan (1997) and to queer geography by contributors to Ingram *et al.* (1997).

16.  I have discussed a similar and related problem in some post-structuralist feminist theory elsewhere, see Roseneil (1995: 141-2).

17.  Martin (1996: 10).

18.  *Ibid.*: 46.

19.  Sedgwick suggests that 'queer' differs from 'lesbian' or 'gay' in that the latter present themselves as 'objective, empirical categories governed by empirical rules of evidence', whereas the former 'seems to hinge much more radically and explicitly on a person's undertaking particular, performative acts of experimental self-perception and filiation'. She hypothesizes that queer 'can signify only when attached to the first person' (1994: 9).

20.  Warner describes queer as 'thorough resistance to regimes of the normal' (1991: 15-16).

21.  This text has much in common with the 'queer cultural studies of history' advocated by Braverman (1996). The 'queer writing practices' he proposes produce hybrid texts which weave auto/biography, poetry, documentary material, theory, personal narrative and critical analyses of structures of domination (1996: 97), and which write history as 'contingent, mutable and ultimately partial' (1996: 127).

22.  The sample was 'snowballed' from a small number of women I knew from my own involvement with Greenham, so that I quickly moved beyond women of my acquaintance. Of the 35 women interviewed, 25 were not known to me prior to the interview. I sought to maximize the heterogeneity of the sample, and chose women with a list of characteristics in mind which I thought were salient to achieve a broad cross-section of the sorts of women who were involved with Greenham. The sample therefore contained a wide range of ages (17 to 71 when first involved), class (self-identified), gate of association, levels of involvement ('campers', 'stayers', 'visitors'), motherhood status, occupation, region of residence and sexual identity before involvement. While the final sample cannot claim to be statistically representative of the population of Greenham (because there was no sampling frame from which to draw a probability sample), it covers a wide range of the sorts of women who were involved, in different ways, at different times in the camp's history.

23.  From my earliest involvement with Greenham in 1982 I had been collecting women's peace movement materials, so that I had amassed a substantial personal archive. I was also given access to those of other Greenham women, particularly Jinny List and Lynette Edwell (who houses the 'official' camp archive). I also consulted the Ann Pettit/Women for Life on Earth Papers at the Mid Glamorgan County Archive, and the Seneca Papers at the Schlesinger Library, Harvard, MA.

24.  For a more detailed discussion of these sources and the methodology of the research see Roseneil (1993, 1994, 1995).

# Chapter 2
# Genealogies of Greenham

*Greenham was the best sort of education that anybody could have. I quite like things like history, and I like politics, but all the things that you learn about are white, middle-class people's history, and lesbian history and working-class history is completely absent from everything. And suddenly you've got all these people who can fill you in.*

*Penny Gulliver*

*I think Greenham was an incredible revolutionary force for women in this country, not unlike the suffragette movement. I think the two things have got a lot in common in terms of how many people they reached. They had similar problems too. I think both were tremendously important.*

*Pat Paris*

*When we were arrested in the Houses of Parliament they put us in a room under Big Ben, and they said, 'Oh, you'll like it here, girls. They put Sylvia Pankhurst here. It's a bit noisy, mind.' And one of the women constables came up and said, 'We had an exhibition about your sort of girls last week.' So we said, 'What sort of girls?' And it was an exhibition about the suffragettes.*

*Carol Harwood*

## Imagining a Past

Social movements do not spring from a void. Ideas and repertoires of action, however novel they may seem, always grow out of what has gone before. Certain ways of thinking and particular modes of expressing political views are culturally available, are 'in the ether' at any moment, because of the words and deeds of others. Individuals' political imaginations are shaped by what they know about the movements and ideas of the past. Those who take part in social movements are usually highly reflexive actors, consciously seeking to make a difference to the world and with a strong sense of their place in history. The collective memory practices of a movement – the creation of a shared understanding of the past – are a central part of its activities. They both build collective identity, and act as a form of cultural and political intervention against the hegemonic history of the powerful.[1]

Greenham women were particularly interested in imagining a past for themselves. They were conscious of connections across time and collectively constructed their own genealogies of Greenham. Leaflets and newsletters placed the camp within the context of long traditions of protest (primarily but not exclusively by women) against women's oppression, injustice and war. Women performed the making of these connections in songs and the enactment of dress – the wearing of witches' hats and black cloaks during actions; the use of suffragette colours (purple, green and white) in ribbons, on badges and in their choice of clothes. Knowledge about this history was shared. It spread through the Greenham network and became part of the oral tradition of the movement. It served to validate women's actions at Greenham and created a sense of what it meant to be a 'Greenham woman', with membership of a radical lineage and a history of proud, defiant outlaw status. When women were stepping outside convention as radically as women at Greenham were doing, feeling that this was not the first time ever such risks had been taken was, for many, very important.

Greenham women saw themselves as collectively descended from, amongst others, the Diggers of the seventeenth century, the witches who were persecuted in early modern Europe and the suffragettes. 'The truth' about the activities of the Diggers, the identities of the witches or the motivations behind the witch-hunts, and the actual similarities and dissimilarities between Greenham and the suffragettes are far less important than the fact that women at Greenham saw a link between these groups and themselves. Because these connections were felt to be real, they *were* real.

However, the influence of earlier ideas and actions is not always apparent to those on whom they act. The histories which were created at Greenham, like all popular memory practices, tended to focus on inspirational role models and on dramatic moments of intense conflict, rather than on unpicking the more subtle legacies of earlier strands of political thought and activism.

Broadly speaking, Greenham was forged from the possibilities created by four interrelated heritages of resistance to oppression and injustice: feminism, anarchism, socialism and pacifism. Over the centuries these bodies of thought, singly and together, have both sustained and been fed by numerous protest groups and social movements. Some of these, such as the Diggers and the Ranters, and the 1960s Situationists, were relatively short-lived; others, such as women's movements and peace movements, have much longer histories, peaking and troughing over the years, and developing their own traditions of thought and action.

Greenham was not straightforwardly or wholly 'feminist', 'anarchist', 'socialist' or 'pacifist'. None of these labels suffices as a characterization of the unique and historically specific creation that was Greenham. Rather it was the product of the interweaving of elements from each of these traditions through the imaginations of the women who constituted it, with a dash of something new added. Feminism, drawing on liberalism, anarchism and socialism, and transforming them through the recognition of the specificities of women's oppression, made it thinkable for women to take action on the global stage, to act as individuals and take control of their lives. Particularly significant was the legacy of the women's liberation movement of the late 1960s and the 1970s. The anarchist tradition contributed its passion for freedom, its opposition to hierarchy and domination, and its belief in a decentralized, self-regulating community of individuals taking personal responsibility for their futures. This was exemplified by the Diggers and the Ranters, and the Situationists. From the socialist tradition Greenham derived a critique of economic exploitation and inequality, of imperialism, colonialism and the profit motive, and a commitment to equality, internationalism and communality. The most important element of the socialist roots of Greenham was the 'New Left', the libertarian, anarchist-influenced radicals of the 1960s and 1970s. Finally, the pacifist rejection of the principle that might is right and the belief in non-violent direct action as a way of pursuing social and political change, contributed to the ideas and actions which constituted Greenham. The pacifist influence was felt through the history of peace movements, particularly women's peace movements and the anti-nuclear movement, through the memory of Gandhi and the philosophy of non-violence of the American civil rights movement.

In keeping with the hybrid postmodern approach I outlined in Chapter 1, this chapter does not seek to chart a linear unfolding of history whereby Greenham ineluctably emerged out of the movements and ideas of previous eras. Nor does it seek to distinguish 'true' history from the myths and stories which were spun at Greenham. Rather it locates Greenham historically by tracing its genealogies through both the past which Greenham women imagined for themselves and through a past of movements and bodies of thought which I believe influenced and shaped Greenham, a past perhaps less obvious to Greenham women at the time.

## Distant Ancestors

When people - whether families, nations or social movements - speak of distant ancestors, a greater leap of the imagination is required than when they talk of closer generations. The likelihood of sentimentality and flights of fantasy is enhanced. All history, including genealogy, is an act of construction, building with the blocks that are available at the time. The ancestors who are caught in a retrospective gaze are interesting not least because of what their invoked presence reveals about those looking back.

Two sets of distant ancestors were chosen by women at Greenham - both largely of peasant stock and both seen to be pursuing admirable ways of life until violent forces of authority began to persecute them. One set was the women who were imprisoned, tortured and murdered as witches in Europe in the fifteenth, sixteenth and seventeenth centuries. The other was the anarchist wing of the revolutionary movement of the English Civil War, the Diggers and the Ranters.

### THE WITCHES

There is now a substantial scholarly debate about the course, extent and cause of the witch-hunts of early modern Europe, but this debate was little known at Greenham.[2] Women at Greenham were influenced particularly by the feminist interpretations of the witch-craze in Barbara Ehrenreich and Deidre English's pamphlet *Witches, Midwives and*

*Nurses*, and in Mary Daly's book *Gyn/Ecology*.[3] Ehrenreich and English suggest that the witch-hunts were part of the establishment of a male-controlled, university-based medical profession, and involved the persecution of women healers and midwives whose knowledge of herbs and women's bodies had been passed down through the generations. Daly argues that the women who were the subject of witch-hunts were not just healers but more generally women who posed a challenge to male supremacy by living outside the patriarchal family: 'women who had rejected marriage (Spinsters) and women who had survived it (Widows)'.[4]

From these sources it seemed that women who stood in the way of men's desire to control life, death, nature, scientific knowledge and the organization of society were to be punished. This made the witches a powerful symbol of women's oppression throughout history. Many who first learnt about the witch-hunts while at Greenham felt a deep connection across time with them. Some chose to celebrate the continuity of feminist resistance they felt with those who had been called witches in earlier centuries. Some chose to commemorate in sorrow their deaths as women who had died at the hands of men. Others read the connection more loosely, with a self-conscious irony and humour about the stereotypical images of witches in popular mythology. A few of those who were more spiritually inclined identified themselves as present-day witches and developed an interest in herbs, rituals and magic.

All were catered for on 29 October 1983, the Saturday before Hallowe'en, and only a few days before the first Cruise missiles arrived at Greenham, when thousands of women, many dressed as witches and carrying broomsticks and bolt-cutters, cut down miles of the perimeter fence around the base, singing:

> We will rise up from the flame,
> Higher and higher and higher.
> Fires' strength we will reclaim
> Higher and higher and higher.
>
> We are the witches who will never be burned
> We are the witches who have learnt
> what it is to be free.

The fire of love is burning bright,
Higher and higher and higher.
Flickering, dancing in the night,
Higher and higher and higher.

We are the witches who will never be burned
We are the witches who have learnt
what it is to be free.

Weave your powers to the wind,
Higher and higher and higher.
We will change and we will spin
Higher and higher and higher.


THE DIGGERS AND THE RANTERS

Casting back to the seventeenth century, women at Greenham also
traced a line of descent which connected them with the Diggers and
the Ranters.[5] The song below, 'The World Turned Upside Down', by
Leon Rosselson, was often sung around the campfire and on actions:

In 1649, to St George's Hill,
A ragged band they called the Diggers
Came to show the people's will.
They defied the landlords,
They defied the laws,
They were the dispossessed
Reclaiming what was theirs.

We come in peace, they said,
to dig and sow,
We come to work the land in common
and to make the wasteground grow.
This earth divided
We will make whole
So it will be a common treasury for all.

The sin of property we do disdain.
No man has any right
To buy and sell the earth for private gain.

By theft and murder they took the land.
Now everywhere the walls spring up at their command.

They make the laws to chain us well.
The clergy dazzle us with heaven
Or they damn us into hell.
We will not worship the God they serve
The God of greed who feeds the rich
While poor folk starve.

We work, we eat together, we need no swords.
We will not bow to the masters
Or pay rent unto the lords.
Still we are free, though we are poor.
You Diggers all stand up for glory,
Stand up now.

From the men of property the orders came.
They sent the hired men and the troopers
To wipe out the Diggers' claim.
Tear down their cottages,
Destroy their corn.
They were dispersed, but still the vision lingers on.

Ye poor take courage, ye rich take care.
This earth was made a common treasury for
    everyone to share.
All things in common, all people one.
They came in peace – the orders came to cut them down.

The Diggers and the Ranters went further than other radicals of the time who were demanding political equality for all men; they wanted common ownership of land, the abolition of private property and an end to the power of master over servant, father over child and husband over wife. Gerrard Winstanley, the theoretician of the movement, began his pamphlet *The New Law of Righteousness* with what was to become a classic anarchist critique of the corrupting effect of wielding power over others:

Everyone that gets an authority into his hands tyrannizes over others; as many husbands, parents, masters, magistrates, that live after the flesh do carry themselves like oppressing lords over such as are under them, not knowing that their wives, children, servants, subjects are their fellow creatures, and hath an equal privilege to share them in the blessing of liberty.[6]

Winstanley's ideal society read rather like a blueprint for the common values of Greenham (see Chapter 6) (if 'woman' replaces 'man', and given that women at Greenham did not raise cattle!):

When this universal law of equity rises up in every man and woman, then none shall lay claim to any creature and say, This is mine, and that is yours. This is my work, that is yours. But every one shall put to their hands to till the earth and bring up cattle, and the blessing of the earth shall be common to all; when a man hath need of any corn or cattle, take from the next store-house he meets with. There shall be no buying and selling, no fairs or markets, but the whole earth shall be a common treasury for every man ... When a man hath eat, and drink, and clothes, he hath enough. And he shall cheerfully put to their hands to make these things that are needful, one helping another. There shall be no lords over others, but everyone shall be a lord of himself, subject to the law of righteousness, reason and equity, which shall dwell and rule in him, which is the Lord.[7]

The Diggers believed, as the women at Greenham were to believe over three centuries later, that the ideal society should be created in the here and now in order to bring about a non-violent transformation in the social order. In 1649 a group of about forty of them set out to put their ideas into practice. They occupied a piece of wasteland on St George's Hill, near Walton-on-Thames, and began to cultivate it. Like the women at Greenham, they were attacked by local vigilantes, arrested and fined by the courts, and their crops and shelters were destroyed. For over a year they refused to be intimidated, or to respond with violence, and they continued publishing pamphlets explaining their philosophy. Some of their number travelled around Britain encouraging the establishment of other communities on wasteland. Finally, however, the persecution took its toll and the squatted community disbanded.

The Ranters, many of whom were Quakers, took Digger ideals further, advocating free love and an end to marriage, and, again like

Greenham, the pursuit of pleasure as an ethic by which to live. They believed that God was within every individual, and that individuals should act according to their innermost desires, drinking and feasting when it pleased them. According to their contemporaries they would 'rant and vapour and blaspheme', and were 'very rude, and sung and whistled and danced'.[8] They formed loose groupings, rather than a structured movement, and although their moment lasted only a few years, their 'exuberant irreverence and earthy nonconformity'[9] anticipated and served as an inspiration for some of the wilder elements of Greenham.

## Great-aunts

The women's peace movement of the 1980s was not the first time women had campaigned against militarism. There is a long history of organized opposition to war and militarism by women dating back at least to the 1820s.[10] The earliest women's peace groups were primarily composed of Quaker women, whose religion inclined them towards pacifism. Neither the Female Auxiliary Peace Societies set up in the aftermath of the Napoleonic Wars, nor the Olive Leaf Circles which spread across Britain in the 1840s and 1850s, could be described as feminist enterprises. They operated firmly within the domestic sphere and the 'separate spheres' ideology of Victorian England, and did not challenge the exclusion of women from the international congresses held by Peace Societies in Europe and the United States, which women could only attend as the wives of delegates.[11] However, the concern of the Circles with foreign affairs and ideas about peace, and their efforts to maintain contact with women in other countries are early examples of the internationalism which characterized later women's peace campaigning.

The real great-aunts of Greenham were the women who, in the early years of the twentieth century, moved out of their homes and into the public sphere to speak against war and militarism. It was no coincidence that - against a backcloth of the spread of feminist ideas and the rise of the suffrage movement - when the Boer War broke out at the turn of the century, women organized publicly for the first time against a war and in opposition to government policy. Feminism made it conceivable for women to set up public meetings to express their views and to face down jingoistic hecklers and physical assaults.[12] At these meetings resolutions were passed expressing sympathy with the women of the Transvaal and the Orange Free State; money was raised to provide relief for refugees.

By the beginning of the First World War the belief was widespread amongst feminists that the struggle for the vote and for women's inclusion in political and social life was linked to the campaign against war. Not all the women involved in the women's peace movement (which emerged in Britain the year following the outbreak of war) identified as feminists, and by no means all feminists were opposed to the war, but the language of the movement wove together feminist and maternalist discourses in a powerful way, one which prefigured the early rhetoric of Greenham.[13] Campaigning began with an appeal for conciliation and arbitration drawn up by the International Woman Suffrage Alliance which was delivered on behalf of 12 million women to the Foreign Office and to the London embassies of the relevant powers on 31 July 1914. The appeal emphasized women's lack of the vote and their duties as mothers:

> We, the women of the world, view with apprehension and dismay the present situation in Europe ... In this terrible hour, when the fate of Europe depends on decisions which women have no power to shape, we, realising our responsibilities as the mothers of the race, cannot stand passively by. Powerless though we are politically, we call upon the governments and powers of our several countries to avert the threatened unparalleled disaster.[14]

What united all those opposed to the war was a spirit of internationalism which sensitized them to the suffering of women in other countries and a belief that women had had no part in the politics which had led to war.

Some women (for example Kate Courtney, Maude Royden and Helen Swanwick) became involved in the Union for Democratic Control of Foreign Policy, a group of pacifist intellectuals from the Liberal tradition, one of the few organizations speaking out against the war.[15] But after years of leading their own struggle for the vote, for education and for access to employment, and with opposition to the war rooted in feminist beliefs, many women were suspicious of male-led groups and chose to work in women's groups.[16] Like Greenham women seventy years later, many who played a central role in the movement were unmarried and did not have relationships with men, surrounding themselves with other women and often having 'romantic friendships', which today would probably be called 'lesbian'.[17] This, together with the fact that both the suffrage movement and the women's peace movement were particularly strong in industrial areas, drawing in many working-class women, appealed to Greenham women who were seeking affirmation of their actions and identities in the histories of other activists:[18]

> People say that there were no working-class women at Greenham, but there was a working-class element there. We were strong. It wasn't only middle-class women; there were a lot of working-class women there … It's like the suffragettes. Middle-class women. But there were also working-class women that were doing things – loads. All the women involved in the women's movement then, they were all sleeping with each other, but no one recognized it because that was what women did, they slept in the same bed together.
>
> *Trisha*

Women peace campaigners during the First World War took a variety of forms of action: at the international level, there was the Women's International Congress at the Hague in 1915; within Britain, rallies and demonstrations, petitioning, writing political tracts and public meetings. The Hague Congress demonstrated the encompassing vision of the movement; it voted to demand an immediate cessation of hostilities, democratic control of foreign policy, women's suffrage and a peace settlement based on justice. The Congress demonstrated its commitment to these goals by sending envoys to the European and US heads of state with their plan for a mediation conference of neutral nations.[19] This action was of great symbolic significance. The largely unenfranchised women of nations at war were demanding to be heard on the issue of greatest international importance, the issue least subject to democratic control. But most importantly the Congress sparked the mushrooming of an international women's peace movement, marking a turning point in women's political history. National sections of the International Committee of Women for a Permanent Peace, which later became the Women's International League for Peace and Freedom, were established in twelve countries to publicize the proceedings of the Hague Congress and to organize another women's congress to influence the terms of the eventual peace settlement.

In the US women were protesting on the streets against the war by the end of August 1914. Rosika Schwimmer and Emmeline Pethick-Lawrence's speaking tours to suffrage groups about the war in Europe stirred up a women's peace movement there before one got off the ground in Europe.[20] Recognizing the potentially important role that the US could play in negotiating peace, Jane Addams put her name to the call for a Women's Peace Congress. It was held in Washington in 1915 and attracted 3000 women from a wide variety of women's societies and clubs - suffragist, settlement, temperance, religious and trade union - from across the country.[21] Out of this congress grew the Women's Peace Party (WPP) which later became the US branch of the Women's International League for Peace and Freedom.

The WPP committed itself to the non-violent resolution of conflict and to feminist internationalism, urging women to 'go beyond' faithfulness and devotion to their country in order to 'maintain true solidarity with the women of other belligerent nations'.[22] It argued for women's greater involvement in the public sphere in order to integrate into the world of politics women's values, which tended to be concerned with human needs rather than commercial profit, and resolved to work for social and economic equality. The WPP organized public debates with arms manufacturers and an exhibition called *War Against War*, which featured an enormous metal dragon representing the war machine and drew up to 10,000 visitors a day.[23] This was remarkably like the visual spectacle at Greenham of a four-and-a-half-mile serpent tail sewn by thousands of women, which was woven in and out of the base in 1983.

Anger at the introduction of conscription, the mounting death tolls and the government's use of draconian Defence of the Realm Act rulings and military tribunals (as well as more mundane frustrations at rising prices and queues for food) widened anti-war protests to include more and more working-class women. Drawing on pre-war women's suffragist, suffragette, socialist and trade union networks within tight-knit communities, a movement named the Women's Peace Crusade spread across the country between 1916 and 1918.[24] It had no official membership, no executive committee or headquarters, and having begun on 'Red Clydeside', it was strongest in the northern industrial towns. The Crusade was loud, confrontational and based on the streets. Demonstrations and open-air rallies against the war and in favour of women's suffrage took place in Glasgow, Manchester, Bradford, Nelson and Leicester, mobilizing thousands of women onto the streets and into local groups, of which there were 45 by November 1917.[25]

The feminist legacy of the great-aunts of the First World War did not pass directly to the women of Greenham. Women's peace campaigning continued at a less intense level during the inter-war years and during the Cold War of the 1950s. During these periods the feminist critique of women's exclusion from international politics was less prominent than a maternalist discourse. The Women's International League for Peace and Freedom (WILPF), for instance, which was the main organization carrying the torch of women's peace politics through the twentieth century, expanded its membership around the world, developed its ideas about non-violence (influenced by Gandhi) and frequently sent women to trouble spots to meet with other women in those places and to attempt to head off conflict.[26] But as it grew, feminism slipped from its agenda.[27] Women's enfranchisement, albeit limited, had not brought the changes in the world order that the WILPF had anticipated, and, with little discussion of other aspects of women's subordination, the link between feminism and peace began to weaken in its literature. Peace and international affairs continued to be considered women's affairs largely because of women's special responsibility as bearers of life.

The specifically socialist women's peace tradition, which had been evidenced in the Women's Peace Crusade, was institutionalized during the inter-war years through the Women's Co-operative Guild.[28] The Guild, founded in 1883 as an auxiliary of the Co-operative Movement, had as its primary concern the education of women (the keepers of the domestic purse) about consumer cooperation. It was thus clearly rooted in, rather than antagonistic to, women's traditional roles as wives and mothers, and was not explicitly feminist. When in the 1920s the International Co-operative Women's Guild was formed, the British Guild became more international in perspective and increased its involvement in campaigning against militarism. It sought to promote international cooperation and understanding through the learning of Esperanto, foreign travel and family exchanges. Ever conscious of the importance of their duties as mothers, Guildswomen campaigned for an annual peace day in schools and against militarist material in textbooks and films. The basis of the Guild's opposition to war was firmly maternalist, as a pamphlet published in 1950 explained:

> Motherhood everywhere carries with it an urge for the preservation of life. This urge, combined with co-operative principles, has inspired the policy on peace which has been so great a part of Guild work over the last 30 to 40 years.[29]

Between the Second World War and the start of the 1980s, women's autonomous peace campaigning continued, but at a much lower level. Of course many women were involved in the mixed anti-nuclear movement of the 1950s and 1960s; indeed a woman is credited with founding the Campaign for Nuclear Disarmament (CND), and the Golders Green branch of the Women's Co-operative Guild played a pivotal role in opening up a political space in which anti-nuclear politics could arise.[30] It was concern amongst the members of this group about the effects on unborn children of radioactivity from weapons testing which led to the establishment of the first Local Committee for the Abolition of the H-Bomb, which was to become the National Council for the Abolition of Nuclear Weapons Tests (NCANWT), and eventually the Campaign for Nuclear Disarmament.[31]

The only new women's peace groups of the Cold War period coalesced around women's concerns about the danger posed to children by nuclear weapons – in Britain, the short-lived Voice of Women, in the United States, the larger and longer-lived Women's Strike for Peace.[32] Both groups were primarily composed of middle-class housewives and mothers who set forth their challenge to the nuclear policies of their nations from their ascribed positions within the nuclear family. There was scant recognition of the relationship between peace and women's freedom which had been so important during the First World War. In many ways this period of women's peace history is similar to the 1840s and 1850s; at both times women were primarily motivated as mothers to work against militarism and in both periods there was no wider women's movement to counterbalance the prevailing conservatism.

Thus it was that the great-aunts of anti-militarist activism closest in age to the women of Greenham were maternalist rather than feminist in their political orientation. However, a firm link had already been

established between feminism, internationalism and peace campaigning. Virginia Woolf's polemic *Three Guineas* provided a crucial link
across the generations. This book was widely read by women in the
early 1980s and served as an oft-quoted inspiration for a feminist
rejection of nationalism and militarism. Most famously, Woolf
declared that the concept of fighting to protect 'our country' is alien
to women as outsiders to male society:

> 'Our country' ... throughout the greater part of its history has
> treated me as a slave; it has denied me education or any share in its
> possessions ... Therefore if you insist upon fighting to protect me,
> or 'our country', let it be understood, soberly and rationally
> between us, that you are fighting to gratify a sex instinct which I
> cannot share; to procure benefits which I have not shared and
> probably will not share ... in fact, as a woman, I have no country.[33]

These words reappeared on banners, posters, leaflets and T-shirts
during the women's peace movement of the 1980s.

## Older Cousins: The Social Movements of the 1960s and 1970s

Rather like older cousins blazing a trail of disruption and critique
through the dense, dark, claustrophobic woodlands of convention and
tradition, the social movements which swept across Europe and North
America from the late 1950s onwards cleared space and opened up
possibilities for Greenham. They introduced new ideas and forms of
action which Greenham was able to draw upon and, though most had
passed their peak by the early 1980s, their presence was still tangible;
they were not yet dead and buried. These movements wove together in
new ways anarchist, socialist and, to a lesser extent, feminist and pacifist
ideas. The peace movement, the civil rights movement, the student
movement, the anti-Vietnam War movement, the Situationists, the
squatting movement, the environmental movement, the gay liberation
movement and, of course, the women's liberation movement – all of
these changed the political and cultural landscape irrevocably. New
vocabularies of politics were germinated in their hothouse atmo-
spheres and new forms of action entered the repertoire of the activist.
Together they laid the ground for Greenham.

ISSUES AND IDEAS

The issues around which this 'New Left' coalesced were wide-ranging. In the late 1950s and early 1960s a peace movement emerged in Britain, initially to contest nuclear testing, and then expanding its remit to call for the abolition of all nuclear weapons, starting with unilateral nuclear disarmament in Britain.[34] Following the gradual decline of anti-nuclear activity in the wake of the Partial Test Ban Treaty of 1963, Britain saw a flourishing of the student movement campaigning, as in the United States and France, for greater academic democracy and against the Vietnam War. In the United States, social movement activity had really begun in the post-war period with the civil rights struggle against racism and segregation.[35] Thousands of people, politicized through this, later became involved in the anti-Vietnam War movement which mobilized around the threat to individual young men posed by the draft and a political critique of American imperialism. In France in 1968 student unrest sparked *les événements* in which students and workers went on strike against capitalism. The women's liberation movement – with roots both in feminist organizations which dated back to the first wave and in other social movements of this period – began in the late 1960s.[36] The police raid on the Stonewall Bar in New York in 1969 marked the beginning of the gay liberation movement in the United States, which spread to Britain in the early 1970s.[37] That decade also saw the burgeoning of the environmental movement and the urban squatters' movement in Britain, West Germany and Holland, taking direct action to immediately alleviate homelessness.[38]

   World peace, internationalism, racism, women's oppression and even concern for the environment, had all motivated collective action earlier in the twentieth century and before, but the movements of the 1960s and 1970s had a new intensity and radicalism in their analyses and practices. In part this was because the world was changing. The nuclear era had brought with it new risks and an unprecedented urgency for those involved in anti-militarist movements. The rapid industrialization of the post-Second World War period, with its attendant pollution and urbanization, had increased the stakes for the environmental movement. The ever-strengthening superpower status of the United States, and its intervention in Vietnam, highlighted the new meaning and salience of imperialism and the exploitation of the peoples of the Third World by those in the West. A new far-reaching critique of the materialism of the first world was formulated in this context. Many in the counter-culture which emerged in this period sought to simplify their consumption patterns and to buy local, organically grown food in order to reduce their impact as individuals on the global environment and the exploitation of the Third World. Campaigns in the late 1950s and early 1960s against nuclear testing and nuclear weapons, particularly in Britain, and in the 1970s against nuclear power stations in the US and Europe, were both the product of, and contributed to, changing attitudes to science and technology. The Enlightenment belief in progress, in the benefits of scientific rationality and faith in experts were increasingly called into question by an ever-growing number of people.

The new movements pushed at the limits of the liberal impulses which had driven most of those who had campaigned about issues of equality among the races and between the sexes in previous decades. A new drive for individual autonomy, self-determination and personal responsibility emerged. As black people became more prominent in the civil rights movement, a black power stance developed in which the importance of black people speaking and acting for themselves was articulated. The women's liberation movement, which emerged out of and in antagonism to the 'New Left', was founded on the belief in the importance of women themselves taking control of their own struggle for liberation, rather than waiting until 'after the revolution'. The Situationists in France in the late 1960s sought to overthrow the mundanity of everyday life and to free the imagination from the tyranny of industrial capitalism. Then in the early 1970s the gay liberation movement was formed, with its confrontational, radical politics which challenged the entrenched heterosexism, homophobia and gender stereotyping of Western societies. 'The personal' - the liberation and development of the self, and its freedom from interference by other individuals or by the state - came to be seen as central to political struggle.

The social movements of this period had fluid and overlapping memberships. The ideas which were developed within the movements percolated out beyond the activists into wider society. The libertarian socialist impulse which fuelled the New Left was part of, and fed into, the decline in deference to authority and a growing belief in each individual's right and ability to control her own life.[39] Linked to this was the central belief running through the movements of the period in the importance of direct participation. In contrast with ideals of representative democracy accepted by liberals and most socialists, this anarchist notion held that power to make political decisions and to take action should not be surrendered by individuals to representatives, however chosen. Rather it should be exercised continuously by all individuals who have an existential responsibility for their own power. This belief in personal responsibility and the involvement of each individual in decision-making was more in evidence in some movements than others. Some, such as the peace movement in Britain and much of the civil rights movement, had relatively fixed hierarchies and leadership structures. Within the student movement there were both groups with leaders and groups which operated collectively. The environmental movement at this time tended to organize at the local level in autonomous 'affinity groups' which liaised with each other through loose networks and newsletters. The women's liberation movement, particularly in Britain (where there was no national organization comparable with the National Organization of Women (NOW) in the US) was structured around locally based, autonomous, non-hierarchical small groups.

The Situationists, a small group of avant-garde artists and intellectuals in France, expressed a particularly potent version of these ideas, traces of which were passed through time to Greenham.[40] They believed that capitalism stifled creativity and suppressed individual actors, and so they sought to overthrow the division within society between actors and spectators, producers and consumers. Every individual in society should construct the situation of her or his own life, and rather than wait for the revolution and the overthrow of capitalism, they advocated the 'spectacular' disruption and reinvention of everyday life. Their vision was of a joyous, playful carnival revolution in the here and now, undertaken by all. They placed pleasure at the centre of social life. Not only was the pursuit of pleasure central to the meaning of life, it was also the means by which revolution should be enacted. Roles should be freely chosen and non-hierarchical; the attitude of revolutionaries should be playful. As one Situationist writer put it:

> An efficiently hierarchized army can win a war, but not a revolution; an undisciplined mob can win neither. The problem

then is how to organize, without creating a hierarchy; in other words, how to make sure that the leader of the game doesn't become just 'the Leader'. The only safeguard against authority and rigidity setting in is a playful attitude. Creativity plus a machine gun is an unstoppable combination.[41]

While Greenham rejected the machine-gun, in its anti-hierarchical, participative ethos and in the spirit of irreverent humour and fun which guided action at Greenham, a clear link with the Situationists is discernible.

FORMS OF ACTION

The forms of action taken by the movements of the 1960s and 1970s were also important in preparing the way for Greenham. Parliamentary routes to political change and the traditional tools of the petition and pressure group were rejected by many and supplemented for others, who chose to take part in civil disobedience. Inspired by the Gandhian movement in India, non-violent direct action was the chosen strategy of many of those in the anti-nuclear movement in Britain in the late 1950s and early 1960s and in the civil rights movement in the US. In addition to the Aldermaston marches and mass rallies in Trafalgar Square, the Direct Action Committee and later the Committee of 100 organized sit-downs in the streets of London to disrupt the city and to draw attention to the threat posed by nuclear weapons. Nuclear bases around the country were blockaded by human bodies and their buildings occupied. In the United States the civil rights movement was sparked off by the individual act of disobedience of one woman, Rosa Parkes, who refused to give up her seat at the front of the bus to a white person. Non-violent direct action, such as the Montgomery bus boycott and occupations of segregated public spaces by groups of black people and by mixed groups became the stock-in-trade of the civil rights movement. Other movements of the 1960s and 1970s also made use of non-violent direct action from time to time. The environmental movement in the UK blockaded the nuclear power station at Torness in Scotland; anti-Vietnam War protesters staged mass sit-downs outside American embassies; the women's liberation movement held 'Reclaim the Night' marches throughout the US and

Britain; and small underground groups calling themselves 'Angry Women' carried out sabotage attacks on sex shops in a number of UK cities.

By the early 1980s there were firmly established precedents in radical circles for the belief held at Greenham that it was acceptable to break unjust laws and that the disruption of 'business as usual' in order to draw attention to demands for change was a useful and morally defensible mode of political action. The proviso was also already established that all such action must be non-violent. No violence should be used by those protesting and they should not respond with violence to violence from the police or others.

## Big Sister: The Women's Liberation Movement

Of all the social movements of the 1960s and 1970s, it was to the women's liberation movement that Greenham was most closely related. Just as the women's liberation movement was formed out of and in reaction to the New Left, so Greenham was shaped and made possible by the ideas and agendas of the women's liberation movement.

The movement emerged to a large extent as a response by women involved in the student movement, the anti-Vietnam War movement and the communes of the counter-culture to the misogyny and marginalization they experienced from their 'brothers'. The emphasis of these movements on personal politics and on self-actualization encouraged women to examine the contradictions of their own experiences in supposedly liberatory movements. What they created as a result was a movement of and for women, autonomously organized around issues of concern to women, where women did not have to do the back-room work for the men who were making the decisions and fronting the campaigns, and where they were not expected to be constantly available to men as objects of sexual desire.

For the women involved in the movement in Britain its first decade was a heady time of intense organizing and life-changing experiences.[42] By the early 1980s the heat of the early years of the movement had lessened and a process of institutionalization had begun.[43] The annual national women's liberation conferences were a thing of the past, largely because the movement had become so large and diverse, but there were national networks of locally based feminist groups and services, such as rape crisis centres, lesbian lines and women's refuges. Many cities had their own newsletters and women's centres, and there were a number of well-established national feminist newsletters and magazines, such as *Spare Rib* and *Outwrite*. Strong friendship networks existed and there were thousands of communal women's households around the country. Predominantly the creation of lesbian feminists, there was also a thriving feminist culture based around women-only discos, women's bands and theatre companies, and a growing literature of feminist novels, poetry and plays published by a small number of women's publishing houses.

The social networks, political spaces and ideas of the women's liberation movement made Greenham possible. The nationwide feminist community helped spread news of Greenham to a potentially sympathetic population and women's centres provided resources and meeting space for newly formed Greenham support groups. Moreover, the women's liberation movement had underlined the importance of women-only organizations and women-only social spaces. It was the availability of this idea which provoked Greenham's transformation from a small women-led but mixed peace camp, into a large, open women-only community and movement. Greenham also took from the women's liberation movement its key principle of organization. Small, locally based, autonomous, non-hierarchical groups were the paradigmatic political formation of the women's liberation movement and they became the model for the camp, its different gates and the wider Greenham network of local groups.

Militarism and nuclear weapons had not been issues of great concern in the women's liberation movement in the 1970s, but there were traces of feminist interest in pacifism, non-violence and war.[44] A small number of women working within mixed peace movement organizations (such as International Fellowship of Reconciliation and War Resisters International [WRI]) organized a women's workshop at the WRI triennial in Holland in 1975 (in spite of considerable male resistance), a five-day-long women-only gathering in rural France in 1976, and the Feminism and Nonviolence Collective in Britain.[45] From these groups a specifically feminist conceptualization of non-violence began to develop.

Following the Three Mile Island incident in 1979 feminists in the US organized against nuclear power and an eco-feminist position began to emerge within the environmental and women's movements. US radical feminist theory of this period, particularly the work of Mary Daly and Susan Griffin, had a strong interest in nature and the environment.[46] The eco-feminist activism of the Spinsters and the Women's Pentagon Action[47] provided ideas and inspiration for Greenham. The women's liberation movement was transnational. Not only were US feminist actions reported in British newsletters and magazines and US writers avidly read, but individual women travelling between the US and Britain brought news and experiences with them.[48] The affinity group structure and the dramatic symbolism, theatricality and humour of actions such as the Spinsters' Web at the Vermont Yankee Power Station and the Women's Pentagon Action encircling of the Pentagon influenced the organization and design of actions at Greenham several years later.

By the time the new Cold War broke out between the US and the Soviet Union at the end of the 1970s and a peace movement began to galvanize across Europe, there were small but significant networks of feminists, already concerned about the nuclear situation, who began to organize conferences and to form groups such as the first Women Oppose the Nuclear Threat group which was set up in Leeds in 1980 and the Women's Peace Alliance (1981). The stage was set for Greenham.

## Dynamic Tension and Conflict

In this chapter I have traced how Greenham borrowed from a host of existing strands of political thought and from earlier generations of protesters. But Greenham was not the direct descendant of any one of these traditions and was anything but uncritical of them. Dynamic tension and conflict with established discourses and modes of action, whatever their claims to radical outsiderness, were crucial in producing Greenham's uniqueness.

The early ancestors – the Diggers, the Ranters, the witches – largely escaped critique, but Greenham women were aware of the romantic nature of their appropriation of these peasant rebels. Many women were also conscious and critical of the lasting power of the maternalist legacy of the great-aunts of the women's peace movement, which continued to frame the motivations of mothers and grandmothers concerned about nuclear weapons in the 1980s. As Greenham rapidly shifted away from the maternalist rhetoric which was in evidence in its early days, there was a determined and often angry distancing by many women from the 'women's special role' position, as Greenham's queer feminisms were developed in its place. Women loudly and publicly rejected attempts by commentators and journalists, particularly of the liberal/left, to understand their actions as those of self-sacrificing, beatific mothers saving the world for their children.

Greenham was also formed in a conflictual relationship to aspects of the social movements of the 1960s, 1970s and early 1980s. Many Greenham women had been involved in these movements (particularly the peace movement, the environmental movement and the student movement) and had found that they were marginalized and assigned secondary roles. Others had been part of the 'counter-culture' and had experienced life in communal houses and alternative communities where they found they were still expected to fulfil traditional women's roles. Anger at this fuelled the determination to make and keep Greenham women-only and anti-hierarchical. The tedium, bureaucracy and dryness of much political organizing on the left, particularly in the newly rejuvenated CND in the early 1980s where many Greenham women first experienced activism, also fed the playfulness, spontaneity and commitment to continuous change which characterized Greenham. In contrast to their older cousins, Greenham women endeavoured not to take themselves too seriously.

Finally, whilst Greenham's relationship with its big sister was the closest of those I have discussed, it was also at times rather fraught, in the way that sibling relationships often are. Greenham was no clone of the women's liberation movement and did not straightforwardly model itself on it; nor was the women's liberation movement uniformly proud of its younger sister, as I discussed in Chapter 1. Greenham rejected many of the categorizations and divisions around which the women's liberation movement tended to structure itself – distinctions between radical, socialist, liberal and lesbian feminism, for instance, and would not be pressured to accept one of these designations. The seven demands of the women's liberation movement, which had been debated and argued over, but ultimately agreed on at national women's liberation conferences in the 1970s, had not included any reference to women's involvement in politics, or to war and peace. Greenham challenged the existing agenda of the movement and the narrowness of what was defined as a feminist issue.[49] In the same way that Greenham rejected the seriousness of much of the left, it also had a younger sister's lighter touch and more of a propensity to laugh at itself and its adversaries than many in the women's liberation movement.

## Notes

1.  Braverman's (1996) agenda for a queer history involves taking individual, collective and popular memory practices seriously as political and cultural interventions in everyday life.
2.  See Hester (1992) for an overview of the debate and a revolutionary feminist position.
3.  Ehrenreich and English (1976); Daly (1979).
4.  Daly (1979: 55).
5.  See Woodcock (1962); Marshall (1993).
6.  Woodcock (1962: 43).
7.  *Ibid.*: 43-4.
8.  Marshall (1993: 103).
9.  *Ibid.*: 107.
10. See Black (1984), Bussey and Tims (1965), Early (1986), Eglin (1987), Foster (1989), Liddington (1983, 1989), Oldfield (1989), Roach Pierson (1987), Schott (1985), Swerdlow (1989), Vellacott (1993) and Wiltsher (1985).
11. Liddington (1989: 16-17).
12. Oldfield (1989: 24-5).
13. There were significant divisions within the suffrage movement over the war. See Wiltsher (1985) and Liddington (1989) for a detailed discussion.
14. Liddington (1989: 77-8).
15. *Ibid.*: 81-3; Oldfield (1989: 25).
16. Wiltsher (1985: 63).
17. Fadermann (1981) discusses, for example, the relationship between Jane Addams, president of the Women's International League for Peace and Freedom, and her 'devoted companions' Ellen Starr and Mary Rozet Smith.
18. See Liddington and Norris (1978) on the suffrage movement.
19. Foster (1989: 2).
20. Schott (1985).
21. Liddington (1989), Schott (1985), Wiltsher (1985).
22. Quoted in Schott (1985: 20).
23. Wiltsher (1985: 168).
24. The Women's Peace Crusade appears to have slumped after an initial euphoric mobilization, but it was boosted by the Russian Revolution (Liddington, 1989: 122).
25. Eglin (1987) and Liddington (1983, 1989).
26. Foster (1989).

27. Spender (1984) argues that it is wrong to see the women's movement in Britain as consisting of two distinct waves; she emphasizes the continuity of feminist ideas and commitment in individual women's lives throughout the century. Her point has validity in the specific case of WILPF, many of whose members were committed feminists in the 1920s and 1930s. Nonetheless, it is still true to say that public feminist action declined significantly after the First World War and in parallel the League's focus on women's rights declined.
28. Eglin (1987: 226) and Black (1984: 472).
29. Quoted in Black (1984: 468).
30. Eglin (1987) credits Gertrude Fishwick with effectively founding CND, but Liddington (1989) argues that it was in fact three Golders Green Guildswomen, Agnes Simpson, Marion Clayton and Vera Leff, who 'triggered the chain reaction which ended in CND'. Other women prominent in the anti-nuclear movement were Pat Arrowsmith, Dora Russell, Sheila Oakes and April Carter.
31. Liddington (1989).
32. Liddington (1989) and Swerdlow (1993). Swerdlow suggests that WSP became increasingly feminist as it entered the 1970s.
33. Woolf (1977: 125).
34. Taylor and Pritchard (1980), Taylor (1988) and Taylor and Young (1987).
35. Williams (1987) and Crawford et al. (1993).
36. Freeman (1975), Evans (1979), Bunch (1987), Jaggar (1988) and Miles (1989).
37. Adam (1987).
38. On the environmental movement see Eckersley (1992), Cotgrove and Duff (1980) and Cotgrove (1982).
39. See Heelas et al. (1996) and Beck et al. (1994) for a theoretical discussion of processes of detraditionalization and reflexive modernization.
40. See Plant (1992), Erlich (n.d.) and Marshall (1993).
41. Vaneigem (1983) quoted in Plant (1992: 71).
42. Rowbotham (1989).
43. Lovenduski and Randall (1993).
44. Liddington (1989).
45. Feminism and Non-Violence Collective (1983).
46. Daly (1979) and Griffin (1978).
47. Linton and Whitham (1982), King (1983), McAllister (1982), Jaggar (1988) and Harris and King (1989).
48. Liddington (1989).
49. See the radical feminists in Breaching the Peace (Onlywomem Press, 1983), who debate whether or not peace is a feminist issue.

# Chapter 3
# Beginnings

## The Mushroom Cloud on the Horizon

I remember when Reagan was elected, I was still at university and we had an End of the World party because that was how we felt. I mean everybody just got roaring drunk for two days because we really felt like that was it, that none of us were going to live to see the end of our twenties ... There was a terrible sense of helplessness. It felt as if the world was being run by maniacs. There was Russia, and you didn't know what the fuck was going on there. And America being run by this cowboy. And our country being run by this lunatic woman who led us into the Falklands War, and if the Falklands had happened, what was going to be next?

*Helen Mary Jones*

For all those who hadn't voted Conservative in 1979 and who hadn't been stirred to patriotism by the Falklands War, the early 1980s was a cold time. Many people sensed that all was not well in the world and were afraid.

In the mid-1970s the global situation had been relatively calm. The Vietnam War was over and a period of détente between the United States and the USSR had begun. President Jimmy Carter began his term of office in 1977 claiming that he wished to achieve the elimination of nuclear weapons. The Strategic Arms Limitation Talks (SALT II) were proceeding. Few women in Britain gave much thought to the problem of militarism or the threat of nuclear war. Feminist attention was directed to the more local and everyday problems of setting up and running women's refuges, rape crisis centres, news-letters and magazines, lesbian lines and groups campaigning for myriad forms of social and political change. Some of the women who would become involved in Greenham were engaged in such activities; others were just getting on with the business of going to school or university, working or bringing up children.

Behind the scenes, however, things were starting to change. In the USA a virulently anti-Communist pressure group, the Committee on the Present Danger, began lobbying the Democratic administration to take the 'Soviet threat' more seriously. Carter pressed NATO to deploy the neutron bomb, a weapon which could wipe out whole populations while leaving buildings and property undamaged. Meanwhile the Soviet Union began to station nuclear weapons (SS20s) in Eastern Europe. In December 1979 Carter persuaded NATO to take the 'twin-track' decision. This amounted to an offer to enter into negotiations with the Warsaw Pact countries about reductions in intermediate nuclear forces (INF) in Europe, while as the same time 'modernizing' NATO intermediate nuclear forces by introducing ground-launched Cruise and Pershing II missiles. The initial plan was to deploy 464 Cruise missiles (on 116 launchers) in Britain, Belgium, The Nether-lands and Italy, and 108 Pershing II launchers in West Germany, beginning in 1983. The public justification for the twin-track decision presented the Cruise and the Pershing as an essential response to the new Soviet intermediate nuclear weapons, and made much of the Soviet Union's supposed conventional superiority. Less publicly, European governments were concerned to 'recouple' the US with Europe, to ensure ongoing US involvement in Europe and the continued existence of the US nuclear 'umbrella'. The US was determined to reassert its dominant position in the Atlantic Alliance.

The twin-track decision marked a watershed in the development of East-West relations for two reasons. First, the new missiles were part of a new 'generation' of 'theatre', or tactical nuclear weapons.[1] Unlike earlier intercontinental 'strategic' nuclear weapons which could travel between the US and the USSR, 'theatre' nuclear weapons were designed for use within Europe. They were to be more accurate and better able to 'penetrate' defensive systems than existing weapons. This meant that they possessed the ability to pinpoint and destroy 'hard' targets, such as command and control sites and nuclear storage facilities. The missiles were also small enough to be transported on mobile launchers; it was claimed that they would 'blend into the countryside' and avoid detection by the Soviets. In all, Cruise missiles were first-strike weapons, designed to make pre-emptive first strikes against Soviet missile silos. The official US nuclear doctrine had shifted from one of deterrence to one aiming to fight and win a nuclear war.

The cusp of the decade also marked a turning point in the domestic politics of both Britain and the US. Margaret Thatcher in 1979 and Ronald Reagan in 1981 were elected on platforms which promised to reverse the liberal legacy of the 1960s and to replace disrespect for authority with the firm hand of real leadership. Both were committed to monetarist economics and the restoration of national prestige (involving increased military expenditure) and both were determined to fight and overcome the menace of Communism. Thatcher had the scourge of socialism to quash in her own country and was also eager to play handmaiden to Reagan's wider global intentions.

Reagan's paranoia about Communist expansionism had been fuelled by the Soviet invasion of Afghanistan. During the first three years of his presidency he increased defence spending by 40 per cent. His increasingly vociferous anti-Soviet pronouncements stirred up further anxiety in Britain and Europe. Soviet leaders, he declared, were not to be trusted because they 'reserve unto themselves the right to commit any crime, to lie, to cheat, in order to obtain their objective ... Communists are not bound by our morality'.[2] The Soviet Union was 'the force of evil in the modern world ... an evil empire'[3] and he repeatedly stated his determination to drive the Soviet Union into economic bankruptcy through an arms race. It also quickly became apparent that the administration believed that nuclear war was winnable (Secretary of Defence Weinberger) and could be confined to Europe, and that Armageddon was inevitable and ordained by God (Reagan). In 1981 the *New York Times* uncovered the 'Five Year Defence Plan', which expounded a nuclear war strategy for 'decapitating' the USSR. A nuclear war in Europe was no longer a remote risk; it was firmly on the US government agenda of possibilities.

### Nuclear Fear

My own awakening to the nuclear issue, like that of many thousands of others, came in 1980 with the British government's 'Protect and

Survive' campaign. This initiative increased public expenditure on 'civil defence' by 60 per cent and backfired on the proponents of nuclear weapons. Booklets were distributed to every home to tell the population about what to do in the event of a nuclear attack. Householders were advised that, on hearing the first nuclear siren, they should whitewash their windows, take a door off its hinges and prop it against a wall, and then retreat into the space between the door and the wall with a substantial supply of tinned food and a transistor radio until the all clear was sounded, which might be up to two weeks later. Rather than making us all sleep easier in our beds, assured that the government had our security interests at heart, 'Protect and Survive' served to bring home just how seriously the government was taking the possibility of nuclear war. It was a propaganda gift to the burgeoning peace movement. The Campaign for Nuclear Disarmament (CND), which had been chugging along at a very low-key level since the Partial Test Ban Treaty in 1963, was suddenly infused with new life and began its own 'Protest and Survive' mobilization.

Across Western Europe, movements began to emerge demanding an end to the nuclear arms race and to the Cold War.[4] The Soviet Union was not excused its part in the global situation and its stationing of SS-20s in eastern Europe was condemned, but the immediate focus for the western European peace movement was the NATO weapons which were to be stationed at US bases across the continent. This deployment of first-strike nuclear weapons was regarded as having two main consequences. It made the countries involved into targets for pre-emptory strikes by the USSR. Every person, and the whole eco-system of Europe, became the potential victims of nuclear war. It also drew every citizen into the moral game of nuclear militarism; if nuclear weapons were fired from one's own country, the moral responsibility rested with the people in whose name the military was acting.

Suddenly many thousands of people could see themselves as both the potential victims and the potential agents of nuclear war, yet they had never been consulted about the involvement of their country in nuclear militarism. Awareness grew that key decisions about nuclear weapons had always, since their earliest days, been the prerogative of small groups of senior politicians, with no public debate or approval and, in the case of the Labour Party, in direct contradiction to professed policy.[5] For Thatcher and Reagan the decision to station Cruise missiles in Britain was a *fait accompli* and was not open to public debate. All this meant that as information about the extent of US military activities in Britain was gathered and disseminated, a sense of subject-nation status arose and augmented anger about the issue.

Popular culture at this time was suffused with the militarism of the Cold War. Espionage novels and films explicitly promoted the belief in the deadly nature of the Soviet threat, while science fiction and horror films spoke more subliminally of the dangers of Communism. Military toys and video games reinforced these messages, demonizing 'the enemy', fetishizing weapons of all kinds and asserting the notion that security is achieved through defence and armament.

With this all-too real spectre of a mushroom cloud on the horizon, hundreds of thousands of ordinary people across Europe were impelled to act. First in Norway and The Netherlands, and spreading to the UK by the spring of 1980, old networks were galvanized and new campaigners activated by nuclear fear. Local groups sprang up around Britain, both affiliated to CND and independent, and marches were organized in Newbury and Caerwent.[6] CND membership soared, the London office took on more staff, leaflets were printed and distributed, public meetings and debates organized, and in October 1981 the first mass demonstration of this new wave attracted over 70,000 people. The movement grew and an oppositional culture began to take root.

At the same time small groups of women began to form women's peace groups. In March 1980 a conference was held in Nottingham on 'Women and the Military', and soon afterwards Women Oppose the Nuclear Threat (WONT) was formed in Leeds. In Scandinavia, Women For Peace collected a million signatures on a petition calling for disarmament; they organized a march from Copenhagen to Paris to demonstrate the strength of feeling across Europe. News was spread through the feminist press, and peace networks and news-letters, and in 1981 the Women's Peace Alliance was set up to facilitate liaison and communication between the various groups in the UK.[7] The numbers of women involved were small and the public profile of the groups was low. Then Greenham burst onto the political scene in September 1981.

## The Beginnings of Greenham

Greenham was never consciously planned. There was no strategic thinking at work, no central committee or great mind was responsible. It all began with the nine-day 'Women for Life on Earth' walk from Cardiff to Greenham Common in late summer 1981. This walk, drawing on the British tradition of protest marches such as the Jarrow and Aldermaston marches, was inspired by the Scandinavian women's march from Copenhagen to Paris.[8] When the women from the Carmarthen Anti-Nuclear Campaign decided to organize a walk from south Wales to the first site for Cruise missiles, the US Air Force base at Greenham Common, near Newbury, Berkshire, they had no plans to even camp overnight at the base, let alone to establish a women's peace camp which would last for years.

The initiators of the walk, Ann Pettit and later Lynne Whittemore, Carmen Kutler, Angela Phillips and Liney Seward, contacted friends and acquaintances and wrote to mixed peace and anti-nuclear groups, women's peace groups (old and new), women's liberation groups, and mixed left-wing and radical political organizations to recruit walkers and to solicit practical assistance in the form of money and accommodation along the route.[9] Advance publicity was secured in *The Sunday Times*, the *Guardian*, and *Cosmopolitan*, in the newsletter of the Women's International League for Peace and Freedom, and in *Peace News*.

Those who offered help or who got involved were a heterogeneous collection of 'alternative types' who shared an opposition to nuclear weapons. They included an anarchist-feminist artist, a Christian feminist, a woman involved in a peace centre, a woman who owned a radical bookshop, a woman from the Centre for Alternative Technology in Wales, a man from Creches Against Sexism, a radical midwife, a woman Quaker, a woman from the Liberal Party, and an anarchist-feminist band, the Poison Girls.[10]

Margery Lewis was one of these 'original' Greenham women who read the article in the *Guardian* about the walk. The daughter of a suffragette, and one-time member of the Communist Party, she was a veteran anti-nuclear campaigner. She had taken part in the Stockholm Peace Petition of 1951, was a founding member of a women's anti-testing group in Loughton, Essex, in the late 1950s, and was involved in the establishment of the CND. However, having four young children had meant that she only joined the Aldermaston marches for a day, while her husband had walked the whole way, and retrospectively she would have liked to have done so too. After she and her family moved from London to Cardiff she found little political activity that engaged her, and walking, bird-watching and voluntary work, rather than politics, came to occupy her spare time. In 1981 she was 64 and her husband had recently died.

> I wrote to Ann Pettit and said, was it a feminist thing or was it a religious thing? And she rang me up and she said, 'No. No, it's people just like you.' And she said, 'So help me organize it from Cardiff'. So then a man here had done an awful lot of work, and he was going away, and I took over from him. And I got thoroughly involved. There hadn't been anything like that. There had been the Copenhagen march. And in a way it presented a challenge to walk a hundred and twenty miles. I liked the idea of it being women. I mean I'm not a strident feminist, but I do like working with women, and as I got involved with Greenham more, I liked being with women much more than I ever thought.
>
> *Margery Lewis*

In all thirty-nine people, mostly women with a handful of men and children, completed the nine-day walk, leafleting and talking to people as they passed through the towns and villages of south Wales and south-west England. Their aim was to challenge 'the deadly peril in which we are put by the escalating nuclear arms race', and particularly, the installation of Cruise missiles at Greenham, which was seen as placing 'the whole of South Wales and the south of England right into the front line for utter destruction in any nuclear exchange'.[11]

The politics of the walk were largely framed within a maternalist 'ethic of care' discourse, which saw the problems with nuclear weapons in terms of the threat they pose to those for whom women care, primarily children.[12] As the mobilizing statement drawn up to recruit participants said:

> Most women work hard at caring for other people - bearing and nourishing children, caring for sick or elderly relatives and many work in the 'caring' professions. Women invest their work in people - and feel a special responsibility to offer them a future - not a

wasteland of a world and a lingering death. Through the effects of radiation on the unborn and very young children, women are uniquely vulnerable in a nuclear war.[13]

In total the statement made six references to the fact that the women organizing the walk had children and were concerned about their children's future, and repeatedly described them as 'ordinary people' and 'unknown women'. This emphasis on the ordinariness, the 'common'-ness of the women involved, was to become a recurring theme in the politics of Greenham, with many women later choosing to call themselves 'Common Women'.

In addition to this maternalism, which has a long history in women's peace movements, the initiators of the walk were also influenced by the socialist and feminist politics which were in circulation in the late 1970s and early 1980s, and used a materialist feminist argument against nuclear weapons in their statement:

> Women bear the weight of cuts in public expenditure - fewer social services, nurseries, less provision for the elderly and infirm, cuts affecting schools.[14]

It went on to address the gender politics of militarism from within a liberal feminist discourse about women's exclusion from political life:

> Most women have played no part in the decisions and delusions that have brought the world to a position where a few people hold the lives of all of us in their control.[15]

Under the heading 'Why Women?' their justification for the march being led by women was one of gender equity in the peace movement and the public sphere:

> The march is led by women to show everyone that women are active and prominent in the peace movement. Men are welcome as supporters, but most of the speakers at meetings and events along the route will be women - some of them already known to the media, most just the unknown women who will be coming on the march to tell the world what they think of our society's priorities.[16]

However, the leaflet handed out to bystanders buried the liberal feminism and emphasized the maternalist politics. It appealed unambiguously to concern for children and fears about nuclear war. On one side the leaflet posed the question, 'Why are we walking 110 miles across Britain, from a nuclear weapons factory in Cardiff to a US base for 'cruise' missiles in Berkshire?' The other side featured a photograph of a seriously deformed baby and the following words:

> This is why. The mother of this baby was exposed to radiation from the nuclear bomb dropped on Hiroshima. 200,000 were blasted and burnt to death. She survived, but her baby, like many others, was born dead and horribly deformed.
>
> The younger you are, the more likely you are to be damaged by radiation from nuclear weapons. As well as deformities in the unborn, this causes cancers and leukaemia.

The nature of the walk's identification with women was more about the work and responsibilities deriving from women's traditional gender identities as mothers than it was about oppositional feminist identities. Feminist discourses were not absent, but they did not occupy a central or dominant position.

The walk was both exhausting and exhilarating, and the walkers bonded strongly in the course of long days of talking en route. However, it attracted very little media attention beyond the confines of the local newspapers of the towns through which it passed. This surprised and angered the walkers, because not only had considerable effort been expended in issuing press releases, but for many the whole point of a women-led walk, taking children, was to attract sympathetic press coverage.

> I think why we had it women only (well of course we did have some men on it) was because we thought that it would attract more attention ... But we felt we weren't making any impact at all. And there we were, women. We were different. We were women, and we were pushing babies, and nobody had done this before, and nobody thought it was outstanding. We thought we were absolutely amazing [laughs], but nobody agreed with us. So as we got nearer to Greenham, that's when we had the idea of chaining

ourselves to the fences, to make some impact, because we were just making no impact at all.

*Margery Lewis*

So when the walk arrived on 5 September, in an action self-consciously reminiscent of the suffragettes, four women chained themselves to the fence of the base to demand a televised debate with the Secretary of State for Defence. A rally was held that afternoon and the base commander came out and said that as far as he was concerned, they could stay there as long as they liked.

So it was at that moment, it was about six o'clock on the Saturday night, that we decided we would just stay there. It hadn't been planned. That's just literally what happened.

*Helen John*

That evening thirty-nine people decided to camp outside the base to support the chained women. On Sunday local people brought camping equipment, as the walkers had none with them, and some decided to stay on. By the end of the first week those who were there had resolved to continue the camp indefinitely, and to march to the CND rally in London in October. Despite numerous further written requests and considerable correspondence with BBC and ITV producers, no televised debate ever occurred. But the camp continued. One day, early on, a woman who was visiting the camp painted the words 'Women's Peace Camp' in purple, green and white (the suffragette colours) on pieces of board and displayed them to the passing traffic; no formal decision was ever taken to name the camp thus, but it stuck.[17] The Greenham Common Women's Peace Camp had been created, and lives had begun to change.

Helen John, a 34-year-old mother of five, was in at the beginning. Having given up her job as a nurse to concentrate on raising her children, she was no feminist, and indeed had never knowingly met a feminist until she joined the walk. She was motivated by the desire to ensure that the world would be a safe place for her children to grow up, yet her maternalist impulses led her way outside the conventional maternal role, sparking radical transformations in her life.

In the process of the ten days of being on that walk and getting very close to other women, and being freed from the responsibility of housework and children and all that for the first time in years, I was able to take a much more direct involvement upon myself as an independent woman. And it changed me.

Just before we got to Greenham four of us decided to chain ourselves to the fence, and it was the first independent action that I had actually chosen to take as an adult woman which didn't represent anybody else except me. It wasn't a question of ringing up and informing the family, or saying, 'Is it okay?' or anything. I knew that there could be incredible consequences brought about because of that. But I felt so strongly about the issue that I decided I would do it. And that's how the other three women felt as well. So we got there and chained ourselves to the fence, and that started the whole impetus to keep the whole thing boiling.

*Helen John*

Caught up in the spontaneity of the decision to stay outside the base, Helen drove back to Cardiff on Sunday to return a vehicle that had been borrowed for the walk, and then turned round and headed straight back to Greenham. For the first ten months of the camp's life she was there most of the time, leaving her children to be looked after by her husband at home. Her life was never the same again.

## Portraits of Common Women

Every woman's route to Greenham was unique and the impetus to get involved was, for everyone, a different combination of the political and personal set within the context of the particular circumstances of her own background and life. Greenham was a community and movement of individuals, premised on the importance of individuality. To speak in generalities about Greenham women carries the danger of submerging the differences and smoothing out the textures. The women whose experiences I focus on resist characterization as 'typical' Greenham women. There was no such thing. However, I believe that the thirty-five women I chose to interview do together encompass the range of differences which existed amongst Greenham women as a whole. In the remainder of this chapter I introduce some of them through their stories of getting involved with Greenham.

WHO WERE THEY?

Into the mélange of Greenham, women came from all over Britain and beyond, from a multiplicity of backgrounds. They had been brought up in middle-class families and working-class families, in material comfort and without. Their parents were Labour voters and Tories, Communists, Liberals and uncommitted. They were employed part-time and full-time, and unemployed; they were students, housewives and pensioners. They came from rural areas and from cities. They were seasoned political activists and novices. They were feminists and not, socialists, environmentalists, trade unionists, Welsh nationalists, anti-apartheid campaigners, student politicians and the vaguely politically discontented. They came with clear ideas about what was wrong in the world. They came as respectable heterosexual mothers and grand-mothers, and as lesbians, dykes and gay women, and as women in turmoil about their sexuality. They came suspicious and enthusiastic, passionate and waiting to be convinced.

Yet there were patterns in this diversity. Obviously it was easier for young, fit, able-bodied women without the ties of children or full-time work and a mortgage to live or spend time at Greenham. Women whose time was relatively flexible were the prime candidates. Illness, infirmity and physical disabilities would have made the outdoor life of Greenham impossible for some women. Sole responsibility for children or sick or disabled relatives prevented others from being involved. Antagonistic husbands and demanding jobs impinged on many. So it was that of the women I interviewed, 60 per cent were under 31, 60 per cent were not in paid employment, and 80 per cent did not have children under the age of 18 at the time they became involved with Greenham.

That said, many women, including a significant number of those I interviewed, did not fit this profile of the young, non-working, child-free Greenham woman. The exceptions were numerous. Women in their forties, fifties, sixties and older got involved with Greenham. Many women, particularly stayers and visitors, had children but successfully negotiated childcare with partners, friends and family.[18] Women with jobs, full-time, part-time and self-employed, made decisions to reorganize their lives to enable them to live or spend time at Greenham. Having domestic and work responsibilities did not inevitably rule out involvement.

In terms of political background, the Greenham women shared, as a base line, a critical attitude towards some aspects of the social and political status quo. Beyond this they were quite diverse. There were considerable numbers of experienced political activists, well versed in campaigning in social movements, pressure groups and political parties. Some were still involved at the time when they first went to Greenham and regarded Greenham as the logical extension of their existing activism. Rather more had become disillusioned, often with the bureaucratic processes and male domination of these organizations, and had withdrawn from them. A substantial proportion had taken part in the peace movement, either in the 1950s and 1960s, or in the new wave of the early 1980s. A smaller number had been involved in left-wing political parties, trade unions and student politics, and, in the late 1970s, in environmentalism, the Anti-Nazi League, and opposition to nuclear power.

As far as feminism was concerned, there was a wide range of previous experience and attitudes amongst those who were to become Greenham women. Some were committed feminists who had been members of consciousness-raising groups and had taken part in feminist street protests, such as Reclaim the Night marches and pro-abortion rallies. The pre-existing feminists were particularly likely to have been involved in campaigning about violence against women and about women's health and reproductive rights. Some identified as radical feminists, others as lesbian feminists, socialist feminists, or just feminists. Far more women, however, while expressing more or less generalized dissatisfaction with the existing gender order, had not been active in the women's liberation movement. Some thought of themselves as feminists, but many did not. To adopt the identity 'feminist' in the early 1980s still required considerable bravery, and 'I'm not a feminist, but ...' was a phrase often on women's lips.

Many Greenham women had been brought up in homes where radical politics of various kinds were the stuff of everyday conversation. Some of the older women were the daughters of suffrage campaigners and others had parents or grandparents who had been active in the Labour Party and in the peace movement of the late 1950s and early 1960s. Growing up in such households equipped women with a political consciousness and a sense of entitlement to engage in politics which tended to set them apart from their peers, and made their activism as adults more likely. But it was not the case that every woman who got involved with Greenham had grown up in a radical or politically aware environment. A number came from conservative families, from military backgrounds, and from homes where politics were never discussed. They often had their first contact with radical politics as students and developed their sense of political efficacy through their education and in the world of student politics.

Almost everyone, however, had some connection to what might be called 'counter-cultural networks' - either overtly politicized, as in the case of campaigning groups, or in a social context, such as groups of friends who were 'hippies', 'alternative types', vegetarians, co-counsellors, feminists, lesbians or punks. The most common way that women were drawn to Greenham was through these connections. The enthusiasm of a friend and encouragement to come along on a trip to the camp or to a local meeting helped to break down the barriers of fear, awe and inertia which could militate against getting involved.

THE INTERVIEWEES

The following tables provide a profile of the women I interviewed.[19]

Table 1   *Age at first involvement*

| Age | No. |
| --- | --- |
| 17 - 20 | 5 |
| 21 - 30 | 16 |
| 31 - 40 | 7 |
| 41 - 50 | 2 |
| 51 - 60 | 3 |
| 61 + | 2 |

Table 2   *Employment status at time of getting involved*

| Employment status | No. |
|---|---|
| Unemployed | 8 |
| Regular full-time paid employment | 7 |
| 'Housewives'/carers | 6 |
| Self-employed | 4 |
| Regular part-time paid employment | 3 |
| Extended travelling | 3 |
| Retired | 2 |
| Full-time education | 2 |

Table 3   *Number of children*

| No. of children | No. |
|---|---|
| 0 | 21 |
| 1 | 1 |
| 2 | 7 |
| 3 | 3 |
| 4 | 1 |
| 5 | 2 |

Table 4   *Self-defined class status*

| Class | No. |
|---|---|
| Middle | 19 |
| Working | 11 |
| Don't know/no reply | 5 |

Table 5   *Education*

| Highest level completed | No. |
|---|---|
| Postgraduate degree | 3 |
| Undergraduate degree | 15 |
| Nursing diploma | 2 |
| School | 16 |

Table 6   *Ethnicity*

| Ethnic identification | No. |
| --- | --- |
| White English | 21 |
| White Welsh | 6 |
| White Irish | 3 |
| Jewish | 5 |
| White Australian | 1 |

Table 7   *Previous political involvement*[20]

| Political campaign/movement | No. |
| --- | --- |
| Peace movement (1950s/1960s) | 5 |
| Peace movement (1979–) | 17 |
| Plaid Cymru (Welsh Nationalist Party) | 3 |
| Communist Party | 2 |
| Labour Party | 1 |
| International Marxist Group | 1 |
| Environmentalism/anti-nuclear power | 5 |
| Women's Aid | 4 |
| Reclaim the Night marches | 3 |
| Women's health/reproductive rights | 2 |
| Student politics | 3 |
| Anti-apartheid | 2 |
| Trade unions | 2 |
| Alternative/left journalism | 2 |
| Anti-Nazi League | 1 |

WHY DID THEY GET INVOLVED?

Women got involved with Greenham for many different reasons and their reasons for continuing to be involved changed over time. Human motivation is a complex matter, involving both conscious thought processes and the less rational, emotional and more submerged impulses which drive our actions. And so it was with Greenham.

Most women, when asked directly, would proffer the most obvious and acceptable reason for their involvement: to protest against Cruise missiles, against nuclear militarism and against the momentum towards nuclear annihilation. Nuclear fear, and the anger this generated, were powerful driving motivators. For some nuclear fear took a maternalist form, focusing on the threat to their children, while for others it was experienced intensely personally as fear for their own life and future. A few went to Greenham with an already clearly articulated feminist position on nuclear weapons and their connection to patriarchal gender relations.

Disillusion with conventional political processes and the traditional methods of anti-nuclear campaigning contributed to women's will-ingness to take the bold steps necessary to go to Greenham. Joining CND, attending meetings, signing petitions and going on annual demonstrations seemed inadequate, given the gravity of the situation. Greenham offered a more direct and radical form of politics, one that captured the imagination and the emotions in ways that the mainstream peace movement did not.

But while opposition to Cruise was the main unifying factor behind Greenham's existence, its importance to individual women depended on their own political and personal priorities. For most it ebbed and flowed. Not everyone was initially well informed about the state of the arms race; some experienced a vague sense of dis-ease and it was only at Greenham that they came to understand its extent and dangers. And there were some women for whom the issue of nuclear weapons was of very little salience as a reason for getting involved. For them Greenham was less a site for anti-nuclear protest and more the chance to live in a radical, queer feminist community. Women did not stay at Greenham, or keep coming back, out of 'pure' opposition to Cruise. Greenham met a whole range of desires, some consciously expressed, others less so. As a women-only community, where women could experience a sense of ownership, participation, and collective and personal power, Greenham exercised a tangible pull towards involvement. The social and cultural facets of Greenham – the strong friendships, the transient encounters, the intense discussions, the singing, dancing and fun of everyday life and the excitement of actions – kept women living there and drew them back. And the lesbian community of Greenham, where love, affection and sexual attraction between women could be freely expressed and where women could explore their sexuality in new ways, was a reason why women got involved and continued to be involved. Some were aware of this at the outset, for many more it became apparent only with time. Greenham was a place where women engaged in projects of self-transformation. In retrospect many saw the desire to enact change in their lives as having propelled them there.

As Penni Bestic, talking about why women went to Greenham, put it:

> I think women came to escape from awful situations at home. I think women came because they were really angry. I think women came because they were powerless, because they wanted to be empowered. I think women came there because it was the thing to do. I think women came there because it was a lesbian society. I think women came there because they wanted to do something. I think women came there because they wanted to be heard. I think women came there because they wanted to have fun. I think women came because they were anarchists. I think women came because they were socialists. I think women came there because they were liberals. I think women came there because it was women. All of those reasons, and two of those reasons, and three of those reasons. And they're all valid.
>
> *Penni Bestic*

PEN PORTRAITS

*Simone Wilkinson*
Simone Wilkinson was a 36-year-old, middle-class housewife and mother of two who lived on the Isle of Wight.

> I had got involved because I did feel that the world was about to end if somebody didn't do something. It came like a kind of

thunderbolt for me. I went into a terrible depression for a while. I had these terrible dreams about what would happen if my children were at school and nuclear war broke out. My whole life was absorbed in this fear that my children, not even that they might die, but that they might actually live and I might be crawling around in some half-life state.

It had started to impinge on my consciousness when I was pregnant with Victoria. And I remember a woman telling me during that pregnancy that in Hiroshima when a woman became pregnant nobody congratulated her; they just waited in silence for nine months. And because I was actually carrying a child when I was told that, that really touched me somewhere very deeply.

Through a friend Simone got involved in hosting a Mothers for Peace exchange trip by mothers from the Soviet Union to the south of England. She felt an immediate bonding with the Russian women, despite the language barriers. This experience crystallized her emerging political consciousness about 'the ideology of hatred' which fuelled the Cold War, and she joined her local CND group. To her disappointment she found that her sense of imminent danger, and her passion and energy, were considered excessive by others in the group, and she was left unsatisfied by the annual march in London. Amongst her circle of friends she felt an outsider.

Looking back on it all, the people that were involved in my social life obviously thought I had completely gone off my rocker, and I suppose, to some degree, I had. I mean, I couldn't stop talking about it. I wanted people to understand and catch that sense of danger. I couldn't understand why people were living normal lives and just getting on with it.

Then she discovered Greenham. It was September 1981 when a woman she knew through Mothers for Peace told her about the camp that had been set up at Greenham five or six days earlier.

I knew that day that I had to be involved with it. It was just an incredible feeling. I got there and I remember saying to Eunice, who was a Welsh grandmother, is it alright if I make a cup of tea?

And she said, you know, of course, it's your camp. And I thought, god, this is amazing, because what she actually said, very simply, was that anybody who comes here is the camp. And that was a really amazing feeling for me. And just talking to women that day and listening to the way that they talked, I understood it because they were talking with the same passion that I was feeling, and nobody had understood it where I had been for the last nine months. They just understood it, and you weren't considered a lunatic if you gave voice to the despair that you were feeling. And women said, yeah, I know what that feels like. And that was such a relief.

And things were never the same again.

I came home that night, and in my household all the major discussions took place around the breakfast table. So next morning I was there with my now ex-husband and two children, and one of the kids said, how did you get on? And I said, it was great, but you're going to have to get used to managing without me, because I've got to spend time there. And it was the first time in my life I wasn't asking permission. I was telling them, all of them, what I was going to do. I just said, there's nothing to talk about, because that's what I'm doing. I'd made up my mind I was going to do it, and I was going to do it. And that was the beginning of my involvement. And so I started going up there regularly, four or five days at a time, and eventually more and more.

*Penni Bestic*
In contrast to Simone, 31-year-old Penni Bestic had been involved in feminist, socialist and Welsh nationalist politics for many years. As a lesbian with no children, and working as a freelance graphic designer in Cardiff, the process of getting involved with Greenham was relatively trouble-free.

I felt that what was happening there was very important, because it seemed to be an effective way of focusing a message. And I also wanted to be part of it, because I was very, very angry, and I had never been in a position to do anything very concrete about my anger. I was angry about nuclear weapons and about military power, and about patriarchy, and men, and all that, and colonialism, and neo-colonialism, and it just seemed that the ultimate expression of all those things that I'd fought against was there in nuclear weapons. They were the most clear and most apparent manifestation of patriarchal power. It sounds like Oscar Wilde: to possess one nuclear weapon is criminal, but to possess how ever many millions of them is just utter lunacy. It seemed to be a complete madness, and it just seemed to show up the madness of men, and all the things that they did, and how they destroy the planet.

She visited Greenham a few times in 1982 and 1983, but it was one particular moment in 1983 when she felt herself being hooked and made the decision to go and live there.

There was just something very magical about it. I went down there a couple of times, and it just seemed to have that extraordinary energy there. If I'm honest about it, it wasn't just the politics, it was about the women's energy, which was just what I needed. A sort of boost. I think a lot of women drew on that energy and put it back in again, as well. It was really exciting. I remember being really, really aware of that at Hallowe'en because I was at the Plaid Cymru [the Welsh Nationalist Party] conference and we knew that they were going to take the fence down. A whole group of women at this conference all knew about it. Sian came back and said, 'It's down.' And all the women there just let out this great huge whoop. And all the men were sitting there, going, 'What's happened?' And we just said, 'The fence has come down at Greenham. And they said, 'Why didn't you tell us?' They turned to their wives and said, 'Why didn't you tell me about this?' It was just tremendous.

And I just decided I was going to go there. So I got on the train, and I got the bus up to Yellow Gate. I hadn't thought much about it, I just knew it was what I was going to do.

### The Porth Women

Susan Lamb was a housewife and mother, living in the small town of Porth, in the Rhondha Valley in south Wales. She and her extended family - Lynne Fortt, Christine King and Lesley Brinkworth - were a tightly knit group of sisters in their twenties, who became aware of the nuclear threat with the decision to site Cruise missiles in the UK. Their propulsion into activism was their fear of nuclear war. For Susan, this took the form of feeling that her work as a mother, particularly teaching her children about the value of honesty, was directly threatened by nuclear weapons.[21]

> The thing that triggered me into doing something was my daughter. We are in the flight path for Heathrow and every plane that went over, she said, 'Mummy, Mummy, they're going to bomb us.' The only way I could calm her fears was to tell her lies, which is not what I want to be doing. So I had to face my own bloody fears about it. So about a week later there was the first resurgence of our CND group and they held their first meeting and I went. It was through that we became involved with Greenham.
>
> *Susan Lamb*

The Porth women joined their local CND group early in 1981 and before long were elected to the committee. Never having thought of themselves as feminists, their anger was stirred very quickly by two things: first by discovering the lack of interest within CND in spreading information about Greenham, which was seen as the marginal activity of a few women, and second by the political inertia and traditional attitudes towards gender roles of the women in their home town.

> We'd done a leafleting drop about making Porth a nuclear-free zone, and then we went back a couple of weeks later to pick up the forms. Everybody had put them behind the clock, and oh yeah, they'd meant to, they had meant to fill them in, and they hadn't. And all these women, I couldn't believe it, I'd knock on people's doors and they'd say, 'Oh, I can't say anything about that, my husband's not in. I leave important decisions like that to my husband'. This was 1981. It was an eye-opener. There was so little positive opposition. It was something like 6 per cent who actually said, well, I actually believe in the bomb. All the rest said it was too depressing, and there's nothing I can do about it. I don't want to think about it, or they signed it, except for this group of women who kept saying, 'Oh, I leave important decisions to my husband.' The majority of women.

So we thought we can't just leaflet people because they just don't listen, they don't read the stuff. So as we got more and more pissed one night, we thought maybe the idea would be to get a group of us and go and live in the open and say, this is what women are doing, and this is why. So we went to Greenham and asked if they thought it was a good idea, well, we asked their permission. They said, oh this is wonderful, this is just what we want. So we did it. We lived in Porth Square for a week. It was November by now. We used the police station's toilet all week, they'd offered us the key. Five of us went down, and six of us stayed all week. And straight afterwards, the local council declared itself a nuclear-free zone. It worked.

*Susan Lamb*

This local Greenham-style action also worked in combating the grip of nuclear fear.

I got involved basically because I was frightened to go to sleep. I kept on having nightmares about nuclear war. And it was so real. I'd feel the heat on my back in the nightmare, and the skin on my back coming off in my hands. It was that real, and I was afraid to go to sleep. So I joined CND, and it didn't go away. I did Porth Square, and it all went away. I never had one of them again.

*Christine King*

After Porth Square, there was no turning back for Susan, Lynne, Christine and Lesley. Although they had complicated childcare arrangements to negotiate with their families, and so little money that they always had to hitch, they started going to Greenham regularly, as well as continuing their campaigning back in their home town.

*Liz Galst*

It was not just women who had children who were driven by their nuclear fear to go to Greenham. Liz Galst was a 20-year-old dyke from New York, just in the process of coming out, who had recently dropped out of the University of Michigan. Growing up in the 1970s in a Jewish family with a liberal feminist mother, she had been interested in feminism and the environment for many years. For Liz the impetus towards anti-nuclear activism was a very real and constant sense of the seriousness of the nuclear threat. Although she had been aware of the nuclear issue for as long as she could remember, it was hearing Helen Caldicott, an Australian doctor and anti-nuclear campaigner, speak at a conference when she was a student which made it all suddenly much more tangible.

> It had this tremendous impact on me. She cites all these amazing statistics which make you feel like any second a bomb is going to explode under your chair, which is exactly how I felt. She provides all this information about near-misses and crazy computer systems, and I just felt incredibly panicked when I heard her. It put a lot of energy into me. And that was around the time when the big demonstrations were happening in Europe about Cruise missiles, and I was really inspired by that.

Like many Jews of the post-Holocaust generation, Liz had grown up with a highly developed belief in each individual's personal responsibility to take action against harmful practices, and this underpinned her determination to do something about the threat of a nuclear catastrophe.

> Bruno Bettelheim wrote that part of the problem with the way that a lot of people dealt with the Holocaust was that they tried to act like everything was normal and that they could just go about their normal business. I had learnt all my life about the Holocaust and had been very carefully brought up to never let it happen again, and that was always my motivation.

At university she had been involved in anti-militarist campaigns against the city's civil defence preparations and had been part of a political film group which programmed radical films and used the money they made to fund their political activities. In the summer of 1983 Liz spent several weeks at the women's peace camp at Seneca in upstate New York. This was an exciting experience during which, for the first time, she met other young lesbians who were concerned about similar issues.

> We got there, and I remember the first night, it was sunset, and we all stood in this circle, and we counted how many people there

were, and there were a hundred people there, and I just felt incredibly moved that people had come from all over the place and really cared, and like we were at the beginning of this big exciting thing and this was going to be a really powerful experience and not just for us. I felt like this is really going to change things. And it was a really wild experience for me in terms of my coming out, because in Ann Arbor one of the reasons why I didn't identify as a dyke earlier was because all of the lesbians I knew were just really boring. They wore flannel shirts and jeans and all had the same short haircut that didn't do anything for them at all, and were only involved in their own world, and were not involved in the kind of political stuff that I was interested in. So at Seneca there were all these incredible women from New York. I was just like a puppy dog. I would just look around with my big eyes and stare at all these women. I just thought, OK, this is it. I'm here now.

Back in New York after Seneca, Liz started working to support the court case which was being brought by a group of Greenham women (including Simone and the Porth women) against the United States government. Increasingly she felt pulled towards Greenham and in December 1983 she and three friends from Seneca flew to England to visit the camp. Liz ended up staying at Greenham for nearly two years.

I felt like, the world is going to explode at any minute and why am I going to college? I mean, why go on with your life in this normal way when you feel like the world is about to blow up? ... A lot of us who were really young then couldn't really imagine anything past five years from then. I mean it's amazing to me that I've made this age of twenty-seven, given the amount of nuclear weapons in the world. It really distorted our perspective on time.

### Rowan Gwedhen

Rowan Gwedhen was a 24-year-old lesbian who had recently moved to London from Plymouth and was on the dole, having previously worked as a clerical officer. She had a generalized opposition to nuclear weapons and an interest in feminism before she got involved with Greenham, but she didn't know much about Cruise missiles.

I was a dyke. I suppose I was a feminist. I always think I was sort of the wrong way round to a lot of people at Greenham because I was a dyke before Greenham, but it was Greenham really where I came in touch with feminism. I did go to the women's centre in Plymouth, and things like that. But I wasn't in any other sense political. Well, I went on Reclaim the Night and Lesbian Strength marches. That's political, isn't it? ... I don't think I knew much about Cruise missiles.

Once you do something like that you do get caught up in it all, and you do get, yeah, we are here to stop Cruise. I became more involved in that sort of thing once I got to Greenham. Rather than the other way round, of people being involved in that sort of thing and discovering women when they got to Greenham it was more to do with it being women living in that way for me.

Rowan was drawn into involvement with Greenham in 1982 by old friends from Plymouth, Skeeter and Babs, who were already living out there.

The first time I had anything to do with Greenham was going to demonstrate outside the High Court in London, which must have been when the first lot of women got arrested at the Easter blockades. I said to one of my friends, are you coming along to the bop on such and such, and she said, I'll come to the bop with you, if you come with me to the demo. So I went along ...

Anyway, on this demonstration Babs got arrested and we all trudged off to the police station. But it ended up with us all getting into somebody's car and going down to Greenham. We all went back to someone's flat, and we thought, let's go there. And we packed a few things together and we went down there. And that was the first time I went down there, and we stayed the night.

I thought I'd come home. It's the closest thing we've ever got to women's land in this country. I just thought, wow, this is it.

Within a couple of months Rowan had decided to move to Greenham. She stayed for three years.

I was living in a shared house with a couple of women who were lovers and it wasn't working out too well. And I was on the dole, and I'd only been in London about six months and I hadn't found my feet. I didn't have a lot of reasons to stay in London. I didn't give anything up to go to Greenham. I didn't give up a job or a house or anything. It was just quite natural. That trunk [pointing] was it for many years – I didn't have any possessions.

### Bridget Evans[22]

Bridget Evans was also an unemployed lesbian when she got involved with Greenham. Having grown up in a liberal Protestant family in a middle-class area of Belfast, she moved to Liverpool to study politics and sociology at university. There she became politically active in the anti-nuclear power movement and then, when she graduated and was signing on, she began working in the Liverpool CND office five days a week. She was 23 when she went to Greenham.

> To be honest I ended up going there really for a totally personal reason. It must have been around the summer of 1983. I really fell in love with this woman and started to have a relationship with her and it was the first time that I had acknowledged that I was a lesbian and I very quickly became amazingly involved with this woman. And what happened was that we went down together to this thing at Greenham … this pulling down the fence and she loved it, she really, really liked it. So a week later she had some holidays from work and she said, oh look I'm going back down again for a week's holiday because I liked it so much. So that was fine and off she went. But she didn't come back … And she then rang me up and said oh look actually I'm not coming back, I'm spending more time here. And then another few days later, and I think this time she'd been arrested or something, and so she was full of it and then she was saying to me, come down and see me. And then she was saying you know there's people from Liverpool coming all the time here you know, get in touch with somebody and get a lift down. So in fact that's what I did. That's what I did. So I rang up and but what was funny was that I didn't tell her why I was only going down to Greenham to see this woman, to see my girlfriend.
>
> What happened was that it became obvious really quickly that she basically wanted out of our relationship. And that she was like very excited and really on a real high about what was happening at

Greenham and had made loads of friends and really liked loads of other women but basically she didn't want to continue our relationship. She wanted like her freedom to do other things and form other relationships. And I was really, really upset about it. Because that wasn't what I wanted at all. I was really, really upset. But as it turned out I actually got a lot of support from other lesbians at Greenham. So by the end of the first weekend I ended up sort of sitting crying at the campfire.

## Notes

1. I use inverted commas in this discussion to highlight the politically loaded nature of the dominant vocabulary of nuclear weapons, drawing attention to how it seeks to familiarize nuclear weapons, while making claims about their role and functions which are highly contestable, often with strong patriarchal overtones (see Cohn, 1987a, b).
2. Knelman (1985: 30).
3. *Ibid.*: 177.
4. Throughout this period there was also a peace movement in Eastern Europe, though its activities were different, and it was generally more clandestine. Connections were forged between peace activists in Eastern and Western Europe, particularly through organizations such as European Nuclear Disarmament (END) and women's peace groups (see Kaldor *et al.* (1989), Kaldor (1991) and Einhorn (1993)).
5. For example, in 1947 Attlee railroaded the decision to develop the A-bomb through a small subcommittee of the Cabinet, and during the 1974–79 Labour government Callaghan, Healey and Owen secretly went ahead with the Chevaline programme.
6. Cox (1981).
7. For a more detailed narrative of this history see Liddington (1989).
8. The term 'walk' tended to be preferred to 'march' with its military connotations.
9. Folder A, Women for Life on Earth Papers, Mid-Glamorgan County Archive, County Hall, Cardiff. Examples of each group: (i) Southern Region Campaign against the Missiles, local branches of CND, END, World Disarmament Campaign, Campaign against the Arms Trade, Medical Campaign against Nuclear Weapons; (ii) Women's International League for Peace and Freedom, Feminism and Nonviolence Newsletter, Women Oppose the Nuclear Threat, Mothers for Peace; (iii) WIRES – the national women's liberation newsletter, Beyond the Fragments Network – a socialist feminist network; (iv) Plaid Cymru, trade union shop stewards.
10. *Ibid.* Letters of support were sent by a number of well-known women who had been asked to participate, including Sheila Kitzinger, Cleo Laine, Janet Suzman, Glenda Jackson and Margaret Drabble.

11. *Ibid.*, Document 8.
12. The notion of an 'ethic of care' has been developed from Gilligan's (1982) work, and is explored by, for example, Tronto (1993), Bowden (1997) and Sevenhuijsen (1998). Greenham's maternalism was a good example of what Ruddick (1990) calls 'maternal thinking', a maternalism grounded in the material reality of 'maternal practice', the work of preservation, nurturance and training, which is involved in childcare. This work is primarily, though not necessarily, done by women.
13. Document 8, Folder A, Women for Life on Earth Papers, Mid-Glamorgan County Archive, County Hall, Cardiff.
14. *Ibid.*
15. *Ibid.*
16. *Ibid.*
17. Harford and Hopkins (1984: 19).
18. I draw a distinction between women on the basis of their level of involvement with Greenham, differentiating 'campers', 'stayers' and 'visitors'. A 'camper' was a woman who, for a period of time greater than two months, made her home at Greenham; a 'stayer' was a woman who stayed overnight at the camp either regularly or for a period of up to two months; and a 'visitor' was a woman who made daytime visits to Greenham and may have stayed overnight on a few occasions. The two-month period which differentiates 'campers' from 'stayers' is somewhat arbitrary but was chosen as reflecting approximately the length of time taken to integrate into the community of Greenham. Within these categories there is considerable variation. For example, the category 'camper' includes women who lived at Greenham for between 2 months and 4 years; women who had no other home besides the camp; those who maintained a home away from Greenham while living there; women who did not leave the camp for months on end; others who went back to their place of origin every fortnight for a few days to sign on and rest, or even lived split weeks at the camp and at home (e.g. because of childcare). The 'visitor' category includes women who visited the camp between four and a hundred times. The level of involvement category says nothing about the level of involvement in local women's peace groups.

    The other problem with these categories is that women's involvement in Greenham tended to be fluid in form and degree, changing over time. Thus I categorized each woman by her highest level of involvement, so the number of visitors interviewed does not reflect the number of women in the sample who had experienced being a visitor. The sample was deliberately skewed in favour of campers and does not reflect the level of involvement of the population of women who were involved with Greenham, which overwhelmingly consisted of visitors.
19. For a discussion of the sexual identities of interviewees, see p. 291.
20. This table does not show involvement with a campaign or movement if that involvement was no more than paper membership. To figure in the totals, a woman's involvement had to have included at least participation in a demonstration, petitioning or regular attendance at meetings. However, the table

does not differentiate between degrees of involvement, so that the level of involvement of, for example, Carol Harwood, who had been imprisoned in the 1960s for peace actions, is not marked out from that of others who merely attended a few demonstrations.

21. The explanation given by Susan Lamb for her involvement resonates with Ruddick's (1990) notion of the contradiction between maternal practice and the effects of militarism.

22. 'Bridget Evans' is a pseudonym, at the request of the interviewee. 'Bridget Evans' was a name often given by groups of Greenham women as an act of non-cooperation when arrested or stopped by police.

# Chapter 4
# Geographies of Greenham

Greenham was at once both a real place and a set of connections across space between people and places. It was a community of women who physically lived together at the camp, and it was also a network of women, an 'imagined community', which stretched across Britain and beyond.[1] Greenham the place, the camp, had a tangible location which can be marked on a map. Greenham the network was composed of local, regional, national and global flows of ideas, actions and women.

While the camp was both the spatial materiality of Greenham and the focal point and centre of the larger Greenham network, neither the camp nor the network were constrained by this and neither were fixed in form over time. The camp was all about its location outside the US Air Force (USAF) base where Cruise missiles were to be stationed, yet its vision and actions were never bound by this. There existed a passion to transcend the physical location, to make links across the globe, at the same time always resisting efforts to forcibly remove its presence from the Common. And Greenham's anarchist ethos determined an openness and fluidity of form over time, a supple dynamism and a chosen chaos in its patterns of (dis)organization. Compared with conventional forms of politics, and even other social movements and alternative communities, both the camp and the network were 'structureless'. Greenham lacked many of the institutions and procedures which serve to freeze communities and political organizations. No constitution, no articles of association, no standing orders to govern meetings, no executive committee, no membership list, no officers, no annual general meetings, no head office existed. This meant that the internal lay of the land was constantly changing, always moving.

## The Greenham Network

The Greenham network as a whole was often likened to a spider's web by the women involved. Playing with popular images of the ensnaring female spider, linked in fairy tales and folklore with witches, Greenham women overturned the fear and loathing of spiders thought commonplace amongst women and embraced the spider and her web as symbols of women's strength. An intricate pattern of individuals and groups, joined together by almost invisible threads, the Greenham web might have appeared fragile, but its strength rested in this supple translucence. The threads which linked the women could not be seen by those who looked for the traditional markers of political organization, but they were clear to those they bound together. They were the ties of friendship, emotional and affective bonds, shared values and an identity forged in common, the identity of 'Greenham woman'. The invisibility of these connections to outsiders was protective; it made the Greenham network hard to locate and almost impossible for its enemies to infiltrate. And like a spider's web, the building of the network was never finished; it was continuously in creation, never static. New women and new groups could be seamlessly woven into its fabric, expanding it outwards, and when women dropped out of involvement, or the activities of local groups lulled, connections could be made around and beyond them.

The network was composed of tens of thousands of individual women throughout Britain, and thousands beyond. Some related directly to the camp, focusing their activities on visits to Greenham alone or with small groups of friends. Most were also involved in local groups and engaged in actions in their home towns, as well as spending time at the camp. Between 1981 and 1987 dozens of groups sprang up across the country, one or more in almost every town and city in England, Wales and Scotland. They were completely autonomous and there was no hierarchy. Each group had connections back to the camp, which was at the hub of the network; those connections were sustained by frequent visits to the camp, by the 'Green and Common' newsletters produced at the camp and sent to contacts around the country to be photocopied and passed on, and, after the arrival of Cruise, by an elaborate telephone tree which was activated when the convoy was brought out on exercise. The camp acted as a clearing house for information within the network.[2]

Although there was no information officer and rarely even a noticeboard or box for incoming mail, some women living at the camp, such as Katrina Allen, took it upon themselves to act as conduits for news.

> I saw Greenham as being a focal point of information, and I used to spend quite a lot of time talking to people who'd come there, trying to keep up with what was happening in other places so that people could know what was going on. At that stage it was very much a centre of what was happening, and people were coming down for weekends, and I felt that if I was a more permanent person there, one of the things I could do was talk about what other people were doing and different actions that people were doing, so that it would be passed around.
>
> *Katrina Allen*

Although the camp was the heart of the network, it was not its headquarters. Ideas for actions were generated at the camp, in local groups and at regional meetings of local groups. Over time the web-like connections between local groups became stronger and information was increasingly passed on by telephone and newsletter; it did not necessarily pass through the camp. Above all the network was sustained by personal relationships among women and the pleasure that women took in each other's company. Friendships existed between women who lived at the camp and women in local groups, and between women involved in different local groups, so that the pleasurable activities of sharing news and gossip with friends, and the discussion and debating of ideas, were also the political activity of the Greenham network.

The local groups were generally embedded in wider networks of feminist, peace and green activists in their localities. Many of them held their meetings in women's centres, advertised in feminist newsletters, alternative bookshops and wholefood stores, and usually included members who were involved with the local women's refuge, rape crisis and lesbian lines, as well as Labour and Green Party branches and the mixed peace movement. They would often use the local CND office and resources.

Like the network as a whole, local groups did not have a formal membership or demand fees. They varied in size from six (as initially in towns like Derby and Northampton) to over several hundred (in Manchester in 1983), with many towns and cities sustaining groups of between thirty and fifty active members by 1983-84 (e.g. Cardiff, Derby, Leeds, Merseyside, Nottingham). Some of the larger groups decided to divide into smaller neighbourhood groups when they grew too large for discussions and decision-making to involve everyone, and there were groups in most London boroughs.[3] There was no single model. Some called themselves 'Greenham Support Groups' and focused particularly on raising money and providing resources for the camp, arranging visits to Greenham and publicizing Greenham in their locality. Other groups were 'Women for Peace' groups and were less Greenham orientated in their actions. Two of the earliest groups to be set up (in Leeds and Nottingham) called themselves 'Women Oppose the Nuclear Threat' (WONT) and in Cardiff there was 'Women For Life On Earth', but all of these later renamed themselves 'Women for Peace'. In general, over time all the local groups tended to focus less on the camp and developed instead their own particular interests. South London Women for Peace, for instance, developed connections with women's groups in Eritrea, while Merseyside Women for Peace focused on the nuclear plant at Capenhurst, the Cardiff group on the Royal Ordinance Factory. The Portsmouth group took to the sea in small boats to protest against naval nuclear militarism. Women's peace camps were also set up for varying lengths of time at other US bases around Britain, drawing attention to the extent of nuclear militarism across the country. The Greenham network spread across Europe to Denmark, The Netherlands, West and East Germany and Italy, and to the United States, Canada, Australia and New Zealand. Individual women travelled from Greenham and from local women's peace groups to women's peace camps inspired by Greenham in these countries, and women from each of these countries (and many others) visited Greenham.

## The Camp

Whilst the *imagined* community of Greenham stretched across Britain and beyond, the *material* community of Greenham was composed of the women who made their daily lives together outside the base at Greenham Common. The base covered an area of approximately

950 acres, and was situated four miles from the town of Newbury, Berkshire. It occupied common land which had been requisitioned by the Ministry of Defence for use by the RAF during the Second World War. It had subsequently been handed over to the USAF in 1950. Inside the base there were scores of buildings – offices, aircraft hangars, sleeping quarters, recreational facilities and shops for the US military personnel. There was an old runway and an air traffic control tower, upgraded for the arrival of Cruise, and plenty of space to build the missile silos. A nine-mile perimeter fence enclosed the base, fencing it off from the rather wild and beautiful common land which surrounded it. In 1981, when the camp was set up, there were eight vehicle gates and one pedestrian gate into the base and a number of gaps (sections of fence which could be rolled back to allow access for vehicles).[4]

THE HISTORY OF THE GATES

At the time of the first major gathering at the camp, the Equinox Festival on 21 March 1982 (in which men were still involved), some of the gates were given names: New Age Gate, Forgotten Gate, Religious Gate, Artists' Gate, Music Gate. The idea behind this was to encourage the involvement of different sectors of the 'alternative scene' by identifying particular places for them to gather at the festival. However, the Equinox Festival had not been popular with many of the women at the camp who focused their energies on the women-only blockade the next day, and before long the gates were renamed using the colours of the rainbow: 'Main Gate' (later called 'Yellow'), 'Green', ('Turquoise'), 'Blue', 'Indigo', 'Violet', 'Red' and 'Orange'. These names stuck and before long even the Ministry of Defence (MoD) police were using them. Very quickly the names came to refer less to the gates themselves and rather to the camp at each gate. When new camps were established at places where there had been no gate in 1982, they were named using this colour scheme. 'Woad' was the name chosen for the camp outside the new gate which was erected in 1985 by the MoD between the old Indigo and Violet Gates, and 'Emerald' was the camp set up in 1984 between Green and Turquoise.[5]

For the first sixteen months in the life of Greenham there was just one camp – outside the Main Gate, which at the time was the only gate in daily use. The camp varied in size during this period from about five women to over fifty, with numbers swelling into the hundreds during the March blockade in 1982 and into the tens of thousands during the weekend of the Embrace the Base/Close the Base action, December 12-13 1982. The month that followed the huge success of that weekend saw an enormous amount of media coverage of Greenham, particularly after the silos action on 1 January 1983, in which women climbed into the base and danced on the missile silos. In the wake of these two actions and all the related reportage, large numbers of visitors and a constant influx of journalists made life at Main Gate hectic and often tense for the women living there. The number of campers was steadily increasing, and although women had started building benders (see p. 93) and pitching tents in the clearing away from the area immediately in front of the gate, the land was becoming crowded.

So on 20 January 1983 a small group of women moved themselves, their possessions and some basic cooking equipment to the woods near Green Gate to set up a new camp. These women explained their motivation in terms of the problems of living at Main Gate, which they felt was overcrowded and lacking in privacy. They wanted to live somewhere quieter without the constant intrusion of male visitors and the press. The physical environment at Green Gate was much pleasanter. The camp was in the woods, about two hundred yards from the fence, and half a mile up a quiet country lane, Brackenhurst Lane, from the busy A339. From its establishment, Green Gate was entirely women-only. Men were not accepted as visitors and were turned away first by notices along the path leading to the camp from Brackenhurst Lane and, if they persisted, by women from the camp.

During a huge influx of women for the week of the July blockades in 1983 two further camps were set up, at Blue Gate and Orange Gate. Women had camped at both during large actions on a number of previous occasions, but it was not until this point that a conscious decision was taken by women committed to living at Greenham to have camps there. The final phase of expansion was in December 1983, shortly after the arrival of the first missiles. During this month hundreds of women stayed at the camp for periods of several days and more, and on 11 December over 50,000 women gathered at the base to protest. Suddenly the number of women living or staying at

Greenham multiplied significantly, and camps were set up at Violet Gate (7 December 1983), Red Gate (12 December 1983), Turquoise Gate (18 December 1993) and Indigo Gate (31 December 1983).

There appeared to be two main reasons for the establishment of new camps:

> I felt it was crucial that we have camps all around. Simply to be visible to the people, the drivers, who went round the north side. Smaller camps were nice as well. And in some ways it was easier to work in smaller groups, to get things like the shopping and the cooking done. You did actually end up working better together, whereas in a big camp, it was just come and help yourself to get things. It was more difficult to get things done.
>
> *Carola Addington*

Following the arrival of the first Cruise missiles in November 1983 many women believed that it was important that women maintain a visible presence outside every gate. Activity within the base had heightened and more of the gates were being routinely used by civilian and military personnel. Having camps right around the base extended the impact of the protest and also enabled women to monitor the operations of the base in anticipation of military exercises. This became increasingly important once the convoy of missile launchers and support vehicles began to be taken out of the base on night exercises. Night watches at camps all around the base meant that the exit of the convoy could be monitored and the 'Cruisewatch' network of activists dedicated to disrupting these exercises alerted.

Perhaps even more importantly there was also the problem of size. As the number of women living at any gate increased, physical space became a problem. It became more difficult to stay warm, as there wasn't room around the fire for everyone, and it became harder to cook communal meals. Much-valued communal living was put under strain. As new women arrived it was harder to maintain a sense of equal and shared involvement in both the chores of daily life and in decision-making. Women experienced the anonymity of larger numbers as tiring and stressful. The close bonds of friendship and shared experience between women who had lived together through intense periods of activism, which were vital in holding the camp together, were weakened. Setting up new camps at other gates helped to renew small-group bonding, at least until, in their turn, the new camps themselves grew too large.

Rowan Gwedhen, who during her three years at Greenham lived at several different gates, explained:

> It did start getting very difficult at Yellow. It got too big. It just couldn't work communally on that scale ... I suppose it still worked, in the sense that we had enough to eat, but it got too big to be a group. I think Yellow Gate became a lot of individual people as opposed to a communal thing.

Towards the end of 1983, with the missiles arriving and the numbers of women at Greenham increasing daily, Rowan and another woman from Yellow (Main) Gate set up Red Gate.

> I wanted to leave the Main Gate. I couldn't cope there any more. It had got too big ... When I moved there, it ... was like a little women's land. It got bigger and bigger. It got so big that you didn't like all the people. And it got to the point where we had Bender City over one side, quote 'long-term' ... So me and Mary went and set up Red Gate ... For me it was about getting away from Yellow Gate. It was about, it was actually about creating a nice place again and getting back to the thing about women's land and community ... And it was all about making a nice environment and eating good food. I don't mean being vegan, I mean eating well ... And we made these lovely benders, and we had a guest bender. And I actually made this big fitted kitchen. There was a bit of old concrete at Red Gate, and we hung polythene from the trees. I think we actually *bought* wood. And I made this wonderful kitchen with worktops and shelves and everything ... Basically I think me and Mary were in a fucking mess. I didn't want to leave camp. I wanted to stay at camp. By then there'd been actions and prisons and evictions, and 20,000 people living in a goldfish bowl at Yellow Gate.
>
> *Rowan Gwedhen*

Once there were camps at all the gates, this form of (dis)organization was not set in stone; as circumstances changed, so the structure changed. Although there were camps at Yellow Gate and Blue Gate until the base was closed, the other camps came and went over time. Orange Gate and Green Gate existed for longer than Violet and Indigo/Woad, and Turquoise, Red and Emerald had the shortest existence. From mid-1984 onwards, these six camps would be set up and closed down as and when there were women at Greenham who wished to spend time there.

The geographical location of each of the gates and their relative significance to the operations of the base influenced the survival of some camps and the closure of others. Yellow Gate and Blue Gate were, for a long time, the two most important entrances and exits and were located closest to main roads. This meant both that women had easier access to these gates from Newbury and that more passers-by would see camps at these gates. The north side gates (Red, Violet and Indigo/Woad), in contrast, were passed only by a B road and there was only a narrow verge on which to camp. They were less comfortable gates at which to live. Women were closer to the fence, to the soldiers, and hence to harassment, and had less privacy. Green Gate occupied by the far the most tranquil and beautiful location (in woods), but when numbers dwindled at Blue Gate, women at Green would tend to feel it important to keep a presence there and so would move to Blue. The camp at Orange Gate was also far enough away from the fence for women to be afforded some respite from the attentions of the soldiers, but by 1986 women from Orange Gate moved to Yellow and Blue in order to keep them open.

THE CHARACTERS OF THE GATES

Most women who lived at Greenham and who spent periods of time staying there, and even many visitors, developed passionate attachments to a particular gate. Their gate was their home, or their connection to the camp, the place where they felt comfortable and really part of a community. Often these identifications to a particular gate developed by chance: many women's 'home' gate was just the first one they visited or stayed at, often because its was a friend's gate. Orange and Blue Gates often recruited because of their locations. Orange Gate became particularly popular with groups of women who visited Greenham in minibuses and coaches, because there was plenty of space to park; these women tended to be older and middle-class, often from the south of England and south Wales. Blue Gate, as the gate closest to Newbury, was the gate at which many younger women first arrived who had travelled to Greenham alone by public transport or hitching; many of them were working-class, from the north of England and Scotland.

Penny Gulliver described how this applied to the women with whom she lived at Blue Gate in 1983-4.

> I certainly think after all of us had been there a while, none of us would have dreamt of staying at any other camp but Blue ... Some women came from other camps, and came to live at Blue, but generally it was people who hadn't any transport who'd come a long way and didn't catch a bus from town to Yellow Gate. They actually walked the signposted way - if you walk the signposted way from the station, you end up at Blue Gate. And I think that's all there is in it.

As communities developed at each gate, a clustering began to take effect. The gates came to be thought of in particular ways and women who wished to live or associate with others with whom they had certain things in common gathered at particular gates. This started with the establishment of Green Gate. Those who left Main Gate because they wanted a quieter, more private life in the woods set a precedent for how Green Gate was to develop. It tended in future to attract women who shared some of the preferences and characteristics of those who were already there - lesbian feminist politics, a desire to be in a women-only space or to live in the woods, a particular interest in environmental issues or spirituality. Those who remained at Main Gate tended to be those who thrived on the buzz of media attention, the constant streams of visitors and a feeling of being at the hub of the camp. A similar spiralling effect occurred at the other gates and very quickly they developed quite distinctive characters. There was, however, only one gate which was explicitly set up on the basis of difference, where everyone choosing to live there was expected to conform. Turquoise was set up by women from Blue Gate who wanted to live in a vegan zone where there would be no animal products of any kind.

One of the favourite topics of conversation around the campfires at Greenham was the character of each of the gates. There, and in the stories about Greenham that women told me, there were clear commonalities in the perceptions held about the different gates. Such characterizations were always tongue-in-cheek and joking, but they were revealing nonetheless about how differences of class, age, nutrition and, above all, sexuality were played out at Greenham.

A Blue Gater:

> There was an image to the different gates, and I think that women often went to where they felt they would be most comfortable. So once Blue Gate had a reputation for being like the Scallies' Gate and the, you know, Piss Artists' Gate and the Frivolous Gate, and it was also the Young Gate and the Lesbian Gate, the Working-Class Gate, then that in turn tended to attract more women. And we were the tough gate. We were on the front line ... We were right on the side of the road, we were right beside quite a busy gate, in terms of things that went in and out of the base, and we were right by the houses as well.
>
> *Bridget Evans*

Another Blue Gate woman affectionately contrasted her own gate with the others:

> There were a few women who moved around and never really stayed anywhere but seemed to fit in everywhere, but they were few and far between. I did spend one night at Yellow Gate by accident ... and it was very different. Very, very different.
>
> SASHA   *How would you characterize it?*
>
> I probably would say, more grown up. More serious. Blue Gate had a hell of a lot of fun. We had a passion bender in the woods and stuff.
>
> SASHA   *And what went on there?* [laughter]
>
> Lots of passion - occasionally, and not for a very long time. It got ripped down by the bailiffs and we didn't rebuild it. And we had a television made out of a cardboard box, with a piece of wire for an aerial, you know [laughter]. There was an element of this is a game and we are all going to play this game and we're going to enjoy it. And we were quite near the pub, and there was quite a lot of drinking, definitely. And that attracted me too. I knew that if I turned up roaring drunk, or got roaring drunk, or whatever,

nobody would say anything. It was fairly normal. And I knew that there were women at Green Gate who didn't drink. I don't know who they were, but I'd heard this rumour. And I knew I wouldn't be happy there. And there was this thing that Green Gate was dead, dead cosmic, you know. And I didn't get to know until much later women who lived there, and I think that's probably incorrect ... Orange Gate was religious, which initially it may have been. The Quakers used to go to Orange Gate. That put us off. Yellow Gate was dead serious, and you'd be in trouble if you did anything naughty. There was a real 'them' – Yellow Gate.

*Jinny List*

Carmel Cadden and Ann Armstrong painted pictures of the particularities of Violet Gate by comparing it with Blue, which resonated with the descriptions given by Bridget and Jinny:

Violet Gate, because we sat in the mud on a slope by the side of the road, had no illusions of grandeur. In fact, we prided ourselves on being matter-of-fact. Each gate got its own personality. Like Blue Gate, Blue Gate were terribly disorganized, there were a lot of young anarchists and punks. They always used to have a lot of dogs around and they were all into having a lot of booze and dope. Not all the time ...

Violet got a reputation for being obsessed with eating and basically having a good standard of living. One of the women had a badge saying we were the right-off gate because we were so ideologically unsound. Because we allowed everything. Also the other thing about Blue Gate was that it was quite seriously vegan, and Green Gate was quite mystical, cosmic. And so Violet Gate kept up this image of being interested in eating and having a good time ... We had such a mixture of women, we had extreme lesbian separatists, who would freeze the moment any bloke came anywhere near – we all did a bit really – and we'd have all the way through to heterosexuals, like me, ... who'd found at least one of them bearable. But that never seemed to get in the way of our personal friendships.

*Carmel Cadden*

Lots of people used to say that we [Violet Gate] were the ones that did all the eating [laughter]. But that was a bit jokey. But we did.

There was always quite a good age range, as well. I always thought Blue were very young, weren't they?

*Ann Armstrong*

Penny Gulliver's memories of the characters of the gates was not dissimilar:

There were a lot of people who came in October, November, before Christmas [1983] and stayed at least until the following summer at Blue Gate. And they were, on the whole, women from the North. There were a lot of women from the North, a lot of women from Scotland and Wales and Ireland, and practically everyone was working-class ...

I always remember the gates as being very different. Like Green was very international – there were women from all over the world there, and I really liked Green Gate. I liked the feel of it. And I also thought it was a really hippy gate, as well, and all the witches jumping over the fires and wishing out the evil, and all that sort of business. And I liked a lot of the women at Orange Gate. It was, I don't know, a lot of older women, who'd been involved since Aldermaston and stuff, a quite middle-class group of women. But much more transient. Women who came regularly, but came like for three days, and then were away for a fortnight ... I really liked that there were particular feelings and groups at different gates. And I used to explain all that to people that visited.

*Penny Gulliver*

Liz Galst, one of a relatively small group of women who experienced living at a number of different gates, offered her guided tour of the base:

The Green Gate was sort of New Age, mystical, kind of, but there were real exceptions to that, like Annie and Jude. But there was something sort of enchanted at the Green Gate. Especially around there I always felt like any second you could see a sort of gnome walk out from behind a tree, and it wouldn't make any difference. And I think the geography of that had a large influence on the character of gates.

But the Blue Gate I remember as being a bunch of really sort of tough working-class girls who broke everything they put their hands on and were just kind of wild, and drank a lot ... I mean it was just really different ... There were different phases and different people were there and it had different characters, but they were kind of a wild bunch.

The Indigo Gate, I don't know what our reputation was. I think we were sort of on an even keel. And it was more about us personally – Annie, Judy and Eleanor – but nothing fazed us too much, and we were all sort of sprightly, I like to think.

The Violet Gate, they were also sort of a sedate bunch, I think. I remember Carola always being very hospitable ... The Red Gate, I don't think we ever had a chance to develop much of an identity ... And Orange Gate was a very cheerful bunch. I dearly love those women from the Orange Gate, we always had these little fun things that we were doing, and it was very pleasant to be there, and I don't mean that in a bad way. It was just very nice, it was like being on holiday at the Orange Gate.

That's my tour of the base for you. So I do think they definitely had different characters. And a lot of it was geography. I mean Blue Gate was forever knee-deep in mud. And I'm not really sure that anybody wouldn't have been wild and broken things there you know. And the Orange Gate was always a very nice place. That part of the Common is beautiful, with all those birch trees and gorse.

*Liz Galst*

However much laced with humour, these comments show that there were firm perceptions that the gates were composed of quite distinctive groups. Blue was young, lesbian, anarchic, working-class. The women there drank and smoked dope. Green was 'cosmic', where women interested in spirituality and women from overseas clustered. Violet was a mixed gate of heterosexual women and lesbians, but women there shared an interest in eating well. Orange Gate was thought to be composed of older, more middle-class women who had been involved in earlier peace movements. Many of them stayed for fairly short periods of time, and Yellow Gate was the home of the 'old-timers' and was seen as a centre of power.

Like all generalizations, it was not actually the case that all the lesbians, or all the young women, or all the working-class women at Greenham lived at Blue Gate, nor that all the women at Green Gate were interested in feminist spirituality. There were lesbians and working-class women at all the gates, a few heterosexual women at Blue Gate, witches at Yellow Gate, and the food at Violet Gate was not always good. Nonetheless, these characterizations undoubtedly tapped into truths.

What is interesting about these generalizations is that they demonstrate that there was a widespread discourse at Greenham which saw the gates as different from each other in important respects. In the case of Blue Gate, for example, this meant that working-class women living there felt an enhanced sense of identity and community with the women around them and were able to distance themselves from some of the aspects of Greenham which they found oppressively middle-class. Similarly many women, aware that Greenham was often thought of as 'spiritual' and 'earth-motherly', rejected that aspect of Greenham and were able to construct the 'cosmic' as other, by locating it at Green Gate.

There were two women, both visitors, who in talking to me expressed disapproval of the behaviour and high visibility of lesbians at Greenham, and sought to disassociate themselves from the 'militant feminism' of some of the women. They were able to do this, in part, by pinpointing gates which they did not visit as problems, thus separating themselves from those features of Greenham which they disliked.

> We [her women's peace group] always went to Orange Gate. We remained attached to Orange Gate ... It was one of the bigger camps and there was land there. It just got established, that's all. Just like the Essex people always went to Red, you know ... It got very divisive, and Blue Gate became very much ... there was just a group of feminists, very, very militant, who were, you know, there were one or two people who were very disturbed, which made it a very difficult place to be ... Anything like that is bound to attract people who are going to use it psychologically, you know, the situation, to work out their own problems. So there were people there who did that. But that's just a slice of life. Some people made an issue of it. I don't because I think it's wrong.
>
> *Ann Lukes*

Our early march [from Cardiff to Greenham] was a homogeneous crew with definite clear knowledge of where we were walking to and what for, but I think there was just a lot of different opinions at Greenham. That was its interest, in a way - that each camp had perhaps different ideas about things ... Red Gate was always a very welcoming gate and Orange Gate was always a comfortable gate. Blue Gate was always full of young people, who I felt uncomfortable with ... I felt when the strident feminists were there, that they blocked out the others ... That's why I never went to Green Gate.

*Margery Lewis*

Conflict at Greenham over power and resources was often formulated in terms of the disproportionate power and influence of Yellow Gate. Jinny List, for instance, saw Yellow Gate as 'more grown-up', 'more serious', 'the grown-ups with money', and Carmel Cadden described it as 'quite remote', 'raised up from an ordinary level'. They were not alone in this.

I never felt happy at Yellow Gate. I was there two or three times. I never spent much time there, 'cause they were always a bit elitist, weren't they? [laughter] ... There were always the sort of stars at Yellow Gate ... One always felt a bit tentative approaching them.

*Ann Armstrong*

I think of a lot of the women at the Yellow Gate as being really entrenched, and a lot of them had been there a long time, you know, the longest, and they were some of the most crazy and sort of threatening and most impossible. And I don't think I was alone in feeling that. It wasn't as if there was an amazing amount of cohesion in their craziness or impossibility or whatever, but there were a lot of people like that there.

*Liz Galst*

Penny Gulliver felt even more strongly:

People were always rude to me when I went to Yellow Gate, from the first time. So I used to go round and get the water and the post and things like that, and there would be all these cars, and we'd walk round and say 'Look, Blue Gate's got no water, and hasn't had any water for a day, can someone ...?' And there'd be a big bloody issue about whether anybody could be spared. And that puts you off people quite a bit. So we really had nothing to do with Yellow Gate because we couldn't stand them. There were one or two people I knew and liked.

*Penny Gulliver*

As the first camp at Greenham, outside the main entrance to the base, Main Gate was the home of many of the women who had been at the camp longest. The post was delivered there, the standpipe for water was there and Main Gate was the first, and often only, port of call for journalists and visitors. This meant that women from the other gates had to visit Main Gate to collect water each day. Resources, in the form of donations of money, food and clothing, tended to be delivered there. So while women at other gates were always aware of what went on at Main Gate, some of the Main Gate women of long-standing never visited the other gates and were perceived as behaving as if Main Gate was still the entirety of Greenham. The symbolic changing of the name Main Gate to Yellow Gate took place at the end of 1983 in an attempt to de-centre Yellow Gate within the camp as a whole. The name change was enthusiastically embraced by women from the other gates and most of the women at Yellow Gate attempted to alter their vocabulary. But a handful of women continued to speak of Main Gate, either deliberately or because they did not consider the issue important.

So, on the one hand, the (dis)organization of the camp into a number of gates served to create physical and discursive space for the management of differences between women at Greenham, and in so doing strengthened the camp. On the other hand, it also opened up lines of fracture within the camp, above all between Yellow Gate and the rest of the camp. This will be seen in Chapter 7 when I discuss conflicts which arose over the use of money and the issue of hierarchy.

# Notes

1.  The concept of an 'imagined community' was formulated by Anderson (1991).
2.  This role was, to some extent, also taken by the London Greenham office, set up by women in London as a base for coordinating London activities and for liaising with the press. The office moved a number of times, often occupying houses on short-term licenses from London Labour Councils. These houses also provided accommodation for women from the camp when they needed a rest and served as an initial point of contact for the press and for women arriving from abroad. From 1985 the Friends' Meeting House in Newbury, which was often used by the camp for meetings in the winter, was loaned to the camp as an office, and showers were installed for campers.
3.  For example, Camden Women for Peace, Hackney Greenham Support Group, West London Greenham Support Group, Balham Women for Peace/South London Women for Peace.
4.  The layout of gates on the north side of the base was reorganized by the MoD in 1985, in order to allow easier access for the Cruise missile convoys when they were taken out on exercises.
5.  Although there was no gate at this place in the woods, it offered a good view of the missile silos and was considered by the women who lived there important for monitoring activities within the base.

# Chapter 5
# Common Living

*At the Peace Camp, Newbury, Berkshire*
*(to the tune of 'An English Country Garden')*

*What are the questions visitors will ask us*
*At the Peace Camp, Newbury, Berkshire?*
*I'll tell you now of some that I know*
*And the rest, you'll surely ask them.*
*'Are there many of you here?'*
*'Is it cold, and are you queer?'*
*'Where do you get your water from?'*
*'Would you die for the cause?'*
*'Do you shit in the gorse?'*
*At the Peace Camp, Newbury, Berkshire.*

*What are the questions the media will ask us*
*At the Peace Camp, Newbury, Berkshire?*
*I'll tell you now of some that I know,*
*And the rest, you'll read them later.*
*'Why did you make this sacrifice?'*
*'Can I talk to someone nice?'*
*'How does it feel now you have failed?'*
*'Can you pose by the gate?'*
*'Hurry up, it's getting late.'*
*At the Peace Camp, Newbury, Berkshire.*

As the visitors to Greenham who are affectionately mocked in this song would ask: What was it like to live at Greenham? How did women cope with the rigours of living outdoors in all weathers, with few comforts? What was it like living with the constant threat of eviction and under the gaze of the media, the police and the military? And how did women deal with each other, in a women's community which was constantly changing and always open to newcomers? How were the problems of sharing the chores of daily life negotiated in these unusual circumstances?

Women's experiences of living at Greenham were varied and changed significantly over time. They were different in summer and winter, when numbers grew and diminished, when there was just one gate and when there were eight. Things changed radically when regular evictions began and at times of major actions and press interest. Women also spent time at the camp in different ways. A small number made it their permanent and only home, moving there completely and divesting themselves of most of their possessions. The first of these were the women who successfully campaigned to join the electoral register and to sign on the dole from Greenham. A larger number considered the camp their home and spent most of their time there, but retained a base elsewhere – returning to their place of origin to sign on, water plants, pay rent and maintain relationships for a few days once a fortnight or so. For women from both of these groups, Greenham was their primary commitment for anything from several months to several years, with a rough average being perhaps ten to twelve months. Another even larger group of women went to Greenham to stay, regularly or irregularly, for anything from a few days to a couple of months. These women had homes elsewhere and usually jobs or other commitments, such as studying or a family, and tended to be active in their Greenham network locally. Depending on the length of their stays at the camp, these women could get a sense of 'living at Greenham', though such experiences were different from those of women who had decided to live there for the foreseeable future. A further group of women, by far the largest in number, made daytime visits to Greenham perhaps staying overnight on a handful of occasions. The categories of 'camper', 'stayer' and 'visitor' were not mutually exclusive; many women first encountered Greenham as visitors, then went on to become stayers and finally campers. Some women, after living at Greenham for a considerable time, returned for short stays and day-long visits.

Living at Greenham was also different in important ways from gate to gate because the gates occupied very different physical locations and had different characters. The difference, for instance, between living at Green Gate and living at Blue or Violet Gates was rather like that between a country estate and a council estate. Living in the woods at Green Gate, a considerable distance from the fence and the gaze of the soldiers, surrounded by trees, with benders and tents spread out over at least an acre of the Common, was quite unlike living at Blue or Violet Gates, sandwiched between the fence and the road, with benders and tents squashed up together on a small muddy verge.

The women who told me their stories were clear that there was no single experience of living at Greenham. They knew that how it felt for each of them changed with the weather, the company, what was going on in the base. And they knew that other women often experienced the same situation differently. They spoke freely of the highs and lows of life at Greenham, the pleasures and the pains. It was not all damp sleeping bags, eye-watering campfire smoke and police harassment. But neither was it just frolicking in the woods, cosy chats over mugs of tea and moonlit meals around the fire. They waxed lyrical about both the positive and the negative aspects of living at the camp and, as we shall see in Chapter 6, about Greenham's successes and failures in living up to its common values.

## First Experiences

For many women the first few days at Greenham were difficult. Living outdoors, particularly in winter, took some getting used to. The experience of arriving at and moving into a tightly bonded community, without a personal invitation, required considerable bravery and determination. Getting involved in the routine chores of daily life and taking part in actions was the route to feeling part of Greenham.

Penny Gulliver, a 22-year-old lesbian who had recently graduated from drama school, first went to Greenham with two of the women with whom she'd been living in a squat in South London. She described her first few days, and the process by which she began to feel part of the camp:

> I arrived on this October night, in the dark, and there weren't many people at Blue. And this woman called Marilyn shuffled up on a bit of plastic and asked me to sit down. And I felt really quiet and I didn't say anything all night. And all I can remember is that

people were fairly quiet, they were talking, but it was strange. I didn't feel comfortable really. And three of us in this tiny tent froze for three nights. Now I think, after that I used to sleep with no clothes on, anywhere, and never got cold. And I took showers in January, and things like that.[1] But for those three nights I was freezing. The next three days were really busy. And because it was wet when we went down, that time in October [1983], it was the continual rebuilding and firewood collecting and drying out which goes on. So I was really busy, and it immediately got better.

The second night we were doing an action – we were painting the runway. They had this meeting the following morning – there weren't many people there, and they were all awaiting court cases – and they said, it's really important to get other people to start doing some actions at Blue. We said, we'll do it. The second day there. And it was a complete disaster from beginning to end, and we got locked up. So the second night I was there, I spent in the nick at Newbury.

*Penny Gulliver*

For Barbara Rawson the process of integration was harder and more fraught. A 52-year-old part-time care assistant from Derby who identified herself as a 'granny for peace', she had no previous experience of involvement in alternative politics or feminism, and found Greenham an alien and frightening world.

There was this caravan with 'Arms Are For Linking', or something like that, on the side, and lots of women's symbols, and I thought, 'Oh dear, this is a bit way out, this.' I think my feelings were mostly feeling out of place and terror at these strong women. And it was noisy, of course, so we didn't get much sleep with stuff churning in and out of the gates all night. I was amazed at the standpipe and things like that. You could actually live like that. I didn't feel comfortable. I couldn't join in. I was dumb most of the time. I just didn't know the language and it was class stuff. That's how I see it. I then got angry at myself, and I put the anger on these stupid middle-class women prancing about. But then I was fascinated with their stories of their actions and what they had been doing – they had just occupied the sentry box … But they frightened me. Not at all consciously; they wouldn't have known it.

*Barbara Rawson*

After this first visit Barbara only went back to Greenham with the encouragement of her friend Leah Thalmann, whom she had met in a co-counselling group and with whom she talked it over repeatedly. This time, however, they went to Green Gate, where she instantly felt more at ease.

> It was softer. I wasn't particularly proud of it, but I needed the trees, the softer atmosphere.

So it was at Green Gate that she and Leah decided to live when they later moved to Greenham.

Jinny List, 20 years old and unemployed since taking her 'A' Levels, was also in awe of the women at Greenham when she first arrived from Nottingham. As she fitted herself into everyday life at the camp, her fear subsided.

> I was terrified. I'd got this picture of very adamant women, very tough. I had a pretty picture of the toughness, an attractive picture, of strong women being very cold and putting up with dreadful things for world peace and a vision of a better humanity. But I couldn't fit myself into that because I was so normal. They were far, far superior to me. I felt very young. I remember feeling very little, and being not sure what was going on ... I thought, what am I doing here? But then there were so many practical things to do, and interesting women to listen to, that I think that went away quite quickly. Like we didn't sit around being strong. We sat around and talked to each other, and made cups of tea. Which then gave me a place to be normal in.
>
> *Jinny List*

## Elemental Skills

Living at Greenham meant living with the elements. The camp was outdoors, without gas, electricity, mains water or permanent shelter. This meant that the ebb and flow of the seasons, the changing weather, the rising and the setting of the sun could not be ignored. There was no central heating to fire, no curtains to draw, no lights to switch on.

Nor were there cookers, fridges or bathrooms. Women had to build shelter from the wind and rain for themselves, and find ways of storing, preparing and cooking food, washing themselves and going to the toilet. They had to use their imaginations, learn new skills and adapt.

Whilst some women were experienced campers and outdoor types (Girl Guides at heart), many had no idea how to pitch a tent, build a campfire, or keep warm by layering their clothes. Women who did not have these skills had to learn them quickly from those who did if they were to survive.

Katrina Allen, a 31-year-old Australian obstetrician and gynaecologist who had grown up taking regular camping holidays, was not fazed by the challenge of living outdoors, but others, such as Carmel Cadden, Penny Gulliver and Helen John were initially rather daunted by it. However, they all adapted and learnt the necessary new skills.

> SASHA: *Had you done much outdoors, manual things before?*
> Yes. Cars - not much, but wood - we'd always had a fire in the house, and we'd always been responsible for chopping the wood. So in that sense I was quite confident about it ... We were all quite confident campers, and it's not unusual in Australia to go off on a camping holiday, so it was only in retrospect that I could understand that women could feel really intimidated by the circumstances.
>
> *Katrina Allen*

I went through a tomboy phase when I was a girl, and when we'd lived in Africa I felt very much I could have been a boy. But when we came to England I became more of a girl, and then my path became much more towards the arts and I couldn't do practical, mechanical things. I remember so well that first time, at Embrace the Base, putting up my tent. It wasn't my tent, I'd borrowed it, so I didn't know the workings of it. But I was also handicapped by a feeling that I wasn't any good at this sort of thing anyway. And I was in a position where it was a big tent, and the other women I was with were looking to me - 'How does this work?' [laughter]. And having to apply your mind to it, and you've got to get it up.

SASHA: *Or you won't have anywhere to sleep.*
Right, and once the position's clear to all six of us, it will go up, we will do it. And it went up, and we did do it ... There were lots of things like that, achievements, which I felt very good about.

*Carmel Cadden*

It was an education, building confidence. I'd never considered myself to be an outdoor person, and I loved it. And I hate camping – I would never go camping now. And I loved camping. I loved the bender building.
SASHA: *Had you ever done anything like that before?*
No. I'd never done anything like it, and I wouldn't have dreamed. I only did it then because I thought, I have to do this. And I loved it; it was brilliant. Building structures and wood collecting.

*Penny Gulliver*

SASHA: *Had you done manual and outdoor things before?*
No. I used to cut the hedge occasionally, and that was it. I didn't like gardening. I wasn't an outdoor type at all. I was just able to adapt because of what was happening around me.

*Helen John*

It was all new. I found that I could go and get wood, and saw it up, get to the standpipe and get the water from the tap. I'd been camping, but in a very civilized sort of a way. I was used to walking and being outside, cycling and things like that, but I wasn't used to not having men around to do things [laughter]. And I liked it.

*Barbara Rawson*

## The Necessities of Life

SHELTER

SASHA: *Did you build yourself a bender?*
Initially I lived in one of those black plastic tunnels by the fire. It was quite pleasant actually because you could wake up in the mornings and stick your head out and somebody would bring you a cup of tea, or if you were really lucky, breakfast in bed. But then I

inherited a bender. It was one of Gill Booth's many bolt-holes, way over in the gorse, in the clearing.

*Kim Smith*

For the first eighteen months or so of the camp's existence, before the first eviction, some shelter for sleeping was available in a couple of small caravans. After these were seized by bailiffs and before the daily evictions began in 1984 a few women slept in vans, but most built themselves 'benders'.

Benders were constructed from large sheets of transparent plastic which were wrapped around igloo shaped frames made from bent-over saplings or dead wood. Well-built benders were watertight and windproof, and if insulated with blankets and equipped with a porch, wooden pallet flooring and often a bedframe lined with straw, they could be warm and cosy. Over time some women became very skilled bender builders, and helped newcomers to make their own, thus passing on the skills of the trade. It was important to choose the right location for a bender – not too close to the fire and the hub of camp life to lead to disturbed sleep, but not so far away as to allow vigilante attack. Some benders were 'owner-occupied', lived in by the women who had built them and furnished with home-made tables, book-shelves, candles and pictures. Others were built by women who stayed in them for a while and moved on, leaving them free for anyone else to take over. The Holly Bender at Green Gate, for instance, built inside a holly tree and invisible, was snug and dark and survived countless evictions, becoming a prized residence passed through generations of Green Gaters.

After the onset of regular evictions in 1984, benders became increasingly obsolete. It was not possible to save the bender materials from the bailiffs and re-erecting benders every night, after the evictions were over for the day, was not practical. From this time on, housing conditions became more basic, especially at the gates on the north side of the base, which were experiencing evictions sometimes five to ten times a day. Communal shelters, like the tunnels described by Kim, could be erected by hanging a sheet of plastic from a washing line strung between two trees, affording some protection from the wind and rain for a number of women. Some women set up tents every night, but many, particularly in the summer, slept under the stars in a sleeping bag inside a Gore-Tex bag or a large plastic survival bag.

SASHA: *That whole period of living at Violet Gate, you never had a bender? You were always just sleeping in a survival bag?*

Mostly in a survival bag. I never had a bender, except briefly at Green Gate in the winter of 1983–84. A couple of people at Violet had benders, and at one stage I had a sheet of plastic strung between trees, but in fact it was somebody else's and I was just using it until they came back. I actually found it less easy to work than just a survival bag. And then I started to use a survival bag and an umbrella, which was actually really nice. We had a great big golfing umbrella, and I used to use that, and I did find it very nice because it would keep the wind and rain off your face so that you could actually sleep out of your plastic bag ... I'd stick my head under the umbrella, pathetic isn't it? [laughter].

*Katrina Allen*

WARMTH

The focus of life at every gate was the fire. Lit every morning and kept going all day even in the summer, the fire was a vital source of warmth on cold days and the means by which water was boiled and food cooked. The fire also played a crucial symbolic role. It was the place women gathered, where they got to know each other, where plans were discussed, decisions made, life stories exchanged. Seating was arranged around the fire. In the pre-eviction days this included battered old armchairs and sofas which had been donated to the camp; later on, tree stumps, old car seats, bales of straw, upturned buckets and wooden crates.

Keeping the fire burning all day, and often all night for the nightwatch women, required a considerable amount of work. One of the daily tasks at the camp was gathering firewood from the Common, and chopping and storing it. This job particularly appealed to some women, whilst others never gave it a second thought.

The thing I did most was collecting wood and that was because I often got off on my own doing that, and just enjoyed being on my own, particularly when Leah and people I felt close to were not there. I knew it was useful and I just liked getting the wood. I couldn't chop but I could saw wood up and I hadn't done that before.

*Barbara Rawson*

There was this picket fence around Blue Gate, and we used to burn it at night. And the next day they'd come and put it up again, and then we'd burn it again. Every day for ages. And it wasn't creosoted - it was nice wood. Wasn't that nice of them!

*Jinny List*

Clothing was also crucial to keeping warm at Greenham. Many women who arrived to stay found themselves inadequately or inappropriately dressed. If a woman was to make the transition from a day visitor, who could get away with city clothing, to a stayer or camper, she had to learn how to dress. Walking boots or Doc Martens, treated with a waterproofing wax and worn with woollen socks, were essential; wellington boots were not warm enough. Clothes had to be layered, and vests, T-shirts, shirts, sweaters and jackets were more suitable than overcoats and mackintoshes which tended to trail in the mud and inhibit movement. Army surplus trousers, or other loose cotton trousers with long johns underneath, were better than jeans, which were generally too tight to be warm and comfortable. And, to the ridicule of the media, woollen hats and fingerless gloves were also vital on the coldest days. Very few of the women who lived at Greenham had expensive hi-tech outdoor clothing made from fabrics such as Polartec and Gore-Tex, but everyone who lived at the camp for any length of time had, by definition, found a way of dressing for warmth and comfort.

I had a knapsack full of stuff and in the winter I wore everything I owned. Constantly. All at once. And that has definitely had an influence on my aesthetic to this day. You know, I still wear three T-shirts sometimes!

*Liz Galst*

FOOD

Food was a central part of life at Greenham. Living outdoors and engaging in strenuous manual labour, such as building benders, digging shitpits and collecting firewood, particularly in the winter, required considerable amounts of food as fuel. Women needed to eat well to sustain their energy but hot cooked food was emotionally as well as physically warming. A good meal followed by a shared bar of chocolate and a bottle of whisky or Bailey's could raise the spirits after an eviction like nothing else.

As with other areas of camp life, food was both a communal and an individual matter. Women from each gate made regular shopping trips to Newbury and bought food from Sainsburys and the local health food store. Paid for with 'camp money', or from a kitty to which everyone contributed, this food belonged to everyone. Breakfasts tended to be on a self-serve basis, with everyone foraging for muesli or toasting bread on the fire for herself. Sometimes, particularly at the smaller camps, one or two women would cook breakfast for everyone, maybe porridge or scrambled eggs and baked beans. Individual women generally prepared their own lunch, usually sandwiches, but the evening meal would be cooked by one or two women for everyone.

Evening meals were the central focus of daily life. Everyone living at the gate would gather around the fire and share the meal. This tended to be the only time of the day when all the campers and stayers came together, and it was a time when news would be exchanged. After dinner there would be hot drinks and often singing or storytelling for several hours. This nightly ritual bound the women of each gate together and helped to integrate newcomers, as well as ensuring that everyone got at least one hot meal a day. By common agreement dinner was always vegetarian and usually vegan so that everyone could eat together. There was no refrigeration (other than that provided by the weather) and storage was a problem, particularly when there were regular evictions, so ingredients were fairly simple. Most meals were based on pasta, rice or beans, but occasionally women experimented with more elaborate fare, making, for example, several different curries and chapatis, or stuffed pancakes, and, by digging an oven under the fire, bread, cakes and fruit crumbles. In the winter preparing vegetables and cooking in the dark could be quite a challenge. Cooking over an open fire for up to thirty or forty women required skills that had to be learnt on a trial and error basis.

> The cooking was a problem at first. We overcame that – Leah and I. Leah found it difficult because she wanted to cook in the daylight, and so we used to prepare the stuff in the daylight. I found it difficult because it was vegetarian, and I hadn't been a

vegetarian. My idea of a meal was meat and veg and therefore I was eager to learn, and said so. I didn't feel bad that I didn't know much about it.

*Barbara Rawson*

## Supporters and Visitors

At that time Greenham was just beginning to get this real blitz of press attention, and there was so much stuff there that had been donated. There were great big dustbins full of bottles. I turned up with a bottle of whisky, and they were, 'Oh yeah, another bottle of whisky. Put it in the whisky bin.' And I opened this bin and it was full of bottles of whisky.

*Sarah Benham*

Supporters and visitors played a vital role in making life at Greenham possible. The camp relied on voluntary donations of money to buy essential resources and on the donations in kind made by people from all over Britain. The total value of money donated during the lifetime of the camp cannot be calculated because there was no accounting procedure. Over the years there were numerous bank accounts but many donations were made in cash and spent without ever being banked. During the peak years of activism income from donations was substantial. The inflow of money depended in part on the level of news coverage. It would increase immediately after high-profile actions and court cases, and at times when the government made concerted efforts to malign the camp. During the period when I was a signatory to the main camp bank account (1984), between £100 and £5000 a week of donations were deposited. This was, however, an exceptional period – Greenham was much in the news and Cruise had recently arrived. At other times, donations were considerably lower, and often non-existent. Money came both from individuals and from groups, particularly the CND and peace groups, as well as trade union and Labour Party branches, raised through collections, raffles, jumble sales and the showing of anti-nuclear films.[2] Amounts varied from the one pound notes sent in by pensioners and schoolchildren to substantial donations of several thousand pounds from famous performers.

Greenham visitors commonly brought food, particularly at Christmas when there was sometimes so much food at the camp that it was passed on to local women's aid refuges. From mid-1984 onwards, as evictions became a regular feature of life at Greenham, a daily 'food run' was established by women from around the south of England, who operated a rota. Every day, in the late afternoon or early evening, hot meals were brought to the camp. As there was no way of knowing exactly how many women would be at the camp on any one day, there was sometimes too much and sometimes not enough to go round; but the knowledge that there would always be a meal relieved women of some of the stress which accompanied constant evictions.

Greenham supporters from all over southern England brought wood, often already chopped, seasoned and ready to burn. During and after the miners' strike of 1984-85, groups of striking miners also donated salvaged sacks of coal as a gesture of solidarity. Other practical donations, often specifically requested by women at the camp in response to questions about what was needed, included sheet plastic for benders, thermal underwear, sleeping bags, tents, pallets, Gore-Tex survival bags and bolt-cutters for cutting the fence. Most of the crockery, cooking utensils, pots and pans used at Greenham were also donations. During the winter of 1983-84, there were dozens of sackfuls of clothing, much of which was unsuitable. Most of the vehicles which were owned by the camp were also donated by individual supporters.

Without this practical support life at Greenham would have been much harder. It is doubtful whether all the wood necessary to sustain camps at several gates during the winters of 1983-85 could have been gathered from the Common. And the luxuries brought by visitors - alcohol and chocolate, particularly - eased the pressures of evictions and warmed our spirits in the rain. The downside of the constant through-flow of visitors and supporters was the expectation of attention from women living at the camp. At times campers found the barrage of questions or just the moral pressure to engage in polite conversation a strain.

One of the reasons for leaving Yellow Gate was I could only give so much. I couldn't constantly have a smiling face on for visitors coming to Greenham, and sitting down: it's the classic 'Where do you get your water from?', 'Where do you shit?' questions eighty-

six times a day. And I think later on most of the women coming
down weren't expecting that initial outburst of hello, welcome, sit
down, have a cup of tea, from everybody, because it was your
home. And you occasionally just want to sit there quietly getting
on with whatever you want to do. You don't want to stand up and
be welcoming constantly. But I guess there were a few people, a
few women who got put off from the place by the welcome that
they didn't get. 'Cause it really did depend on your mood. I mean
if you'd been sitting out in the freezing cold and pissing rain for
six hours you didn't feel like putting on a smile and getting the fire
going.

*Kim Smith*

The times I enjoyed living at camp most were times when there
was a fairly fixed group of us. It wasn't at the times of big actions
when there was an enormous amount of coming and going. It was
those Wednesday mornings, when there was a solid group of eight
or nine women who you started to get to know quite well. I did
find it difficult when new women came ... Although once
someone had been there for even a week, she was a fixture and
part of your life. It didn't take long for women to be absorbed.

*Carola Addington*

## Campwork

Like any household, the camp required a certain amount of routine
work to keep it running. But 'campwork' was rather different from the
housework which besets ordinary domestic life. Campwork was *queer*
housework. The tasks it involved, the manner in which it was done
and how it was thought about were all decidedly unusual, outside the
norms of late twentieth-century Western home-making. Dirt, disorder
and messiness were part of life at Greenham and could never be
vanquished by campwork. If women were to live happily at Greenham
they had to come to terms with the dirt of the earth around them, the
disorder and messiness of life outdoors. They had not just to tolerate
it, but to enjoy it and revel in its difference from clean, tidy normality.

The absence of running water, electricity and gas at Greenham
returned tasks to those of the pre-industrial era. Water had to be

fetched (albeit in plastic containers and by car or van); wood gathered from the Common and then chopped and stored; fires laid and tended throughout the day; washing-up done in bowls with water boiled over the fire; and shitpits dug and covered. Other tasks were those of twentieth-century Western life writ large: shopping in Newbury for between four and fifty women, catering for vegans and lacto-vegetarians, and then cooking for the same number over an open fire.

Campwork was also (dis)organized very differently from the housework which is done in most homes and this can be seen as queer feminist political action. Since the 1960s struggles about housework have been central to straight feminism. Feminist research-ers have argued that housework should be taken seriously as *work* and heterosexual women in their everyday lives have fought endless and often fruitless battles to make the men they live with do their share of housework.[3] But the evidence suggests that little has changed. Men have proved remarkably reluctant to do more than 'help out' around the house and women have continued to do almost all the work to keep homes clean and tidy to the standards which are socially acceptable.[4] The decision that the camp should become women-only was made in the context of this feminist politicization of domestic work, in part because the men were not doing their share of the washing-up and cooking. This indicated that the politics of the camp was moving beyond straight feminism; instead of engaging in a protracted struggle to change men's behaviour, men were asked to leave. Greenham's queer feminism could then say 'fuck housework'. Traditional femininity tends to fetishize housework, often carrying it out to a standard that is much higher than hygiene and comfort require.[5] Straight feminism has focused on the problem of who does the housework but has failed to disrupt the importance attached to it, for fear of seeming to attack the women who do it. In contrast, in the women-only community of Greenham, the importance of women's traditional work could be radically repositioned and traditional ways of organizing it challenged. Conscious efforts were made to minimize the investment of time and energy in routine chores in order to free women to engage in more enjoyable and politically significant activities.

Although campwork was performed by women, as housework still predominantly is, this was by choice – the result of the women-only decision – rather than being the product of a traditional division of labour. It was not the work of one woman, mother and wife, on behalf of her family; rather it was (dis)organized on a communal basis. And, unlike most communal houses, chores were performed by individual women according to their choice, not as determined by a rota. This meant that women were able to work when they wanted to, at the tasks at which they wanted to work, rather than either having to do everything (like the housewife), or to do a particular job at a time not of their choosing (as in many communes and kibbutzim). Campwork was not accorded any more importance than other contributions to the life of the camp, such as singing or having ideas for actions, and there was space for women to choose to make their contribution in any way they saw fit.

> I think the communal living worked really well. Sometimes I'd notice that certain women didn't do anything, but there was always some contribution that they made, whether it was singing or, they would have an outstanding contribution they would make in a different way. I felt it worked really well, and I liked the idea that you contribute what you feel like when you feel like contributing
>
> *Jenny Heron*

Camp jobs would be done by whoever chose to do them, with women tending to do those at which they were particularly skilled, or which they particularly enjoyed. If someone hated cooking, it was unlikely she would ever lift a knife to a carrot; if she found digging two-foot deep holes in the ground too strenuous, she would not take charge of the shitpits. Those jobs requiring skills which women are not traditionally encouraged to acquire - for instance, chopping wood and car repair and maintenance - tended to accrue the most status, but, as part of the ethos of openness to change, skill-sharing and learning new skills was common practice. Women who had not done a particular task before Greenham would tend to join in when it was being performed by an 'old-timer' and would learn the ropes; this was particularly the case with tasks such as cooking which required the adaptation of old skills to new circumstances.

Women at Greenham tended to spend as little time as possible on those domestic tasks which require constant repetition and which have little satisfaction attached to their achievement. In part this was a sensible adaptation to the environment at the camp. It would have been impossible to replicate the standards of cleanliness and tidiness considered normal in a house. The leaves and dust could never all be swept away, the ground could not be prevented from turning to mud when it rained, there could never be storage places for all the crockery and food. When there could be no permanent shelters, standards had to be different.

Guiding this (dis)organization of campwork were the common values of Greenham. Every woman was expected to take personal responsibility for the collective recreation of daily life at Greenham, to see what needed to be done and to do it. In the spirit of non-hierarchy, there was no centralized allocation of duties. However, differences in interest, aptitude, experience and temperament were respected, and women's decisions not to do particular work were rarely challenged. The other side of this principle of personal responsibility was that women were expected to take responsibility for *not* doing work as much as for doing it, to make sure that they did not become 'martyrs to the washing-up'. In other words, women were expected to exercise agency in the realm of campwork, whether this meant undertaking it or refusing it.

For some women, particularly older women who were mothers and/or wives, realizing that they could make a choice about whether or not to do such work was a transformative experience. Helen John, for instance, who had been a housewife prior to her involvement with Greenham, spoke of how she had to make a conscious decision not to take on too much of the domestic work and how she found the low priority given to domestic work at Greenham liberating.

> For all the time I was there, I stopped having, you know, a council house mentality. I gave that up because a lot of the other women who were in my age bracket, they cracked up because the younger women - and the younger men who were there initially - I mean, these women were good housewives, you know, would wash all the dishes and go to bed at night and be horrified when they woke up in the morning and found them all covered with mud and filthy and everything'd been used and nobody'd washed them. And I very quickly decided I hadn't come there to mother people, that if they wanted to get up and have dirty cups and saucers, that was great, that was their decision. It wasn't my responsibility. So it freed me from a lot of that. And you know, it's like cutting a big knot around your neck. I was away from that.
>
> *Helen John*

In a similar vein, Leah Thalmann described how she stopped taking on too great a responsibility for domestic work:

SASHA: *Do you remember whether you felt happy about the way work was done and chores were divided?*
I found it rather strange at first. I can remember an experience, before I was living but when I came to stay early on at Yellow, and there was a group of women eating somewhere down by the road, and they had lots of dirty pots and cups lying on the ground. I went over to them and said, 'Would you like me to wash up?' They looked at me amazed: 'You don't have to do that sort of thing.' I crept away, feeling really awful ... And when I went to Yellow, I used to do the washing-up. It was incredibly squalid. I used to do mounds of washing-up in all this mud. All the while I was doing it, more women came and put dirty dishes down, and cups and things, and plates full of food, and there were cakes being trodden into the mud. I thought, this is terrible. I've got to do this washing-up, why does she have to come and just dump? It was endless. This seemed to be the sort of chore I could do - I felt capable of doing this particular chore. I'd wash up endlessly. I don't think it was until I went to live at Green Gate that I realized that you didn't have to be like that. I still often did the washing-up, but I realized that you didn't have to, and that I was choosing to. If I wanted to wash-up eighty mugs - and if you remember we had that mug tree with eighty mugs on it - then I was choosing to do it. I think I realized one night when I was lying in my tent and I knew that the shitpit was virtually overflowing, and I thought, god, somebody has got to build a shitpit, nobody's going to do it, and we're not going to have a shitpit. Then at dawn I woke up and I heard this noise and it was women digging a shitpit. It didn't have to be me. All the chores still get done, and you can choose what you want to do, and that is quite a revelation. That was really good. I still did the washing-up quite a lot, but I chose to do it. I didn't have this resentment about it. That was amazing.
*Leah Thalmann*

The women I talked to were overwhelmingly of the opinion that the organization of campwork at Greenham was successful. Many commented that it worked much better at Greenham than in the communal houses in which they had lived, before or since. This was generally explained in terms of the fact that Greenham was outdoors and therefore 'different', removed from many of the pressures associated with traditional expectations of daily life.

> At the times when the gates were really big, I actually think that they worked incredibly well, in relation to living in households. Shopping, and things like that. I found that on the whole it was quite remarkable how it did seem to get sorted out, and it was relatively rare that you came to the end of the day and there was no food. Usually somebody would manage to get it together to go and do the shopping, and somebody else would organize the cooking. And I think it did work very, very well, without really trying. There wasn't a system for it, and there certainly weren't a lot of discussions about how it should go or whatever.
>
> *Katrina Allen*

Most women considered it inevitable that the anarchy of the system led to some women doing more domestic work than others, with a few women doing very little. The value placed on personal responsibility and individual autonomy was such that these problems were seen to be outweighed by the benefits of the flexibility and freedom inherent in the system.

> I think that people tried to give each other as much freedom as they could, and not restrict each other. And sometimes that was problematic because there are people who just don't do shit. You know, they didn't clean up after themselves and they weren't confronted because of that. Because people were trying to give people as much slack as they could, and not do that. And I think that could be a problem, but I think it was also really a very good experience for a lot of people, including me.
>
> *Liz Galst*

> SASHA: *Chores, did you feel that they got done fairly evenly?*
> No, but they got done. Blue Gate didn't seem to worry about that kind of stuff so much. Every so often we'd have a clean-up. But when we were being evicted every day, the bailiffs would just do it for us. We just used to leave the rubbish out [laughter].
>
> *Penny Gulliver*

Deprioritizing domestic labour meant that the camp was often untidy, strewn with unwashed dishes and half-eaten stews in pans, and this annoyed some women, but only two believed that domestic work should have been a higher priority at Greenham.

One of these was Nell Logan, who as a life-long member of the Communist Party disliked the anarchy of Greenham and believed that the untidiness made a bad impression on the outside world. She explained differences in attitudes to domestic order in terms of age:

> Jane and I and Ursula, we were older you see, and we were going round picking all the papers up. We didn't like the mess that went on. Some of them were young, they thought it was a picnic, in a way. And it wasn't. It wasn't a picnic, by any means. We did tidy up, and we had to do that because we didn't want visitors coming and seeing all the mess, you see. It was alright. People would pass remarks about it, but then, I'd say, I'd rather be in this mess than in that mess in there [the base].
>
> *Nell Logan*

The other woman who found the lack of emphasis on 'housework' at Greenham problematic was Pat Paris. She became aware of the mess around her at Blue Gate only when she brought her young daughter to stay at the camp. She was the only woman I interviewed who spent significant periods of time at the camp with a child. This suggests that the high level of tolerance of the relative domestic disorder at Greenham may have existed, at least in part, because they were few young children around whose health and safety had to be considered.

> Of those of us who ran around clearing up, it was people like me and Chris who had kids and homes and knew if you left the lid off the jar long enough, then all these flies got in and you'd be poisoned. Little things like health hazards. I took Rowan once and that was the first time I ever really looked at Blue Gate and thought, oh my god. It was in the summer. The kitchen was on pallets somewhere. There were knives covered with all sorts, knocked onto the floor, picked up, put back. All those tins that had been opened, with sharp edges, and I just saw Rowan, two-and-a-half, and I thought, she's going to be killed here, and if she's not going to be poisoned, she'll be cut to pieces. That was the

weekend that I really lost my rag and we had one of our meetings, and I said, 'I can't go on. I'm not going to be able to bring Rowan. I can't cope with it. It's too dangerous.' So we had periodic sort outs.

*Pat Paris*

However, the situation did improve.

SASHA: *Did women respond to this?*
Oh yes, yes. For a couple of days. Most of the time it never felt like a major problem, but it was never organized. It was very laid-back. It got better when we got given the kitchen, the kitchen on wheels, and we could actually keep things in their place. It had two wheels and a handle at one end. It was rather like a fast food stall. It was wooden and had shelves and a roof on it, and deep wooden pockets, so the wooden pockets took all the archives. And when the bailiffs came you just wheeled it off.

*Pat Paris*

## Uncommon Activities

I thought, it's wonderful. Here's these big strong women who can chop wood, and chop up cars, and mend vans.

*Carola Addington*

Although the mundane chores of daily life were not prioritized, considerable energy and imagination were expended on activities which were less traditionally designated as female. Some of these tasks were essential, such as building benders and chopping wood; women had to learn them if they were to survive at Greenham. Other activities were not strictly necessary but were, for many women, driven by the desire to learn new skills and to develop a sense of self-sufficiency, independence and autonomy.

The maintenance and repair of camp vehicles was one area in which women developed new competencies. A handful of women at Greenham had some experience of car mechanics and many more were keen to learn the skills which teenage boys acquire without a second thought and which give them the freedom to roam the country without much money. The battered old cars and vans which had been donated to the camp were vital, particularly to gates on the north side, for daily tasks such as fetching water and shopping. They were the only safe place to stow camp and personal possessions when the bailiffs arrived for evictions. Camp vehicles were invariably in need of attention and there was plenty of time available for trial and error. Without the servicing and attention provided by those women who were interested in cars, the camp could not have afforded to run many of the vehicles.

Women found themselves able to play with cars at Greenham unimpeded both by men's interruptions and by the 'men in their heads' who told them that they couldn't do it. Katrina Allen, for instance, was not a novice at car mechanics, but she found it different at Greenham:

> One of the things I liked about Greenham was the way you just got on and did stuff, and although that wasn't a complete revelation for me, there were times when I was just really happy that there wasn't anybody else that was going to muscle in and say, I'll do that - about the cars particularly. Because usually there's a bloke around and he usually feels himself more confident about the car, even if he's not necessarily more competent, and that's enough to make me feel it's not worth doing. And if I don't know how to do a thing, then I tend not to want to do it. And it was actually really, really useful for me ... Even if there was a woman who knew more about it, she would come over and talk to you about it. You wouldn't feel that you were ignorant and she was competent. Remember Polly, she was really good with cars, and she'd just come over and say, why don't you try such and such, and you'd just get on with it. It's very different from the sort of heavy feeling you get when blokes are around and they take over. And it may be that the blokes were taking over and I gave up that space to them; I think it's a bit of both. And I think that was a really good thing about Greenham, which made it a positive experience for me to stay, was just the fact that you were with a group of other women who were all doing everything for themselves, often for the first time in their lives.
>
> *Katrina Allen*

Women tried their hands at a whole range of new activities. During periods when evictions were infrequent a number of women, particularly at Green Gate, devoted themselves to making furniture from scrap wood and bundles of sticks. Women built mobile kitchens on wheeled pallets in order to be able to save food from the bailiffs, and Liz Galst at Indigo built a bender on an old supermarket trolley base which could be wheeled away during evictions. Women at Green, Blue and Orange Gates built earth ovens to bake cakes, breads and puddings. Others forged grills and sandwich toasters from pieces of the fence which they had cut down. At Green and Blue Gates showers were rigged up from trees, and for a period of time at Green Gate women exercised their creativity by digging shitpits in the shape of women's symbols, peace symbols and doves.

Many of the women I talked to spoke of experiencing a new sense of creativity and practical competence at Greenham.

> It was a space for me where I felt more creative. I did all this stuff that I hadn't ever done before in my life. I just started making things all the time. First I had this idea for making a boat. I had made a lot of stuff before, like postcards and silkscreen stuff and posters, but I just really felt like I could do anything when I was at Greenham and it didn't have to be for any particular reason other than that I wanted to do it ... And I built all this furniture, and I had no idea how to build furniture. I built a rocking-chair because we'd gotten this wood that had an edge, a kind of edge and I thought oh that's really nice. And I built those benders on wheels. I learned to knit, and I learned to spin, and I painted those big banners and made postcards. It was a very great experience.
>
> *Liz Galst*

> I did like the amazing creativity at camp. If you hadn't got what you needed at the time, you invented one. I used to think that lots of the things that we invented were brilliant.
> SASHA: *What sort of things?*
> People would put shelves in their bender for their books and bits and pieces, made from string and bits of undergrowth. All the things that we used on the fire, ways of supporting pots and pans. Some of the ovens that we built. We made apple crumble. We just buried it under the fire basically, but it came out and was

absolutely perfect, blackcurrant and apple crumble. It was surprising what you could do with very little resources, we always managed to find something that would fit the hole or do the job.

*Pat Paris*

Seeing other women doing such uncommon activities inspired many to try it for themselves.

I remember thinking when I was sitting at camp, if the car didn't work, then you had somebody who knew bits about it and you learnt things and you fixed it and you fixed all sorts of things and we were totally self-sufficient, really in almost every way you could think … It was just incredible what women could do. It was amazing. I didn't actually think I was a lot like them, but it gave me the confidence to try, and also it was a safe place to try because people were into learning and telling you things and showing you how to do it. And it was fine. They didn't expect you to know it. They were into passing on skills.

*Pat Paris*

Another woman, who had struggled to put up her tent on her first night at the camp, was challenged to push herself:

Lots of times you were in a situation where you couldn't look around and say, well I can't do it. You just know that that's not on, you would have to do it. Or you could say you can't do it, but you actually should try to figure out a way of doing it … Greenham was the only aspect of my life where I was doing anything like that. And even though I knew women can do all these things, all the time you're seeing examples of women doing things which are amazing. She's amazing, she's taking this vehicle apart, and putting it together. And all the time you came into contact with women who were quite staggering, at least to me … But you didn't feel you couldn't have anything to do with them, that they were on another level from you. It *was* possible, you should be able to do these things yourself, if you wanted to.

*Carmel Cadden*

**The Pleasures of Common Life**

> I always had this thing in my head, that anybody who actually lived at Greenham liked living like that. You know, we weren't into self-sacrifice there. If you actually lived at Greenham, then you liked cooking on a campfire, and camping and being out of doors.
>
> *Rowan Gwedhen*

> I really loved the winter at the camp. It was really, really busy, and there were a thousand things to do, and it got dark at 4 o'clock, so we had yet another disgusting vegan stew that half a tree had fallen in, and you didn't know until you were eating it, then we sang all the songs, and it was bedtime.
>
> *Penny Gulliver*

Life at Greenham undoubtedly had its downside - evictions, vigilante attacks, violence from soldiers, arrest, imprisonment - but there were many pleasures. For those who chose to live at the camp these far outweighed the pains.

> I really hated being wet. I hated being in benders where you couldn't stand up ... But there were parts I really loved. Like I loved being outside in the nice weather. I loved walking, you know, I love to walk, and I walk all over the place, and it was so nice for me to walk. And especially before all the big evictions started happening all the time, I used to walk around the base nearly every day. And there are parts of the Common that are just so beautiful. I loved to sit under the stars to see the harvest moon just really low over the Common. It was really beautiful to wake up in the morning, and just sitting round the fire. I have never again felt as in touch with nature as I felt at that time. I always knew what the weather was like and I always knew what phase the moon was in and I always watched the constellations move across the sky.
>
> *Liz Galst*

And, as Jinny List pointed out, women tended to remember the good things.

I don't think about the fact that sometimes I'd wake up and my sleeping bag would have leaked, and I'd be wet through and cold and miserable, and there'd be no toothpaste, and no coffee, and somebody had just used the last bit of water to wash their hair. Those kinds of things don't stick. What sticks is being there, with women, and being able to do what I wanted to do, and be accepted and acceptable.

*Jinny List*

Above all what women enjoyed was each other's company.

I enjoyed the women's energy. And I enjoyed the humour. There was tremendous humour, and that I think drew me back as much as anything. I think a lot of people missed that when they were reporting on Greenham; they didn't bring out the humour that was there. And there were a lot of agonizing times too, a lot of traumatic times. And some women, particularly after Christmas, in the first six months, seemed quite traumatized. They were quite loud and angry, and they were difficult, I suppose. But they were also funny too. They had a lot of humour; they would laugh and cry ... I enjoyed the pace, being able to spend time talking. We don't do that enough in our everyday lives. I really appreciated that. And just meeting so many different women from all over the world. I found that very exhilarating, wonderful. Of course there were times when it just got too much, and you didn't want to talk to anyone. But I really did like that communication going on.

*Carola Addington*

For all the problems that happened in the spring I really loved it. I loved all the excitement and I loved all the actions and all that. It was great. And mixing with a big group of women which I'd not mixed with before. Actually living at camp with a group of working-class women. I was the only southerner for a long time. There were lots of women who came and went from the south, and more women after the winter that came and stayed. I really had a good time and liked it and enjoyed it. And that's why I stayed. I think if I'd been miserable I would have found reasons for, I would have left, 'cause I'm not a sticker. I don't stay at things

I'm miserable at. I stayed because I liked it, and I did feel that it was important as well.

*Penny Gulliver*

I loved it. I really liked it, even though it drove me mad a lot of the time ... All that energy was amazing. I was in my thirties then, and I hadn't been around women who were 16, 17, 18 with ideas like that or energy like that, some of the things they did were so brilliant I couldn't resist them. They did absolutely lunatic things in the base ... Even though it was all deadly serious, at Blue Gate there was always this element of, you could be deadly serious but you could have a good time at the same time. They never planned anything that did not have this built-in element of lunacy. I think I just found them, they opened my eyes with a vengeance. I was loathe to give that up and I was prepared to put up with a lot.

*Pat Paris*

## Notes

1.   A cold-water shower made from a plastic water container with a watering-can spray hose was sometimes hung from a tree at the more secluded gates (Green and Turquoise).
2.   While small anonymous donations of money were received at the camp several times accompanied by stationery from the White House (suggesting dissenting opinions among US government staff) no money was ever received from the USSR, despite British government propaganda to the contrary.
3.   Ann Oakley (1974) was the first feminist sociologist to make this case.
4.   For a review of the relevant literature, see Jamieson (1998).
5.   In Friedan's (1963) now-famous dictum, 'housework expands to fill the time available'. For discussion of the domestic labour of wives, see Oakley (1974), Hardyment (1988) and Delphy and Leonard (1992).

# Chapter 6
# Common Values of a Queer Feminism

As much as it was a place, Greenham was also an attitude to life, a set of ideas and ways of thinking about how we should live, both as individuals and as a community. These beliefs about what is morally right and good provided the ethical underpinning of Greenham's experiment in alternative ways of living and they shaped the actions which women took there. This chapter explores the common values which bound the camp and the Greenham network together.

Exploring the particular configuration of values which fuelled Greenham is worthwhile for a number of reasons. The very existence of an elaborate code of values created by the women at Greenham underlines that ethics are negotiated by ordinary people in their daily lives, and that they are not just the prerogative of professional philosophers. Greenham's common values were a unique example of a set of ethics informed by feminism in a postmodern context which had been developed, tested and refined in practice, not just in theory.[1] They provided both a model of community and politics and a model of self, and so engaged with one of the dominant themes in contemporary discussions of politics and moral philosophy - the relationship between the individual and the community. They also developed a distinctive position on the issue of how communities should deal with difference and diversity - another central question in recent political and philosophical debates. In these areas and others the values developed at Greenham were an articulation of a new approach to feminist politics, an approach which can be described as a queer postmodern feminism.[2]

## Inventing Values at Greenham

In our uncertain postmodern world, where tradition has less and less hold over us, we are increasingly forced to create our own codes for living.[3] We have collectively lost our faith in the moral absolutes claimed by religion and in the answers of meta-political ideologies; scientific truth and reason no longer offer legitimation for our beliefs. The typically modern desire for the certainty which is derived from a cohesive and universal set of principles grounded in reason gives way to a more fluid approach to an ethics, which is self-consciously ambiguous, local and contingent.

So it was in the early 1980s for the women who came together at Greenham. They could not appeal for legitimation of their politics to the very ideologies which they saw as having brought the world to the brink of nuclear annihilation. The unhesitating self-confidence in their own truths of techno-scientific rationality, communism and capitalism was seen as the problem; absolute truth claims grounded in ideology could not, therefore, be the solution. Greenham's critique of this meant that its politics were always understood to be about values rather than about claims to truth. These values were recognized to be the *chosen, invented* values of the women at Greenham, rather than an expression of an ultimate universal truth about how people should live their lives. Their fluidity and specificity, and indeed their 'messiness', were embraced.

The values which grounded Greenham's politics were not taken off the peg from other social movements. The situation faced by women at Greenham was unique, and their project – to build a community of women opposing nuclear weapons and challenging dominant gender relations – required a novel approach. There was no ethical framework readily available to tell them how they should live together and how they should confront the threat of nuclear war. What they had were the political traditions of feminism, socialism, anarchism and liberalism, of which many had been part and through which all had been, indirectly at least, formed. And they had the experiences and histories of other social movements to draw on. But none of these was adequate to meet the situation at hand and each had its gaps and problems. Women at Greenham had to invent their own set of values to guide their actions.

The process of creating these values began on the walk to Greenham and continued throughout the existence of the camp in the everyday practices of life there. Discussions about the right way to do things were an integral part of daily life, both informally in conversations over the washing-up and around the fire, and in meetings dedicated to considering matters such as the morality of cutting the fence around the base, or how to spend camp money ethically and effectively. The physical separateness of the camp (four miles from the nearest town) and the obvious differences between camp life and 'normal' life aided the construction of a new set of values. Greenham was *liminal* space, a created world where many of the rules and values of the rest of society were consciously questioned, reworked, transformed or discarded in favour of a new set of beliefs. Greenham was outside normality, outside 'the real world'.

> I always said, there was the real world, and there was Greenham. Partly that was a bit of a joke, but partly it was very true and it still seems like it was a different world. In a positive way.
>
> *Jinny List*

Many women spoke of how to live at Greenham, or even to visit the camp, was to experience a sense of liberation from the constraints of traditional ways of thinking and acting. In particular, living outdoors created a highly productive intellectual openness:

> You'd get this sort of freedom to let your mind wander outside its normal confines, which you can't do if you're confined by a building, and your thoughts are shaped by that building. If you sit around a fire, it's dark, and after a while you could be living in any century, and any country, and your whole being is totally free from those restrictions ... Women felt outside normal behaviour.
>
> *Carmel Cadden*

The common values of Greenham were never consciously or explicitly laid out in the form of rules, guidelines or policies, and were flexibly and loosely held.[4] They were not a doctrine to which newcomers had to subscribe in order to join. Women would become aware of them as they spent time at Greenham or were part of the Greenham network. Then through their participation in life at Greenham they became part of the process by which values were transformed.[5] But the values were no less real for being unwritten and implicit. They constituted a powerful moral discourse which shaped life at Greenham, providing continuity as women came and went, and forming part of the core collective identity. To be a 'Greenham woman' meant to accept, to a greater or lesser extent, Greenham's common values.

In speaking about Greenham's values, many women struggled to express the seeming paradox of, on the one hand an absence of any clear-cut rules and an explicit anarchist rejection of the attempt of a collectivity to control the behaviour of individuals, and on the other the existence of a strong set of shared principles by which women were expected to live.

> ... communal living, shared responsibility, anti-authoritarianism, feminist principles. Basically everyone not having to do any more than they wanted to, but keeping the place ticking over. Taking some sort of responsibility for your own actions, that was a pretty essential ethic. There were certain things that were acceptable and certain things that weren't acceptable, and you were aware of them, whether they were said or not. Like, for example, we have no leadership. That was said all the time. It wasn't acceptable to go round saying, 'I am a leader', or 'She is a leader'.
>
> *Sarah Benham*

> As far as rules were concerned, there was that [vegan food only at Turquoise Gate], and not having men there after dark. There were lots of things, but a lot of them were unsaid and it's just how we lived. We didn't say, we're not going to vote on things, or we won't do this if one person's unhappy about this.
>
> *Penny Gulliver*

> SASHA: *Do you think that there was a set of ethics or principles at Greenham?*
> Yes ... that everyone has their own opinion. That was the big ethic. There were the obvious ones, about violence in the camp and about always talking, always trying to talk things through ... But there were no agreed principles in the way that there have been within the women's movement, the seven demands of the women's liberation movement ... In a sense, the ethic of Greenham was, there are no rules, although I suppose there was one rule: no men.
>
> *Penni Bestic*

I've never heard of anywhere else where there were absolutely no rules at all and there were no rotas. The only rule at Greenham was no men, and you could do exactly what you liked, and yet one ate jolly well at camp. It worked ... there were no committees, or anything like that, and everything was done by consensus. And it actually worked.

*Rowan Gwedhen*

I think that people tried to give each other as much freedom as they could, and not restrict each other.

*Liz Galst*

I think it was partly the principles and ethics that attracted me really. There was no pressure on women to do anything that they didn't want to do, and most of the time that was actually put into practice. Sometimes it wasn't, but mostly it was. And the ecology bit; women tried very hard to hold on to that as an important principle. Non-violence was adhered to. And supporting women was a strong principle, giving support when women were in need of it. Sometimes those things didn't work, but mostly they did. And it was an unsaid principle really that it was fun as well. Nobody said, right, this is going to be fun. But fun was never far away.

*Jenny Heron*

I'm not sure that they were worked out enough to be called ethics. I think that lots of women had principles, and people had many, many different personal reasons for being there, and there was agreement over some things as well. And I think there was some acceptance and some agreement about not having leaders, but there were forces that did make leaders anyway.

*Bridget Evans*

## A Model of Self

Greenham had at its core a set of beliefs about how individual women should seek to be in the world. These beliefs constituted a postmodern feminist model of self. This model moved beyond the sameness/difference dichotomy within which modern feminism has become entangled.[6] This dichotomy represents feminism as forcing a choice between either seeking for women an autonomously individual self, modelled on the 'male' self, or valorizing the traditional difference of the more relational, less individuated 'female' self.[7] The model of self developed at Greenham sought neither to make women more like men nor to reinforce traditional femininity with its propensity to always put others before the self. Rather, it overturned this dichotomy and struggled towards an integration of autonomy and relationality.

AUTONOMOUS INDIVIDUALITY

To explain this more concretely, Greenham worked with a principle of personal autonomy and personal responsibility which was derived from anarchism. This principle assumed and required that women act as autonomous individuals, asserting their moral agency in the world. Greenham was premised on the notion that individual women should take it upon themselves to oppose the deployment of Cruise and to withdraw their consent from military decisions which had been made in their name but to which they (as ordinary citizens, and particularly as women) had not been party. This principle was rooted in a belief in the importance of individual agency in the creation, re-creation and transformation of society. An acceptance of personal responsibility was seen as a refusal of victimhood and as a refusal to cede power to the state. Each individual was expected to look to her own conscience and desires to decide on her actions. From decisions about whether or not to do the washing-up or cook dinner, to whether or not to cut the fence, attend court, pay a fine or go to prison, there was no external arbiter. The onus for action lay with the individual and was not to be placed on others; women expected each other to make their own decisions and not to wait for leadership.

Just the initial decision to go to Greenham and then to stay there required that women exercise their autonomous agency as individuals. Each woman who got to Greenham had taken a bold step, as an individual, often acting against the wishes or advice of family and friends, risking social disapprobation in choosing to be there. As we saw in Chapter 3, many women spoke of how deciding to go to Greenham was the first decision which they had ever really made for themselves in their adult lives.

I just decided I was going to go there. My contract at this place I was working was expiring and they said, do you want to renew your contract. And I said no. So I didn't. It was great because it was the first time I felt like I'd actually made a decision to do something. I'd always done things by proxy. I knew a few women down there, but not really … It was the first time that I felt empowered about doing something. It was great.

*Penni Bestic*

Jenny Heron summed up what the Greenham philosophy of autonomous individuality meant to her:

For me it means taking into my own hands what I want to change, as well as working in groups. It's seeing yourself as part of society, but also as an autonomous person who can have quite a bit of control over my own life. It's about not being a victim of capitalism or patriarchy.

*Jenny Heron*

The expectation that women at Greenham would act out of a sense of autonomous individuality contributed to ensuring that this happened. In seeking to 'live up' to the Greenham model of self, women developed a new self-confidence and sense of individual purpose and self-determination.

I've become more autonomous. I am less fearful of doing what I want to do, if it's not what society would approve of. I understand the consequences of that sort of action more fully than I ever did. But in a way having braved those consequences, I am more prepared to do what I want to do. I sort of feel like I can weigh that thing up and decide, yes, I actually need to do this thing. And I need to do it either openly and probably get caught, or I need to try and get away with it. But either way I'm more clear about what I might need to do and more able to weigh it out. Instead of saying, oh I can't do that, it's against the law, I sort of think, that's only one factor, and there might be other things that are more important.

*Katrina Allen*

In the context of a society where dominant expectations of adult women are still that they will put the needs and desires of others before their own, that women's sense of fulfilment will come through relationships rather than through the pursuit of their individual life projects, Greenham's valuing of autonomous individuality was profoundly feminist. It engendered in women a feeling of power, as individuals and collectively as women, and challenged the fear which many women experience of setting oneself apart as an individual.

> I think it has changed me. I mean, I think it's meant something to me in terms of the power that women can have. And that I have power ... I think it's almost for me, once you become aware of that, that feeling never goes away. That feeling of power, that women can have.
>
> *Bridget Evans*

> It's made me brave. I deliberately use it sometimes if I feel afraid ... I think, come on, you're a Greenham woman. So that aspect of it was important to me. It dragged me up a bit more, out of doing as I was told and thinking everyone else knew what to do and not me.
>
> *Barbara Rawson*

> I think Greenham changed me enormously ... I felt at the beginning that I could push the world over, almost. I felt less afraid than I'd ever been.
>
> *Margery Lewis*

RELATIONALITY, REFLEXIVITY AND PERSONAL CHANGE

However, an emphasis on autonomous individuality could, if untempered, have produced a collection of raging egos, each determined to pursue her own path, firm in the belief in her own rightness. Rigidly autonomous individuals operating with a sense of self which is stable, unchanging and tightly bounded would find it difficult to live and work together. However, the postmodern bent within the common values of Greenham meant that its model of self had a fluidity and openness. The valorizing of autonomy was counterpoised by an emphasis on the importance of being with and for 'Others', that is, an emphasis on relationality.[8] There was an expectation that individuals should be reflexive, that they should question and monitor their own behaviour, and that they should be prepared to change. An openness to and concern for the opinions and desires of others, and a flexibility and fluidity of ego boundaries were valued in preference to a rigid sense of self and one's rightness.[9]

> Greenham was always about being open to new ideas, about being prepared to look at yourself and at your politics and change and not believe that you have things absolutely right. It wasn't about 'We are Greenham women, and everything we do here is the best and the most important.'
>
> *Sarah Benham*

Because Greenham was a space carved outside 'normal society', but to which women came moulded and formed by that society, it was a place of change. Major upheavals in self-identity were expected. There was a postmodern acceptance that identities are fluid and open to question and that attitudes, beliefs and politics shift. The autonomous individuality that was valued at Greenham was not that of the isolated, free-floating, fully and irrevocably formed individual, but rather that of an individual open to change through self-reflection and interaction with a community of others.

This model of self was an ideal and of course individual women at Greenham did not always feel fully autonomous or ready to take personal responsibility for transforming society. Nor did they always face the challenge of personal change with equanimity; relinquishing old beliefs and behaviours was often resisted or feared. Everyone had their off-days and weak moments, some more than others. But Greenham's model of self was not an impossible one; it did not require that women set themselves superhuman goals of personal behaviour.

## A Model of Community and Politics

Greenham's model of community and politics was a postmodern experiment in living according to queer feminist values. In many respects these values built on the ideas and practices of the women's liberation movement, particularly its more radical and anarchist tendencies.[10] But they brought a new edge to them, a postmodern and queer delight in upheaval, dissent, diversity, difference, ambiguity, obstreperousness, pleasure, parody, emotionality and spontaneity.

VALUING AUTONOMY AND SELF-DETERMINATION: A DEMOCRACY OF THE PRESENT

As well as being valued at the level of the individual, autonomy, reflexivity and openness to change were a fundamental part of Greenham's model of community and politics.

Greenham was, from the outset, an autonomous action and community, accountable only to those who were actively involved at the time. It was never affiliated to any organization or political party and accepted direction and orders from no external body. Many outside observers assumed that Greenham was an arm of the Campaign for Nuclear Disarmament and a few, including a number of MPs and journalists, suggested that it was under the control of the Soviets. Although donations of money and goods were accepted regardless of who sent them, no influence over what happened at the camp was thus secured. This produced a democracy of the present, both in the sense that only those present mattered in decision-making and in the sense that it was how things looked in the present rather than how they had been seen in the past which informed discussion and decisions.

A central aspect of Greenham's commitment to autonomy and self-determination was a valuing of women's autonomy from men. In asserting its independence of other organizations, political parties and groups, Greenham was asserting women's collective right to organize politically and to live outside the control of men. The decision to make Greenham women-only, which was taken in February 1982, was initially a response to the problematic behaviour of men who had been living at the camp. Their failure to share equally in campwork and a number of violent outbursts they directed at the police and at women precipitated the decision. This was seen as a way of undermining traditional gender relations and preventing their performance at Greenham. The women-only 'policy' was the only hard and fast rule at Greenham, and it became central to the camp's collective identity. Being exclusively for women was a strong statement of valuing women, of prioritizing women's desires, ideas and choices in a culture which tends to prioritize men's desires over women's.

## VALUING REFLEXIVITY AND CHANGE

Greenham's democracy of the present contributed to an ongoing reflexivity which was intrinsic to the ethos of the camp and the network. Decisions, routines, patterns of behaviour, plans and beliefs were always contingent, open to question and amenable to re-orientation as circumstances changed and new ideas emerged. Nothing was handed down unquestioned. Dissent and disagreement were seen as potentially productive and dynamic, as producing movement and change and preventing ossification. The modernist desire for order, discipline and predictability, which accompanies a worship of reason, had no place at Greenham.

Carola Addington explained how she believed that Greenham's democracy of the present and openness to change, which meant that there was never an overall policy or strategy, was positive:

> Because there was never one particular group in charge, everyone contributed, and it changed. So often people say, Greenham women are like this, they were all so horrible, and they all shouted at me, and that was it. But go back a week later, maybe you got them on the wrong day. There was no overall policy. Even trying to say where are we going, what are we doing? We could never agree on that. And loads of women decided to close the camp and leave, and they left and still it was there; all that sort of thing. So you can't talk about it in terms of formal strategies like a political party or Greenpeace ... That's why it was so exciting, so exhilarating, because you could go in any direction ... It was more open to women putting in something. If you've got strategies all the time, whoever's got ideas won't put them in because they won't think they're valued.
>
> *Carola Addington*

## VALUING PARTICIPATION, EQUALITY AND COMMUNALITY

I think Greenham was organized around some sort of belief in everybody's contribution being valuable. It was definitely organized around non-hierarchical ideas. So not having a leader, not having leaders were principles. And following on from that is that therefore everybody's contribution is valuable, and there isn't a hierarchy of contribution, that says, if you live here full-time you're contributing something that has a value of ten and if you come once to a big action you're contributing something that has a value of minus something, or point three.

*Vee Wright*

The ethos of Greenham was fundamentally participative. To be a Greenham woman was to participate in Greenham. It was recognized that participation took many different forms and that individual women had different abilities, circumstances and desires which meant that their involvement took different forms, but there was no sitting on the sidelines and no paper membership. Women understood that Greenham was continuously recreated through their own actions and that the participation of each individual mattered.

There was a strong discourse of equality and anti-hierarchy, and an anarchist rejection of leaders and 'stars'. Hierarchy based on the length of time women had been at the camp, and between those who lived at the camp and those who visited for different lengths of time, was explicitly rejected. Greenham's democracy of the present demanded that the opinions of the newly arrived be treated with as much regard as those of the long-term residents. There was a desire to maximize participation in camp decision-making and to take decisions collectively, openly and by consensus. There was a commitment to talking, often at great length, in order to involve everyone who wanted to be involved, and a code of behaviour for meetings - everyone was given an opportunity to speak - in order to produce decisions with which everyone was happy. A positive value was placed on the airing of dissent and disagreement.

There were definite rules about listening to people, about not interrupting, about accepting people's ideas, about being democratic.

*Vee Wright*

Very often there was really good argument, with women treating each other with enormous respect, and listening to each other.

God, that was the difference between Greenham and mixed politics. Alright, women might not always get it right, and occasionally they end up shouting each other down, but the assumption is, from the beginning, that you should be listening to each other.

*Carol Harwood*

Along with the emphasis on participation and equality, an ethic of communality provided a counterweight to the autonomous individuality of Greenham's model of self. The sharing of daily life, its necessary work, its pleasures and pains, was central to Greenham's values. Yet this was a communality that operated within an anarchist moral framework of personal freedom. Women were not forced to be communal. There were no rotas to determine the equal allocation of tasks and individuals were free to opt in or out of communal meals and actions. Most of the necessities of life were consumed collectively and individual possessions tended to be kept to a minimum, but women were free to buy their own food, cook it themselves and live as separately as they wished. Yet most women chose to live communally in all important respects and valued the pleasures of communality: the exchange of life stories, the retelling of histories of the camp to newcomers, the giving of emotional support, the participation in communal entertainments such as singing and dancing.

## VALUING INDIVIDUALITY, DIFFERENCE AND DIVERSITY

We did talk a lot about where we'd come from and who we were. There was an incredible tolerance. I think that was an ethic of Greenham. That you were tolerant of people who turned up, as much as you possibly could be, and way beyond the call of duty sometimes ... Nobody was ever rejected out of hand or not given the space even to be difficult ... We allowed people to be who they were. And there was so much difficulty involved in being in a group of between 30 and 50 women, because the age range was from 16 to 60, and every type of woman you can think of and every sort of lifestyle and background. And those issues had to be dealt with ... A lot of time got put into talking about who people were, and why people were vegetarian, why they were vegan, why they lived in collective houses, why they did this, so that women could understand better who they were working with and to take the edge off the tensions ... And I think that people really began to see that you didn't have to be any other way than you wanted to be really. And I still think that that was Greenham's biggest strength – the incredible diversity of women that you met.

*Pat Paris*

Greenham's more modern values of equality and communality went hand-in-hand with a postmodern valuing of individuality, difference and diversity. The desire for equality and communality did not produce, as it did in state socialist countries, an imperative towards sameness or attempts to erase difference, to smooth out the rough edges, textures and tensions which occur when people come together. From the outset Greenham operated with a coalitionist imperative, seeking to draw in and make space for women from a wide variety of backgrounds, with a range of political and social experiences, of different ages, classes, ethnicities, nationalities and sexual and political identifications. Because Greenham did not require women to sign up to a particular 'line', to adopt a particular brand of feminism, and because its common values were fluid, it could accommodate different *reasons* for being there and different *ways* of being there. Because of the value placed on reflexivity and personal change, women were not seen as fixed forever in their difference but as complex individuals who were open to change; salient differences could change, and the meaning and importance of differences could change.

To make it possible for such a heterogeneous group of women to live and work together, respect across difference was vital. Difference was a source of tension, as we shall see in Chapter 7, but it was accepted as inevitable and seen as a resource and strength, rather than being suppressed or ignored. There was a commitment to discussing differences rather than denying them and many hundreds of meetings were spent building understanding and common ground. This was deemed as important as the outward-directed actions against the base.

As well as respect for social differences of experience, background and political and sexual identification, the tolerance of individuality, of the quirks, preferences, creativity and specificities of each individual woman was also seen as important. Attempts to flatten out even the most difficult personality, to mould women and make their behaviour more acceptable to the group, were frowned upon. Maximum freedom for women to express their individuality was sought.

In practical terms, the valuing of difference meant that it was central to the ethic of Greenham that women should be free to participate in the ways in which they felt able. So for instance, Bridget Evans, who because she came from Northern Ireland did not feel able to take part in actions which might result in arrest, saw her role as supporting those who did take part in such actions and talking to them about her experiences of the British military.

> The other thing that I liked about Greenham was that there was an acceptance that people could contribute things on different levels. So although I was never somebody who did loads and loads of the action type things, I didn't ever go inside the base or do much of the cutting of fences, but I always felt that it was accepted, really accepted by other women that I didn't feel able to do that. And nobody put any pressure on me to do that or said that I wasn't contributing anything. I was really allowed to contribute other things. And in fact my role was in supporting other women who did want to do that, and in being an educator from Northern Ireland about security.
>
> *Bridget Evans*

## VALUING LIFE, NON-VIOLENCE AND THE ENVIRONMENT

At the core of Greenham's ethos was the value that it placed on life, in contrast to the focus of nuclear militarism on death and destruction. Opposition to Cruise missiles, and to the military and political practices which were behind them, was perhaps the ultimate unifying theme. Greenham was an expression of 'life politics' against a politics of death.[11] To Greenham women the preservation of life was of greater value than the protection of a particular political regime. They rejected the arguments of nuclear strategists and the Cold War governments that it was necessary to be prepared to use nuclear weapons in order to preserve 'peace and security'. Nuclear weapons could never be justified by a higher cause.

It was a principle of Greenham that no violence should be used either in daily life at the camp or in the course of actions, even when faced by violence from police or soldiers. This principle had its roots in Gandhi's commitment to non-violence and the civil rights movement in the United States. Violence was rejected as a mode of power, not just at the macro-level between nation states but also between individuals. This commitment was specifically feminist and involved a recognition of the (socially constructed) differences between men's and women's relation to violence – the fact that men are far more likely than women to use interpersonal violence and that women suffer huge amounts of violence at the hands of men. Contrary to critical commentary about Greenham there was a firm belief that men's violence, individual and collective, could be prevented, that it was not biologically determined. Women were not believed to be 'naturally non-violent' as radical feminist Lynn Alderson suggests.[12] Rather, non-violence was seen as a political principle, to be consciously chosen and actively pursued, which challenged the widespread legitimacy of the use of force and violence in society.

The implications of the principle of non-violence were the subject of considerable debate at Greenham. In particular, before a new action, such as cutting the fence, was done for the first time there was often lengthy discussion about whether it was likely to provoke violence from police or soldiers, or whether it was in itself a violent act. The question of whether non-violence constituted an adequate or appropriate politics for all situations was also much debated. Few women were absolute pacifists and many firmly supported the armed struggles of revolutionary movements such as the African National Congress, the South-West African People's Organization and the Sandinistas. However, it was universally accepted that actions at Greenham should be non-violent.

For some women non-violence was a general philosophical principle which was about the recognition of the humanity of those one is opposing and rejecting the use of violence against them.

> For me non-violence is knowing that the person you're confront-
> ing is just another human being ... What I like about non-violence
> is that you're trying to get through to people who are apparently
> on the other side. Most times they're not really. It's just a job. A lot
> of people do think about things you say to them, and it's like
> drops of water, and it does in the end have an effect.
>
> *Carmel Cadden*

For others, non-violence had a specifically feminist and personal derivation.

> My basic political philosophy is based on the idea that pain is bad and pain should be avoided at all costs, and that violence is painful, and that our experience as women, as victims and survivors of violence, should very much influence our political action. And the other thing is that I have never been able to win in a violent situation, so I never felt like that was a real option for me. Most of all I don't think that we can beat the state with violence. And I think violence is a bad thing, that violence fucks people up. I think that the option of violence really makes people not think about what the options are, and that violence makes people think in terms of winning and that winning is not really what life is about ... There are times when I personally would fight for my own body, and I think that you should not let people hurt you, because you are a valuable person and you don't deserve to feel pain. But I feel like sometimes you have to swallow that because it's not expeditious.
>
> *Liz Galst*

To others it was a question of local, context-specific tactics. In the particular situation of Greenham where women were opposing the British state and the United States military, violence was unlikely to achieve anything.

> Violence always backfires; the establishment can always use it against you. But I couldn't go up to a Nicaraguan and say, you're wrong. That doesn't mean to say I think violence works.
>
> *Penni Bestic*

> What I used to say at camp about non-violence was if I was in Nicaragua I'd probably have a gun in my hand. But I believe that it was absolutely totally right at Greenham. It could not have been otherwise. And I am not a violent person. Non-violence is a privilege; it was a privilege that we could choose to be non-violent. But I'm not into self-sacrifice. If witch-hunts began again, and they were out for dykes I don't think I'd let myself be shot. I don't have this absolute dogma about non-violence, that if the tanks roll

down the street coming to get you, you should let them roll over you. But that doesn't mean I believe in violence.

*Rowan Gwedhen*

Many women found the ethic of non-violence particularly difficult to live up to when faced with violence from police and soldiers, but breaches were very rare.

I believe in non-violence, but I find it difficult. I've never been inclined to hit anybody, but it's been there in the background.

*Barbara Rawson*

Non-violence did seem very important at the time, but you got to the stage where you were being arrested so much and chucked about by the police so much, and you felt, how did this philosophy of non-violence actually fit in with feminism, which often involved you as a woman being on the receiving end of a lot of shit from men, because sometimes you just wanted to lash out physically. I still do think that you get a lot of strength from not playing on their terms, just doing things on your own terms – which was non-violence.

*Sarah Benham*

Another aspect of the value Greenham placed on life was concern about the environment and about minimizing the harm done to the immediate eco-system of the Common. This ethic arose gradually through the experience of living outdoors at Greenham and was refracted through the discourse of eco-feminism. Eco-feminist ideas were brought to Greenham by individual women (particularly American women who had been involved in the Women's Pentagon Action) and in the writings of Barbara Deming and Susan Griffin which were widely read at the camp. Living in the open, on a beautiful piece of common land (at least for those at Green and Orange Gates) made women increasingly aware of the effect of their presence on the ecology of the area. The experience of having to deal directly with the waste products of one's own existence for the first time (without running water, sewage systems and regular refuse collection) also impressed upon women the importance of environmental issues. Combined with the ethic of personal responsibility, this created an impetus for each woman to attempt to minimize her impact on the environment. Thus Greenham women generally used biodegradable detergents, exercised care not to damage trees or to leave traces of their presence on the Common, and, in planning major actions, considered the implications for the eco-system of the presence of large numbers of women.

> I saw most of the women - and remember that I was at Green most of the time - I saw most of the women caring for their surroundings, thinking about what was happening to the woods when we were living there, being vegetarian.
>
> *Barbara Rawson*

## VALUING THE 'NON-RATIONAL': EMOTIONALITY, PASSION AND PLEASURE

> I think I became less empirical, demanding less empiricism and understanding a lot more.
>
> *Penni Bestic*

> There was this magic about it. I could *feel* it was real. I've got a firm belief in magic after Greenham.
>
> *Susan Lamb*

Modernist politics, including modernist feminism, has tended to ground its arguments in reason and to rely on strategic and rational calculation of relationships between means and ends. At the heart of Greenham's postmodern politics was a rejection of one of the core beliefs and practices of modernity - rationality. There was an explicit recognition amongst women at Greenham that the rationality and bureaucracy which organized the millions of tasks required to enact the extermination of millions of people in the Holocaust had parallels with the rationality and bureaucracy of the modern nuclear state and its military in preparing for nuclear war. Both required, in Max Weber's words, 'precision, speed, unambiguity, knowledge of the files, continuity, discretion, unity, strict subordination, reduction of friction and of material and personal costs … a discharge of business according to calculable rules and "without regard for persons"'.[13]

The ethos which was constructed at Greenham and which guided the way life was led and actions were taken there was in sharp contrast to the bureaucratic rationality of the modern state. In its opposition to nuclear militarism Greenham opted out of the modernist discourse about nuclear weapons which was accepted both by the military and by the mainstream peace movement, and refused to engage with the techno-strategic discourse of the defence establishment. It did not seek to argue that there were more effective or rational modes of defence than the acquisition of first-strike nuclear weapons. It refused the terms of the discourse of the Cold War which demanded attention to military forms of defence. Against this Greenham ranged an expressive politics of the emotions which focused on the dangers and damages of military technology.

At Greenham the realm of the 'non-rational' was revalued. Emotionality, intuition, 'gut feelings' were accorded significance as sources of knowledge on which to draw in decision-making and in daily life.[14] An integral part of discussions about how life was organized at the camp and about planning actions was attention to the feelings of the women involved. For one woman to say that she 'felt uncomfortable with' or 'had bad feelings about' something that was happening or planned at the camp would carry as much weight and be taken as seriously as someone saying that she thought the same thing was ill-judged.

Valuing the non-rational was a self-conscious attack on and transcendence of the Western philosophical dualisms of reason/emotion, mind/body, male/female, which many feminist philosophers have pointed out systematically devalue the side of the dualism which is constructed as female.[15] It was not that women at Greenham were implying that women are *naturally* more emotional, intuitive or closer to nature than men; rather they were pointing out that the non-rational is an important realm of human experience, and that it should be admitted as a resource in political action. Here again Greenham drew on eco-feminist ideas. Some women were also influenced by feminist/matriarchal spirituality and carried out rituals and practised magic.[16] Other women, however, rejected this interest in spirituality and tended to ridicule what they called 'cosmic' practices and ideas.

Emotional relationships, caring, affection, friendship and love between women at Greenham were strongly valued. The strength and pleasure which women derived from their relationships with each other were seen to be a vital wellspring for the energy of the camp and the network, rather than just a by-product of living and working together.

It was an environment where you felt very supported, and women would know what was happening for you, for me. And you'd go and sit on your own and think what a shit world it is. But then somebody would turn up with a cup of tea and a piece of vegan chocolate, at some point, or a cigarette, or something, just to show that thought was there, and they cared. And they really did. And I'd do it too for other women, even women I didn't like very much … You'd try and find out what was wrong, and you'd talk about it, and you'd behave civilly, and be supportive.

*Jinny List*

It was also felt to be important that living at Greenham and carrying out actions there was a positive and pleasurable experience:

I think one of the things I learnt from Greenham was that thing about it's not a revolution if I can't dance at it.[17] I actually think Greenham gave me that. I mean that is not a trivial quality that a political action has got to reflect you and it's got to nourish you as well as taking from you.

*Clare Hudson*

Traditionally politics is seen as the serious and sober business of men in grey suits. Those engaged in oppositional politics tend to take themselves equally earnestly, often veering towards pomposity. Greenham stood as the complete obverse of this. Whilst the women involved held passionate beliefs about what they were doing, it was a principle that actions should be as enjoyable as possible and that they should not entail suffering or martyrdom. In the tradition of Situationism, it can be seen as a parodic response to the deadly seriousness of the global situation and to the pomposity and earnestness of many in the mixed peace movement. Many women were conscious of wishing to challenge the portrayal of Greenham women by the liberal press as ordinary housewives and mothers who were heroically making sacrifices to save the world for future generations. They strove to overturn the construction of self-sacrifice, altruism and vulnerability as feminine virtues.

Many of the actions which were carried out at Greenham were designed to mock, parody and deflate, and at the same time to be fun to enact. For example, the Teddy Bears' Picnic of Easter 1983 in which several dozen women dressed as bears, bunnies and jesters and climbed into the base to have a picnic, was pleasurable for those taking part, made an ironic statement about the deadly seriousness of the global situation and was a pointed gesture to CND, which had refused to respect Greenham women's request that they not organize a major mixed demonstration at the base.

> I thoroughly enjoyed Greenham. Perhaps it was being a naughty child. A wicked girl. There was something of that about it. So many of the things that we did at Greenham were silly and fun. We always used to laugh so much. And I did try to explain in court one day, how laughter is the only antidote to the nuclear madness that was going on.
>
> *Ann Armstrong*

Clare Hudson saw Greenham's use of humour as a non-violent means of protest:

> I think there was always a shared view that we were finding new ways of doing things because we were women, and I do think that non-violence was pretty sacrosanct. Not totally but pretty nearly – as near as you could get and that wasn't just a tactic. It was what we were about and that informed everything we did. And what followed from that were actions that made you laugh, or even made them laugh, or made them look silly. All those things were very much part of how we tried to dismantle the structures that were part of militarism in our society.
>
> *Clare Hudson*

Women sought to demonstrate that their involvement with Greenham was anything but self-sacrificial and altruistic. Living at Greenham was, much of the time, great fun. Humour was an important part of life there and often took the form of self-mockery, irony and parody. One of the best examples of this was Gill Booth's song 'Down at Greenham on a Spree' which played with many of the most common stereotypes and characterizations of Greenham women:

> Down at Greenham on a spree,
> funded by the KGB,

dirty women squatters in the mud.
Mostly vegetarians,
except when we're devouring men,
foreigners and other kinds of crud.

Mr Andropov provides us with our vodka,
Mr Castro makes sure we're kept in dope.
All the women here are outside agitators,
who can't see that Ronald Reagan brings us hope,
                              brings us hope.

What a bunch of layabouts,
who don't know what it's all about,
how we need deterrence for the best.
Lighting fires and burning toast,
bringing Communism close,
threatening the safety of the West.

In the bushes a cache of guns is waiting,
with sealed copies of Karl Marx in plastic bags,
                              in plastic bags.
All our children live in misery with rats and
                              deprivation.
But what can you expect from queers and hags?

Down at Greenham on a spree,
funded by the KGB,
laughing, singing, dancing in the rain.
Nowhere signs of sacrifice,
making do or being nice,
and most of all we're not accepting pain.

'Cos we're trying to be done with games and
problems,
with hypocrisy, dishonesty and fear.
So, don't be getting shirty,
Cos it's us that's getting dirty,
And because of us
We'll all be here next year.[18]

VALUING THE PRESENT

Greenham's emphasis on pleasure and enjoyment of the process of opposing nuclear militarism was part of a broader philosophical position which placed great value on the present. Radical modernist politics have tended to operate with a fundamental orientation to the future, a utopian vision which sees the goals of struggle in the far distance and the present as a time of necessary sacrifice for the cause. A long road is mapped out, leading by stages towards a better life. In rejecting this modernist view of political change Greenham was not abandoning the ideal of a more just, equal and free society. Rather it was seeking to create that society in the present through the ways women lived their lives at Greenham and by taking direct action which would have a clear and immediate practical and symbolic impact. Choosing to act in the present, rather than developing long-term strategies and pursuing a parliamentary or party elite road to social change, was an expression of impatience, of the urgency that was felt to exist. It represented a refusal of the modernist belief that rational calculations could be made of the probable outcomes of strategic action and was grounded instead in a belief in the inseparability of the means and ends of social and political transformation.

> There was a realization that how you did something was as important as what the job was. I think that was an important quality about Greenham. It was the process itself and how we acted that was just as important as the end result.
>
> *Simone Wilkinson*

This belief that the route to change is as important as the desired goal was derived from the anarchist/Situationist tradition, in which the reinvention of everyday life is considered a revolutionary act.[19] It is not just that the means determines the end, but also that the present matters in and of itself. Processes of discussion and debate were valued and (unlike traditional left-wing politics) personal change, non-oppressive organizational structures and, above all, transforming gender relations were not to be deferred until 'after the revolution'. The belief in the inseparability of means and ends was also part of Greenham's opposition to the military discourse which held that peace in Europe could only be guaranteed by the acquisition of a new generation of nuclear weapons and by preparation for war. The means (the arms race, with all its consequences for public expenditure and the risk of accident) was not seen as justifying the ends (the maintenance of 'peace', or the geopolitical status quo).

The valuing of the present can be seen as the summative principle of Greenham's postmodern queer feminism. As well as reorienting action away from an excessive concern with the future and allowing an often unruly spontaneity of action, it also sought to free women from the past. This operated at a collective level in terms of Greenham's democracy of the present, which as I have already discussed meant that prior decisions and camp routines and traditions were always open to question and reformulation. Previous generations of Greenham women could not dictate how things should be done. It also meant that although there was interest in the traditions of radical activism which had preceded Greenham, women did not feel bound by them. Feminism in particular could not operate as a tradition with the power to control and constrain women's actions. There was a disrespect and scepticism towards all authorities and traditions, and a belief in the importance of the self-creation of moral and ethical codes. At the individual level, Greenham's emphasis on the present allowed women to construct for themselves a break with their own pasts (if they so desired) and opened up space for the reinvention of the self. Ways of thinking and being, past relationships and identities, could be re-evaluated and left behind much more easily where what mattered was not who one had been but rather who one was at that moment.

## Notes

1. There is now a considerable amount of literature on feminist ethics (e.g. Ruddick, 1990, Frazer, 1992, Held, 1993, Tong, 1993, Tronto, 1995, Bowden, 1997 and Sevenhuijsen, 1998), though few writers engage with feminist ethics as practised by actual communities of feminists, preferring instead a theoretical discourse.
2. Like Smart (1993), I am suggesting that feminist politics and ethics/morality are inseparable.
3. See Bauman (1993, 1995), Smart (1993) and Weeks (1995) for discussion of ethics and morality in postmodernity. Their sociologically grounded consideration of postmodern ethics challenges the widespread idea that a postmodern approach to ethics is one which celebrates the 'demise of the ethical' (Bauman, 1993:2). As Bauman puts it: 'the novelty of the postmodern approach to ethics

consists first and foremost not in the abandoning of characteristically modern moral concerns, but in the rejection of typically modern ways of going about its moral problems (that is, responding to moral challenges with coercive normative regulation in political practice, and the philosophical search for absolutes, universals and foundations in theory)'(3-4).

4. However, there is some discussion of principles of action in writings by Greenham women (e.g. Cook and Kirk, 1983; Harford and Hopkins, 1984).

    In the first few months of the camp's existence, a number of the women who had been involved in the Cardiff to Greenham walk drew up a list of rules. These included asking for a financial contribution from those staying at the camp and banning the smoking of dope. However, the rules were never taken seriously or followed, and they soon disappeared altogether.

5. The exception to this was that on occasions of major actions (such as 11 December 1983) the principles of non-violence, caring for the environment and valuing the 'non-rational' were set out in leaflets for those visiting the camp. However, these leaflets tended to be produced by CND or local support groups, not by women at the camp.

    The general informality and lack of codification of principles contrasted with the Seneca Women's Peace Encampment in the USA, where a list of 'respected policies' was drawn up and given to women as they arrived. For a discussion of the 'governance' of Seneca and a list of the 'respected policies' decided by national planning meetings and general meetings at Seneca, see Linton (1989).

6. For discussion of the equality/difference dichotomy within feminism, and attempts to move beyond it, see Bacchi (1990), Scott (1990) and Bock and James (1992).

7. There is no space here to outline the debate which has arisen from Gilligan's (1982) work on women's 'different moral voice' and the notion of an ethics of care. See, for example, Tronto (1993) and Sevenhuijsen (1998).

8. This is not dissimilar to Bauman's (1993) call for a postmodern ethics based on 'being with' and 'being for the Other'.

9. Benhabib (1995) argues for a feminist ethics, politics and concept of autonomy which shows similarities to that developed at Greenham.

10. See York et al. (1979) for a statement of radical feminist principles of organizing.

11. Giddens (1991) contrasts 'life politics' with 'emancipatory politics'. Greenham combined the two.

12. Alderson (1983: 12).

13. Gerth and Mills (1970: 214, 215) quoted in Bauman (1989: 14). See Bauman (1989) for a discussion of the role of rationality in the Holocaust, and Roseneil (1999) for further discussion of Greenham's Holocaust consciousness.

14. This is a principle shared with one strand of radical feminism, exemplified in the writings of Griffin (1978) and Daly (1979). See Jaggar (1988) for a discussion. It was also the target of criticism by radical feminists (e.g. Onlywomen Press, 1983).

15. Griffin (1978, 1989) and Lloyd (1984).

16. See, for example, Spretnak (1982).

17. 'If I can't dance, it's not my revolution' is attributed to Emma Goldman at an anarchist ball (Marshall, 1993: 409).

18.  The song refers to the frequent allegations by government ministers and the press that Greenham (and CND) was in receipt of Soviet money and that there were Soviet agents at work at Greenham. It also comments on the tabloid press coverage of Greenham women as dirty lesbians and inadequate mothers, and on the liberal broadsheet coverage of Greenham women as self-sacrificing women suffering for their cause.

19.  'It is plain that the goal of the revolution today must be the liberation of daily life. Any revolution that fails to achieve this goal is counter-revolution. Above all, it is *we* who have to be liberated, *our* daily lives, with all their moments, hours and days, and not universals like "History" and "Society" … There can be no separation of the revolutionary process from the revolutionary goal' (Bookchin, 1971: 44–5).

   'No revolution can ever succeed as a factor of liberation unless the MEANS used to further it be identical in spirit and tendency with the PURPOSES to be achieved' (Goldman, 1977: 161).

# Chapter 7
# Differences, Debates and Conflicts: The Politics of 'Women' at Greenham

*There was a lot of conflict. There were just so many different types of women there – heterosexuals and dykes, Catholics and witches, upper-middle-class, lower-working-class, different backgrounds, different beliefs, different reasons for being there. I think there must be conflict in something like that. Because that was the thing about the place being open to anybody who would turn up. And yes, by the time you're getting 16-year-old street runaways, and by the time it got to hundreds, and women were just turning up with a myriad of reasons. All of us there had our different reasons for being there, and a whole myriad of different attitudes and beliefs and ways of behaviour. I think obviously there were going to be conflicts and arguments, and not being able to stand each other sometimes. There was a nun on one side and a lesbian anarchist vegan on the other. Yet there was a unity there, and it was OK.*

*Rowan Gwedhen*

Greenham was a highly politicized environment, one in which debate and conflict were the stuff of everyday life. Rather than being seen as dangerous signs of schism and disunity, discussion and dissent were embraced as core to the existence of the camp and the movement. Greenham's queer feminism was neither a political programme nor a coherent political philosophy, but rather a broad approach, a code of values within which there was ample room for disagreements and differences of opinion and orientation. In seeking to live by a set of ethics which valued participation and equality and which opposed hierarchy, women considered it vital to scrutinize the power dynamics and political implications of (almost) everything they did. The value placed on reflexivity and openness to change meant that there was a belief in the importance of constantly re-examining and challenging routine practices and ways of thinking. And the emphasis on individuality and difference encouraged the exploration of diverging opinions. There was a general acceptance of the inevitability of conflict and a commitment to seeking to allow it proper expression, in the belief that this would channel it into productive change. Given the wide range of backgrounds, motivations, beliefs and lifestyles of the women who were involved, and the fact that most were strong-minded, determined, articulate and passionately idealistic, it was hardly surprising that life at Greenham was anything but a tranquil idyll of peaceful, beatific women living together in harmony.

The debates and conflicts which I focus on in this chapter, and which I consider to have been the most significant at Greenham, hinge on the question of the meaning of the designation 'women'. 'Women' were named as the actors and owners of the 'Greenham Common Women's Peace Camp', the identity invoked in a celebratory, oppositional and seemingly essentialist manner, as the women of the camp set themselves against the men of militarism. Yet as everyone quickly discovered, however powerful and exciting it was to mobilize as women in a cultural context which devalues women and their connections with each other, 'women' is not an unproblematic and inherently unified category. The category of 'woman' has come under much scrutiny recently in feminist theory, particularly from post-structuralist and postmodernist perspectives, but its assumed coherence has also been contested in everyday feminist practice, particularly since the early 1980s, and Greenham was as much a site for debates about the meaning of 'woman' as it was about other arenas of feminist politics.[1] Questions about who the women of Greenham were, who was included, who excluded, who the *real* Greenham women were, about degrees and hierarchies of being Greenham women, and how the identity of 'woman' was to be performed at Greenham were the issues which constituted the internal politics of the movement. Together they raised questions of gender identity, sexual identity, class and race, the key concerns of contemporary feminism.

> As time went on I think questions like, why are there so few black women at Greenham, what's the place of, you know, Welsh women, Irish women, Scottish women at Greenham, about class – all the things that were happening in the women's movement, all those tensions that were growing in the women's movement

through the eighties from the sort of simplistic, and I don't mean it dismissively, but the very simple view that if only we could get women together it would be all right - from that sort of feminism in the seventies to a much more complex view of whole sort of patterns of multiple oppression and how as women we can actually be contributing to each other's oppression. All those kinds of questions that were being raised in the women's movement generally were being reflected in what was happening at Greenham.

*Helen Mary Jones*

By exploring the particular ways in which these debates and conflicts were framed at Greenham, the differences of opinion which existed and the rather different ways of thinking about and responding to them which were developed there, the distinctive politics of Greenham are brought into focus. The five debates and conflicts which I discuss are those about the women-only decision, the queering of Greenham, the problem of hierarchy and the insider/outsider distinction, the distribution of material resources and the King's Cross affair.

## The Women-only Decision

The first major issue of debate and conflict in Greenham's history was about what it meant that the camp was called a '*women's* peace camp'. In order to understand the substance of this debate the context within which the camp was established is important. The Women for Life on Earth walk from Cardiff to Greenham had been initiated and led by women, but a small number of men had taken part and stayed on to live at Greenham when the camp was set up. At the beginning, 'women' did not mean 'women-only'. The politics of the walk were, as I suggested in Chapter 3, largely maternalist in orientation and the initiators did not identify strongly as feminists, although they did tap consciously into feminist networks and were influenced by and used feminist ideas. The women who took part in the walk were from a wide range of backgrounds, and many, including Ann Pettit (the instigator of the walk) saw it as a 'women's walk' largely as a way to attract publicity.[2]

I think why we had it women only (well of course we did have some men on it) was because we thought that it would attract more attention.

*Margery Lewis*

However, once the camp had come into existence and news spread through networks of radical activists around the country, several of the new women who came to live there were feminists who were drawn there by its designation as a *women's* peace camp. Within the women's liberation movement by this time the principle of autonomous women-only organizations was well established; indeed it had been fundamental to second-wave feminism. Consciousness-raising groups, women's health groups, feminist collectives running women's centres, women's refuges, rape crisis lines, newsletters and magazines, for example, all operated as women-only groups. Many women who had been active in left politics had disengaged from mixed organizations as they battled with men for the right to organize autonomously. These new women brought with them feminist discourses about the importance of creating women's space away from men as part of the process of women's liberation from patriarchal control and constructions of femininity. Some of these women left very quickly when they found that their ideas were not shared by everyone, often because they did not wish to return to working and living with men.[3] Those who stayed were party to regular discussions about the issue of women-only versus mixed actions during the first six months. Matters finally came to a head when women living at the camp organized their first women-only meeting in February 1982. They decided, after lengthy and heated debate, that all future actions should be women-only, that only women should live at Greenham and that the camp should always attempt to deal with women representatives of the authorities and women journalists. Men were to be allowed to visit the camp only during hours of daylight.[4]

As Helen John (who had been on the original march and who was at the camp at the time of the decision) tells the story – the women-only decision was underpinned by Greenham's emphasis on promoting the voices of 'common women'.

It was the fact that there were going to be evictions – the first series of evictions by the council. And it was decided that it was absolutely important that it should be women dealing with representatives of the council and that only women should deal with the authorities so that we could prove that you did not have to be an expert, that you did not have to have specialized information or qualifications, that we were able to make decisions in the face of the danger that we were being faced with.

*Helen John*

The men living there at the time were asked to leave, and it was suggested that they might camp on another part of the Common, which a handful of those who opposed the decision did for a brief period of time. This was an epiphanic moment in the emerging politics of Greenham.

Helen was one of the women who changed her mind during the course of that meeting.

I started off not really giving two hoots and feeling that men had a right to be there, but when it was put to me by others that we ought to have women only facing authority and presenting a clear, decisive women's view, I accepted that view wholeheartedly and have never gone back on it ...

There were eleven of us living there, eleven women and a number of men. And Jayne Burton, who is an incredible woman, was the one who really actually put it into words that that should be the policy. So she was the one who actually formulated the theory, and the others of us agreed. She said that it should be women only living there and confronting and dealing with the authorities, that men should in no way be allowed to have a presence in that sphere, that if men came to the camp it should be in a supportive role only.

And the problems arose because there was a group of individuals who had come to babysit the camp whilst we did a walk to London to join a CND demo, and some of these individuals, who were non-violence trainers, went completely off their heads when they were informed that the decision had been taken, and they were asked to remove themselves. They couldn't cope with that and felt it was a terrible insult, and they went absolutely potty. There was one chap - we had a huge dome-shaped construction just by Yellow Gate and they'd erected this tripod in the middle to have water heating – and I was just sitting in a seat like this, and the guy who was the non-violence trainer actually threw the water all over me, and at that point he had no idea whether it was boiling or what. He was in such a rage and took it out on me personally, though it wasn't my decision. And he would not accept that it was a group decision. I was covered in water from the waist down, which was tepid, mercifully, but he had no way of knowing that. And then he took a handful of coins out of his pocket and screamed that there was a woman's face on that and that we were ruled by women not men, and threw these coins at me. And another chap who had erected a brand-new teepee there was living in it with a woman who had agreed that it should be women-only. He was furious and said that we were behaving like governments. He wouldn't acknowledge that we had the right to make that decision; and he took his teepee away.

And so the very next day three women tried to go back on that decision and so it caused a big division. And that split led to a lot of unhappiness, I think, for a lot of women. It was a tragedy. Because they had made the right decision, but in the face of pressure from some of the men they couldn't stand up to it.

*Helen John*


Several further mixed meetings then took place at Greenham and at the Green Gathering at Glastonbury that spring at which the decision was revisited, but the policy was never overturned. Some of the women who had been on the initial walk to Greenham, but who were not living at the camp, repeatedly spoke against the women-only decision, arguing that it was divisive, that it would weaken the peace movement and that men should be encouraged to be non-violent and to change, rather than being excluded. Ann Pettit, in particular, believed that her vision had been betrayed and continued to actively oppose the decision for many years, often coming with her male partner to camp on the Common in their van. The policy remained extremely controversial within the peace movement and left circles, and was debated at length in peace groups around the country, with many CND groups teetering on the brink of splitting over the issue. Resolution was often reached by the women who supported the policy leaving to put their energy into women's peace groups and Greenham support groups. Those activists, men and women, who wanted mixed peace camps turned their attention to setting them up at other nuclear installations, such as Faslane, Burghfield, Molesworth, Alconbury and Upper Heyford.[5] But with the exception of Ann Pettit and a handful of other women who from time to time expressed their opposition, the policy became one of the two foundational principles of the camp (the other was the commitment to non-violence), and it ceased to be a source of conflict within the camp. Those who didn't agree stayed away.

It was after the women-only decision that Greenham really started to grow in size and influence as new constituencies of women were attracted to the camp and as the debate about Cruise heated up. Every woman who got involved in Greenham after February 1982 contributed to the reaffirmation of the women-only decision – her participation signalled her agreement with it. There were few Greenham women, whether campers, stayers or visitors, who were not called upon many times during the course of their involvement to explain, justify and defend the policy to friends, family and acquaintances. Very quickly the original reasons for the decision became less important than those given by women as explanation for their support of the policy. There was, in effect, a plurality of reasons why Greenham was women-only, with each woman constructing for herself – from the ideas in circulation at the camp and in the context of her own experience – her own explanation of why it was the right policy. Under the rubric of the policy there was room for a wide range of political positions in relation to feminism and a wide range of ways of thinking about relations with men.[6]

A popular argument, particularly in the early days, was that only women should take part in actions as a means of promoting the non-violent nature of the protest because men were more likely to have recourse to violence. The violence and aggression of some of the men who had been living at Greenham quickly became part of the oral history of the camp, passed on in conversations around the fire. This added to the weight of many women's everyday experiences and observations of men's violence and bolstered the policy. Well aware of the critiques and dangers of an essentialism which saw the origins of men's violence in biology, these arguments would often emphasise that men's propensity for violence was learnt behaviour which could and should change, but that meanwhile men should work on these issues with each other, rather than relying on women to show them how to change.

I know it [the decision] was to do with violence. I think this boy Derek who'd been on the first march, I think he lashed out at somebody, or something happened. But women we felt we could control. That has always been the feeling at Greenham. That women are not going to start beating up anyone.

*Margery Lewis*

I think it [Greenham being women-only] made a tremendous difference when you were involved in the direct action. It definitely made a difference. I've always found it very difficult to be in any non-violent direct action with Ray [my husband], for example. He would always be over-protective of me, you know. If a policeman got hold of me, he would have hit him, you know. That sort of situation, I think most men would. Violence so easily comes. It's so difficult too, perhaps some are OK, but most will get stuck in if somebody's doing something to a woman that they love or feel protective towards. I think that's difficult.

SASHA: *Do you think that it's just natural for men, or do you think . . .?*
I don't think it's natural. I think it's how they're brought up. I mean women police behave just as badly as the male police, so it hasn't got anything . . . I mean I think it's very difficult to behave non-violently. I mean a lot of women can't do it either, but I think generally there are the situations that would be awful with men.

*Ann Armstrong*

Another feminist argument, drawing on stories of the first six months of the camp and on women's own experiences in mixed left politics, suggested that working with men was often problematic. Men were seen as having been a drain on the camp in the early days, as not having taken responsibility for their share of the domestic labour and as having pushed women back into traditional housewife roles. Critiques of the style and culture of debate within male-dominated politics were adduced as further support for women-only space.

But it is always noticeable, if you have a meeting when you're all women, the different way women behave. They will let each other have their say. And then you go to a mixed meeting, even though it's supposed to be a peace one, you find some man telling everybody what to do. I went to an amazing march once, which was organized by a couple of men, and it went from Newbury to the racecourse, actually down to the camp and round the base. It was supposed to be some sort of support for them during evictions. There was this couple of men actually running it, and they were telling us what to do. And you got to the camp, and they said, you may talk to the women [laughter]. It was just incredible. We left them, and went our own way [laughter]. They were organizing them, and I believe that's how it was in the early days at Greenham, when it was mixed. The men actually told the women what to do, and you know, the women did the cooking, and they said, we'll go out and do this and that and organize things.[7]

*Ann Armstrong*

I felt pissed off with the left and the peace movement, which I'd had some dealings with in Leeds. What pissed me off? Loud, bearded men kind of making pronouncements. I just found it a bit irritating the way the men always took up so much space really. And did all the talking and that it seemed to continue the sort of traditions we were supposed to be opposing.

*Clare Hudson*

Even back in the sixties I knew that there was something absolutely flawed about any political movement that was mixed, unless men changed their ideas ... The idea that women were very peripheral went right through the peace movement. There's no question ... I knew that there was something really radically wrong with politics because I knew that men were playing their own power games within radical and left-wing and peace and alternative politics ... I think all you have to do is observe the way that men behave and then reverse it [laughter]. I'm being quite serious about that; you just have to look at the way that they organize and behave and then do the opposite. But this idea that women are inherently more gentle, more this, more that, I think is a bit dodgy really. Whatever you think about Thatcher, she's proved that a woman Prime Minister is not a soft option.

*Carol Harwood*

The explicitly feminist explanation frequently given was that the women-only policy was a symbolic action drawing attention to the gender politics of militarism and its support from the state: women peace activists facing men soldiers, police, bailiffs, local and national politicians. Women-only Greenham was seen as highlighting women's exclusion from mainstream politics and as a clear statement of opposition by women to political decisions to which they were not party.

> I'd come to see militarism more and more as a product of patriarchy, if you like. I'd done a lot of radical feminist reading in the course of that year. Most of which or much of this I now think is crap actually. But at the time it had a very very powerful effect and I could see and I still do see the connections between the way that little boys are taught to behave, and the way that men relate to each other and to women, and the way that men then relate to the world in terms of creating war. And I thought the symbolism of women resisting male violence was important. I also came to feel more and more that it was important to have women-only spaces. But I didn't feel, and I still don't feel, that the peace movement is a women's job. It's not women's business … It's difficult to describe but I felt that women should be resisting that because it was a male thing and it was part of male power. Both in terms of the way people were perceiving it but also in terms of the actuality of the situation of what was really true. I'd also found that it was a situation where a lot of women who'd never been political were prepared to be political and I thought one of the reasons why they were prepared to do that was because they felt fairly safe. I mean not safe in a physical sense but safe to assert themselves in a supportive atmosphere and I think that was very important.
>
> *Helen Mary Jones*

And, as with Helen Mary, the argument often proceeded to state that working within a women-only environment was empowering and transformative, offering women opportunities and experiences which they would be unlikely to take or have in mixed-sex environments. Overall this argument was the most frequently made amongst the women I interviewed.

> It's very unlikely I would have got involved with a mixed peace camp, very unlikely. Particularly because the big action with the

silos was already being planned when I first went down, and it was so soon, and I think it would have been unlikely had it been a mixed thing that I would have dared to get involved. I can imagine a mixed thing where men would have planned the whole thing. I wonder if I would have so quickly taken the decision to participate. I think I would have held back, and I would have held back a lot had it been a mixed thing. I don't think I would have stayed or got involved.

*Carola Addington*

And the fact that it was women-only really made me feel that I could have a chance to operate freely. I wouldn't feel, I mean I was on a mixed collective on the Leveller. It wasn't that I had difficulty working with men, it was just as most women say, it's just easier when you don't have that factor around, because you have all that in your head anyway. You censor yourself from saying things. I wouldn't have got involved if it hadn't been women-only. It was that strong, really. Because there just would have been so many other complications. I wouldn't have felt so safe either.
SASHA: *Safe?*
Physically, from sexual harassment, and men can get themselves into fights so easily.

*Carmel Cadden*

And the other thing that women were exposed to at Greenham was being in an all-women environment. And I think that that also had a profound effect on a lot of women going to Greenham that was about self-confidence and about understanding what happens in their world if they assume that men are more competent than they are. And if you remove that factor, you can neither give it to the men, nor can they take it. And so you suddenly learn all sorts of things about stuff that you can do.

*Katrina Allen*

Turning the focus on the exclusion of men on its head, women often argued that what was important was not the exclusion of men but the inclusion of women, the space that was created explicitly for women.

I had hostility to it being women-only, plenty at Greenham with people, men visitors.

SASHA: *How did you deal with that?*

Well, Helen John came out with a very good quote which I used to quote quite a lot: it wasn't discriminating against men, it was positively promoting women. Really it was trying to allow women to have the space to develop themselves and to express themselves and to say that there is an alternative way of working and maybe to run the world.

*Carola Addington*

I did write an article about the 10 Million Women when I got back to France and I sent it to *Nonviolence Politique*, a magazine they have there, and that got published ... I was trying to explain to all these people why Greenham wasn't anti-men but pro-woman. And the usual question, why is it women only? I used to say, it's not to keep men out, it's just to allow women the opportunity to make a contribution ... This whole thing of anti-men, I would say, it's not against men, it's really for women.

*Carmel Cadden*

In the context of their enthusiastic support for Greenham being, women-only, women positioned themselves in a variety of ways in relation to feminism and had a range of different attitudes to men and to 'separatism': from Rowan Gwedhen's 'cradle dyke' complete disinterest in men to Ann Lukes's contingent acceptance of separatism as a symbolic strategy. Although every woman I interviewed was in favour of Greenham being women-only, no one claimed the identity of 'separatist', although Rowan came closest, and some saw other women at Greenham as separatist. Most were more interested in talking about the positive experiences of living and working with women than in labelling themselves in this way, or in engaging in debate about the meaning of 'separatism'. Greenham's women-only policy had real everyday implications and meanings in their lives and it was this that they found significant. A few women made a point of expressing their unease about separatism, and sought to distance themselves from separatism - as an all-encompassing, permanent lifestyle - and feminist politics. Two stressed that they did not 'hate men'. But most avoided discussing men in general terms and focused instead on women. This can be understood as a consequence of the displacement of the centrality of heterorelations which Greenham enacted in their lives. Greenham can perhaps therefore be seen as *a separatist moment*, a particularly long-lasting and politically significant moment, and considered by those who made it politically necessary, *even essential*, at that particular historical moment. As a collective action, it may be seen, therefore, as an example of what Gayatri Spivak has called 'strategic essentialism'.[8]

> I've never been a separatist. But I thought Greenham had to be women-only. I wasn't a radical feminist. I'm a member of a political party so I couldn't be a radical feminist.
>
> *Penni Bestic*

> There is no way – you know about you saying was it more women than Cruise – I would never have dreamt of going there if men had still been there. I wasn't involved with men at all. I'm a cradle dyke. Or whatever the term is. I'm one of those things that don't exist. Born dyke. One of the things everybody's been running around for the last ten years saying don't exist. 'We all chose to become lesbians.' But yes, I'm one of those ... I didn't have anything to do with men, in the sense that I never have had.
>
> *Rowan Gwedhen*

> I spent a bit of time at Emerald,[9] when I was just going for short periods, and to adjust to men coming and sitting down by the fire, it was alright, but it was different, and I liked it at Green. I was sometimes disturbed by some things that were feminist and I didn't know if I could accept them or not, and that still happens of course.
>
> SASHA: *What sort of things?*
>
> I know now, although I didn't know when I was at Greenham, that it's a sort of being separatist, completely separatist, which Green Gate was, but that didn't bother me, but I still find the concept difficult. The person who helped me with it most was Jif and also Katrina. One of them said, have you never felt that deep anger about what men do? And I had to say, no. I can get angry about men, but I knew what she was saying was a different thing. And because Jif isn't a separatist either, she knew where I was and she

was relating to me. And I can see that need now amongst women to be completely separate from men as valid for them, and I can accept that. But that's one of the things that I did, and still do a bit, find difficult. Most of my friends were housewives, women who worked to make some money towards the household. I use the term 'keeping their heads down' and that's what I'd been doing. I've had a lot of jobs and nothing that I've trained for, and the women that I've worked with wouldn't see themselves as feminist, even now, and would see it as a threat.

SASHA: *Would you call yourself a feminist?*

Yeah [laughs]. Yes. Although I like men and have men friends, when the chips are down, yes. I think most people know I am too. I enjoy being with women best.

*Barbara Rawson*


Once it became women-only I only felt comfortable with women being there. And any action I've done subsequently I prefer not to do it with men.

SASHA: *Why?*

I don't feel comfortable. There seems to be a strength or a feeling of trust that you have with women, and as I've grown older, my friends are women friends. I find them more interesting. I think there's absolutely no logic in the way I feel. So I don't try to look for logic, but I know when I was younger I liked men an awful lot. It isn't that I dislike men now, but I go out walking a lot and I always find that I'm walking with women. They are my friends. I go out with them if I go to the theatre or something. I don't seek companionship with men.

*Margery Lewis*


There was other stuff going on in Nottingham that I could have quite easily gotten involved in, but was mixed. I don't know that then it was that clear to me. And the women's group that I was in too was quite a big part of it. Having discovered that there were other dykes around, I wasn't going to waste my energy working with men. Because what I needed to do was meet other women and find out what the hell was going on in my life, and the only way I thought I'd find that out was looking at what was happening in other women's lives. I went through, I don't want to say phase, but it probably was, an incredibly separatist phase … not wanting to have anything to do with men, other than give them my bus fare, really. Now I have two or three friends that are men, but they're only really friends because the women that I live with know them.

*Jinny List*

One of the criticisms that could be levelled against Greenham was that it was very white and feminist as opposed to womanist. And that it wasn't aware of the different relationship that black women have to black men, as opposed to the relationship that white women have to white men. And that therefore some of the separatist arguments that were very popular within Greenham, I have some difficulties with, in as much as I don't think that they're applicable across the board. And I think that there are many reasons why black women can't be as comfortable that they have a dislike and don't want to relate to men on any level at any time because of racism that black women share with black men. In a way white women have less to feel in common with white men. But also Greenham didn't even think about the relationship between lesbians and gay men. I think that's quite interesting. I didn't think about that at the time, whereas what I've gone on to do since, particularly around Clause 28, I'm much more thinking about those dynamics. And that doesn't sit easy with radical separatist lesbianism, which was quite a dominant strain within Greenham.

*Bridget Evans*

I understood very well the way that the women there felt that you did need reverse discrimination. The men didn't need the space, they didn't need to be able to show their own ability and the women needed it to show that there is something other than the way things are worked in the hierarchical male-dominated society that we have. And I agree with all that, but on the other hand I didn't really agree with the militants who were not doing it from that sense but were doing it from an anti-man sense. They weren't doing it because they were being supportive of other women, they were doing it because they were anti-men. And I felt that was wrong.

SASHA: *Would you call yourself a feminist?*

It depends what category of feminist. I would say I identify with a lot of the aims of a lot of feminists' movements. But I don't identify totally with the feminist idea of separatism. I think the way forward is for men to change their ideas. And for all this male hierarchical structure which is so destructive to go. But I divorce that from men, from men as men, as people. I think they're just as much the victims as we are. I think they're victims of a power structure in the same way that we are. They react differently, on the whole, but not always. And therefore I feel that it should be a way forward together. I don't think separatism is the answer.

SASHA: *Do you not think Greenham was separatist?*

I think it was, but I think the need for that symbol at the time justified it. It was symbolic separatism because the women were symbolizing, because the thing they were going against was the absolute converse. It was male. Power dominated. And the missiles there are the highest symbol of that thing, so it needed that.

SASHA: *So you think in certain times that separatism is justified?*

Yes. It is. And if it's not used for other purposes.

SASHA: *Used for what sort of purposes?*

Well aggressive purposes and not used symbolically. I know a lot of women there who were getting their own back at men ... I mean I met some women who said all men are potential rapists. You know, they've got to be just because they're men. And when you have that sort of attitude, which there was a very large group of women who had that attitude there, you know, they're sort of damaging. Because it couldn't conceive the idea that there could be cooperation. It couldn't conceive of the idea that this was just a stage, just a step, that the ultimate emancipation of men and women was what was necessary.

*Ann Lukes*

So it was that the women-only policy of Greenham encompassed a wide range of justifications and beliefs.

## The Queering of Greenham

Whilst Greenham was always a place open to considerable diversity of political orientation, social background, motivation and lifestyle, there were discernable changes over time. One of the most significant of these may be summed up as the 'queering' of Greenham. By this, I am referring to a shift in the dominant politics of the camp from the maternalism of the walk and the early days to the much stronger feminist politics of anarchist, lesbian, radical, socialist and eco-hues which began to take hold after the women-only decision was taken. The queering of Greenham also involved a gradual transformation in style from polite and hesitant (if still direct and outside the bounds of traditional politics) to confrontational, uncompromising and 'in your face'. The women adopting this style cared little for convention or public opinion, and indeed often deliberately sought to shock and to disturb complacency and traditional ideas about what were considered proper ways of making political statements or of performing femininity. These shifts were brought about by a changing constituency of activists at Greenham from the predominantly heterosexual group of women – many of whom had children, who had had little contact with feminism, who were on the walk and who lived at Greenham in the early days – to the generally younger, child-free, more radical, anarchist and feminist group who later lived at the camp, many of whom identified as lesbians.

These were shifts in emphasis, however, rather than complete, revolutionary changes. They can be thought of as 'queer tendencies' which lived alongside Greenham's 'respectable tendencies'. The co-existence of the respectable and the queer was symbolized at the Embrace the Base gathering in December 1982 when women decorated the fence with (amongst other things) both nappies and used tampons, photographs of children and lesbian symbols. But however strong the ethic of tolerance of difference, conflict was inevitable, the ground having been laid by the debates which took place over the women-only question. The decision to make Greenham women-only marked a significant shift in power and influence from the more maternalist, respectable group to the younger, more anarchist, feminist and lesbian group: the shift from nappies to tampons. It was around this time that the first open tensions about lesbianism surfaced as more lesbians got involved and women who had not previously identified (either to themselves or publicly) as lesbians, became more confident and open about their sexuality.

> There was a blockade and Fran d'Ath came along with this group of women, and she hadn't given up the idea of re-mixing the gates. She'd come with this group of women to argue the point, and in doing so whipped up a lot of shit. They started attacking the women at the camp who were lesbians. Before that the camp was a mix of heterosexual and lesbian women, except nobody was discussing their sexuality. And then there was this big confrontation at the gate, and it was the first time that people had come out and said, yes, we are lesbians, and they were made to defend that position. It was appalling, and then a lot of the heterosexual, well, most of the heterosexual women who had stayed at Yellow Gate, which was the women-only gate, left.
>
> *Christine King*

Tensions between Greenham's queer and respectable tendencies continued after this. The queer tendency was much more in evidence amongst women who lived at the camp; the respectable tendency was represented more amongst the wider Greenham network who occasionally stayed at or visited Greenham, particularly amongst those who were also involved in the mixed peace movement and CND rather than in women's peace groups. However, there were some 'respectable' campers who took similar positions, such as Helen John (see pp. 158-9), and those of the queer tendency did not all always identify as lesbians, and those of the respectable tendency did not always identify as heterosexual. Broadly speaking the differences coalesced around sexual identity and age cohorts, but there were many exceptions to this pattern – older women who took queer positions and lesbians who took respectable positions.

In general the respectable group expressed concern that Greenham should not appear too alien and different to the general population. They worried that potential support for the case against Cruise might be lost by the media's outpouring of stories which focused on the feminism and lesbianism of Greenham. A report commissioned by CND in 1983 added fuel to these concerns:

> The Greenham women are burying a potentially popular cause in a tide of criticism levelled against them on personal grounds. They are discrediting a cause to which they profess allegiance.[10]

Whilst few who actively participated in the Greenham network would have fully endorsed this opinion and would have argued that Greenham women were doing far more good than harm to the anti-nuclear cause, regular exposure to such opinions within the peace movement and from colleagues and acquaintances in their daily lives perhaps contributed to the criticisms they expressed. They voiced their anxieties that 'ordinary women' would be put off by some of the things that went on, such as public displays of affection, explicit discussion of lesbian sex, nudity, drunken high spirits, dope smoking, and 'rudeness' to/or confrontational encounters with Newbury residents, police and soldiers. They would also argue for the importance of impression management and the need not to detract from the 'real issue' of Cruise missiles. When interviewed by journalists, or making public speeches or dealing with the public, they often played down or denied the presence of lesbians at Greenham and emphasized the mothers and ordinary housewives. This meant that there were sometimes open clashes of cultures between queer Greenham and respectable Greenham as vociferous women of the queer tendency defended their right to kiss their girlfriends, smoke dope, drink alcohol and behave as they wished, mobilizing variously Greenham's ethic of diversity and individuality, anarchist feminist critiques of bourgeois respectability and lesbian feminist arguments about the importance of challenging compulsory heterosexuality.

Helen John, who had got involved with the walk to Greenham out of concern for her children's future and who became a lesbian while at Greenham, represented the respectable tendency within the camp. Pat Paris, who remained in a heterosexual relationship throughout her involvement with Greenham (coming out as a lesbian later, see Chapter 10), describes the tensions within her women's peace group. These two women illustrate how positions on the queer/respectable continuum could not be read off from an individual's own sexual practice.

> There was a lesbian on the original walk and she was very nice and she was a committed feminist, but lesbians were a bit thin on the

ground then. And then there came that time when it was entirely
lesbians and that in a sense produced another set of problems
because a lot of heterosexual women felt very intimidated about
going there. And I know it was important that lesbian women
should have somewhere where they were completely identified
and could be completely at ease with each other. I think a lot of
women learnt to respect each other and a lot of heterosexual
women learnt to live with lesbian women and vice versa ... But
there was a time when I regret to say I thought it was the bald-
headed brigade. You know, when there were so many young,
vocal, very vigorous young lesbian women there. I didn't identify
with any of them. There was a big generation gap. I didn't identify
with their music, their manner. So there was a big block off for me,
and I didn't want to be associated with them ... Green Gate
became a real hot-bed of lesbian activity, and I didn't identify at all
with that. I wasn't opposed to it happening but I didn't identify
with it. And I could understand how a lot of heterosexual women
were intimidated. That was their problem, I also understood that,
but I could realize what the problem was. I could understand if I'd
got off the bus having left the kids for the day and made an effort
to come up there and suddenly walked into the Wild West as it
were, and it wouldn't have had a positive impact on me. But then
again, if young women have found their identity and they're all
cock-a-hoop and so forth, good luck to them.

*Helen John*

As time went on the group [Nottingham Women for Peace] was at
least half, if not slightly more than half, lesbian. And the
heterosexual women, particularly the more middle-class women,
were suddenly looking around and thinking, oh my god, everybody's going to think I'm a lesbian. I didn't find it a problem if
people thought I was a lesbian. There were some heavy discussions
in that group and some of those women left. They went into mixed
CND groups and stuck very much to the peace thing.

*Pat Paris*

Penni Bestic and Penny Gulliver recounted their memories of tensions
between queer and respectable Greenham.

SASHA: *Do you think there were conflicts between lesbians and heterosexual women at the camp?*

Yes, inevitably, though not with the women who lived there. I think women who came did find it very difficult because it was so open. I think it was the usual thing. Heterosexual women are prepared to tolerate, if they're liberal with a small 'l', lesbians, as long as they don't have to look at it. But when you actually have to sit there and watch two women snogging, it's a bit much. And there was some quite outrageous behaviour. Some of it was in the spirit of Greenham, and was winding up, quite deliberately.

SASHA: *Do you feel that was wrong?*

No. I don't feel it was right either. I feel non-judgemental about it. It was part of the non-rules of Greenham that there were no rules about that.

*Penni Bestic*

SASHA: *Did you ever feel there was any conflict between lesbians and straight women at camp?*

No, I don't remember it between women who lived at the camp. But I do I remember one night there being a bad row at Blue when some visitors had come and they were heterosexual, and we were being really rowdy, and they were really really angry with us. And they said, it's true what they say in the papers, you're just a bunch of rough aggressive bloody dykes. No wonder people say these things. And we'd been down the pub and we'd come back and we'd sung and we were being really rude about the Skulls[11] really loudly, because they'd been chucking bricks at us the night before. People just went off to bed - oh, I can't cope with this. And a couple of women tried to explain to them, we live here. It is not possible to be quiet good girls for 24 hours a day when people chuck bricks at you, eggs, maggots, blood, and you're getting arrested and beaten up. It's all very nice to think we can all be on our best behaviour but we can't. And these people chuck bricks at us, so why can't we keep them up to one o'clock in the morning occasionally. And they wouldn't have it, and they left. They'd come to do the nightwatch, and they refused to do it and went home. I think visitors were quite often shocked because quite often we'd talk about sex - it was really mind broadening for them.

*Penny Gulliver*

Penny Gulliver also identified tensions about appropriate camp behaviour which she saw as related to class and which were about the attempt to present a respectable Greenham to the outside world.

> At Blue there was conflict because the middle-class women that were there thought that drinking was bad and that being loud and raucous was bad, but they said, oh you just put everything down to class. But they shoved their class down your throat all the time, but because they didn't label it, or recognize it, they just thought it was the working-class women who had discovered their class and were obsessed with it.
>
> There were people who were very nice and very reasonable at Yellow Gate, the people who did a lot of media speaking and touring talks and that sort of business who I felt just as unhappy about. They did it because they didn't look like or sound like what the press led people to believe Greenham women were like. And I talked to one of them and she said she knows she kept speaking and always spoke to the press but she thought it was important that they got an opposite to the stereotype that they had made about the rough aggressive lesbian dirty dykes at camp ... I only once tried to explain to her that I thought that that was wrong, and actually it didn't matter if a grubby aggressive Blue Gate lesbian talked to people, that's about everyone taking responsibility and everybody having some sort of power.
>
> *Penny Gulliver*

Of the thirty-five women I interviewed there were only three who expressed a personal discomfort with or political objection to Greenham's queer tendencies – Helen John (pp. 158-9) and two women who did not live at the camp. Ann Lukes, an occasional visitor from Cardiff, did not explicitly pinpoint lesbianism as the problem. But her coded references to 'militant feminism' at Blue Gate are probably best understood as referring to the particularly sexually and politically up-front culture of Blue Gate, given that 'militant feminism' was, in the popular press discourse of the time, inextricably linked with lesbianism. But she also made clear that she did not see the matter as a straightforward division between lesbians and heterosexual women.

It got divisive, and Blue Gate became very much a group of

feminists who were very, very militant, and that made it quite a difficult place to be.

SASHA: *How do you mean there were militant feminists?*

Well, militant feminism really is, I suppose, people who will want to get men out of power by whatever means, and they will include aggression ... They were very aggressive in attitude ...

SASHA: *What did you think about the fact that there were a lot of lesbians involved with Greenham? You don't think that there was division between lesbians and heterosexual women who were involved?*

I don't think there was. I mean, our group here is a very mixed group. No, I felt much more of a division about the women who were militant feminist. I mean, a lot of lesbians, perhaps there are proportionately more lesbians in the sort of militant feminism anti-men group than there are lesbians who just feel that you, know, it's the right of the individual and a personal matter.

*Ann Lukes*

Another visitor was also cautious about identifying the problem as one of conflict between lesbians and heterosexual women, but expressed similar discomfort at Greenham's queer tendencies, although she focused on Green Gate rather than Blue Gate.

I can remember going to Green Gate when it was a very feminist era, stridently so. I remember a funny occasion when I went into the sanctuary and I walked in with my clothes on and they were all starkers. And they looked full of animosity towards me, so I had to pretend, I almost had to pretend I had no clothes on, without taking them off, and hope they accepted me. They were all much younger than me. And there was one meeting around that time when they were talking about feminism and Elizabeth Gough, who would never mince words, said, well, I can see it from the other point of view. I'm a heterosexual. And my golly, it was like dropping a bomb. She'd said the wrong thing ... I felt when these strident feminists were there they blocked out the others.

*Margery Lewis*

Occasionally the tension worked in the other direction, as was sometimes the case at Violet Gate which had the reputation of being rather more heterosexual than the other gates.

When I came back from Australia things had changed quite a lot at Violet Gate. There was a Violet Gate contingent that was very friendly with the soldiers. Being friendly is OK. It's the common pleasantries of life. I didn't talk to the soldiers. I mean, I'd say hello if one said hello to me. It takes a lot of energy to ignore somebody. And there was that level when I went to Australia, but when I came back Violet Gate did seem to be going through a heterosexual revolution, that occasionally seemed to also include flirting with the soldiers, which I found quite offensive ... But it wasn't straightforwardly a heterosexual–lesbian thing, because Veronica had difficulties with some of the things that were going on.

*Rowan Gwedhen*

But another lesbian who lived at Violet Gate was not bothered by this.

At Violet Gate we had the meat-eaters and the hets [laughter], so it was a group of all the leftovers. So I didn't feel that there was a tension at Violet Gate. I was in the minority, and I was used to it. They were in the majority and they were used to it. It was fine. But I know that it was a tension in other places.

*Katrina Allen*

Over time tensions about sexuality and 'respectability' ebbed away as anti-lesbian views were increasingly rarely expressed and the diverse queerness of Greenham became normalized. Many of the women who objected to the queering of Greenham ceased to be involved or gradually altered their perspective. Greenham's queer feminist culture was a safe and joyous space for lesbians as well as a place where open-minded heterosexuals were able to feel comfortable.[12]

Greenham was something of a dyke enclave, but I don't really remember too many conflicts between lesbians and straight women, and especially at the Orange Gate, it was quite a mixed group. And at the Indigo Gate and Violet too. There are a lot of straight women who are put off by dykes, but I don't remember that being so much of an issue because those people probably never even made it to the camp, so we didn't have to deal with them.

*Liz Galst*

I was accepted as a heterosexual woman. If anyone felt bad about me being there it was never made clear to me. I felt I was accepted.

*Barbara Rawson*


## Hierarchy, Insiders and Outsiders

Central to the common values of Greenham were an opposition to hierarchy and an ethos of participation and equality. It was an often-stated motto that every woman at Greenham was a 'Greenham woman', no matter how long she had been there. What this motto tried to capture was the belief that the right to participate in camp life and decision-making did not have to be earnt by serving time or passing through rites of passage. Within this context, there was a high degree of sensitivity about any hierarchies which seemed to be forming, about groups of insiders and outsiders and the inequalities of power which related to membership of these groups. Conflict and tension therefore arose in situations where hierarchy and inequality were minimal in comparison with conventional political organizations and living arrangements. There was much discussion about these issues and many meetings were devoted to collective analysis of the problems, particularly as they were seen to relate to the cultural resources of class. Greenham's commitment to reflexivity, self-scrutiny and open discussion helped prevent the entrenchment of disputes, and the constant through-flow of the population of the camp served to ease tensions, but at times conflict about these issues was very intense.

In part, hierarchies were constructed by external factors beyond the control of the women involved. The press, in particular, would not accept that Greenham had no leaders and so designated as leaders a small number of women who had been involved with the camp for a considerable length of time and who had previously given media interviews. Reporters tended to see the Main Gate (later Yellow Gate), as the decision-making centre of the camp. Sarah Bond, for instance, in the *Daily Express*, identified four Yellow Gate women as 'the gang of four who pull the strings'.[13] This had the self-perpetuating effect of sending journalists repeatedly in search of the same women. It also meant that these women were often the ones asked to speak at conferences, rallies and public meetings as representatives of

Greenham. Another effect of media concentration on 'leaders' was that visitors often wanted to meet these women rather than anyone else. They wanted to talk to a 'real Greenham woman' and invariably asked everyone how long they had been there in order to find the woman most qualified to discuss the camp.

Most of the women highlighted for media attention attempted to deflect it, sometimes refusing interviews and suggesting journalists talk to other women, but undoubtedly being a 'peace personality' had its attractions. Its downside was, at times, a certain degree of hostility from other women who believed that the sought after women should have done more to disabuse journalists of the notion that they were the leaders. If anything, their influence within the camp declined in direct proportion to the amount of outsider attention they received.

The hierarchies that were seen to be 'real' within the camp were not so much concerned with the few women labelled by the press and visitors to be leaders - women living at Greenham knew that they were not. Rather, they were the hierarchies and inequalities of power which were formed on the basis of length of involvement, level of involvement and, more intangibly, personal and cultural resources. Women who had been living at the camp for a long time, who knew its history and had been part of major actions (such as the Silos Action), and women who had been feminists prior to Greenham and who had access to feminist discourse, were particularly likely to be respected within the camp. Many of these women, though by no means all, were middle-class and were strong speakers, which posed an additional political issue where hierarchies on the basis of class were being consciously critiqued.

> I think there were women who were leaders ... Well, no, leaders is the wrong word. More like catalysts ... They were women who were very, very strong, very bright. I think if they wanted something to happen, then it would happen. It would be very unusual if it would happen without their consent. I think things probably did happen without their consent, but on the whole not. You have to acknowledge that. If you don't acknowledge that, there are problems. We have to acknowledge that there are particular women, and men, in the world, who have particular gifts, and we have to use those gifts, not fight against them. And part of the problem is that some of the women who have those

particular gifts were middle-class, because it's partly about learning the tricks of being articulate, and it's to do with self-worth. So I think the majority of the women who were outspoken were middle-class, but not all of them.

*Penni Bestic*

The terms 'delegates' and 'minions' were coined, jokingly but pointedly, to highlight these inequalities.

There was the hierarchy that Pauline pointed out: the 'delegates' and 'minions', which caused hilarious fun with everybody except the 'delegates'. You could tell who the 'delegates' were, because they didn't laugh. It was good that she pointed out the hierarchy that everyone tried to pretend wasn't there, and she did it in this hilariously funny way. I mean, visitors were lower than 'minions' … I was a 'minion'.

*Jenny Heron*

'Delegates' were the women who tended to do the 'speaks' and to travel abroad as Greenham women. They were the women whose opinions were particularly valued within the camp.

When a decision had to be made, everyone had their say. But it was never really talked about that you might just give a one-word answer and the person next to you might go on for half an hour. Everyone took what the group of 'delegates' said very seriously.

*Sarah Benham*

One of the hierarchies which caused the most conflict within the camp was that which was perceived to exist between Yellow Gate and the rest of the camp. Almost every woman I interviewed who had not lived at Yellow Gate referred to tensions about the power which was exercised by some of the women who lived at Yellow Gate.

It was only a handful of women from Yellow Gate doing it, but it was an elitist power situation, and we took a long time to tackle it. I think it was partly the media thing – the fact that it had been called Main Gate and the media treated it as the main gate. I think it was the fact that it was the first gate. There were some very strong individuals at Yellow Gate, and they were by and large older, which is interesting. I think they had quite a lot of collective power between them, because they were all not dissimilar. They were all very powerful women, and I think it was difficult for other women to challenge them.

*Pat Paris*

To some extent it was inevitable that such hierarchies should develop; the length of time a woman had been at the camp *did* matter, not least because newcomers had much to learn about how the community worked and about its philosophy and values. Friendship groups grew up amongst women of the same 'cohort' on the basis of the shared experience of being at the camp. These were not always open to newcomers. It was also the case that being at Greenham facilitated women's self-confidence and so the longer a woman had been there, the more powerful she was likely to appear. However, as Jenny Heron recognized in retrospect, the power and strength of the 'delegates' also rested on attribution from the 'minions'.

I didn't feel I fitted in with the big shots … They were all much more everything than me. They were funnier, they were more attractive, they were more experienced, they had more to say … But I haven't put women on a pedestal since then.

*Jenny Heron*

There were also tensions between women who lived at the camp and those who were involved in the wider network. Although the slogan 'Greenham women are everywhere' was widely quoted, and although the collective ethos of Greenham valued the contribution of every Greenham woman and deplored hierarchies between women based on the level of their involvement, women did not always live up to their ideals - or indeed always believe them.

We used to say at the camp, 'Every woman's a Greenham woman, even if she's only come for an hour.' It depends what you mean by a Greenham woman, doesn't it? In the sense that we meant that every woman who comes to Greenham, even if it's only for an hour, is interested and probably has a similar political outlook, maybe in that sense she's a Greenham woman. But when you look more closely and separate the wood from the trees, I don't think you can say that. It was a bland phrase that felt good at the time. It was good to make people who just came for an hour, to say that to them, to stop them feeling like a visitor, and they hadn't anything to contribute. But I think there must be something different between someone who has lived there for some length of time and somebody who's just come for the afternoon and is going back to make her husband's supper and couldn't stay overnight. Not that she couldn't but that she hasn't taken that jump.

*Leah Thalmann*

There were the stars at Yellow Gate, and I always felt a bit tentative about approaching them. I always felt that I didn't have the credentials because I didn't live at camp.

*Ann Armstrong*

Sarah Benham, who regularly stayed at Greenham after having lived at the peace camp at Faslane, recalled attending a meeting about the women's peace movement at which women from Greenham and from other peace camps were present:

I just remember Greenham women looking a certain way, having very much a Greenham look about them, and acting in a self-important way, and talking about 'Camp' ... and I was thinking, there are Rosyth and Faslane, these are both camps, but we don't talk about them as 'Camp' ... There was a real arrogance: *we* are where the women's peace movement is at. And that was never really challenged.

*Sarah Benham*

However, she went on to acknowledge that there were reasons why hierarchies developed within the Greenham network.

I think that once you'd been to Greenham you were a Greenham woman – you couldn't get it out of you, you couldn't not be a Greenham woman. But some women were more Greenham women than others. It was easier for some women to go to Greenham than for others. For us it was a five-hour journey and we used to often get there at midnight on Friday and be really tired, but some women used to zip up from Brighton and I think it was a lot easier for them to be more involved in Greenham. And there was always a hierarchy given how much you were involved.

*Sarah Benham*

Some women were inclined to blame the insularity and the lack of real commitment to challenging insider/outsider hierarchies of those who lived at the camp. Others, however, were less critical of the women who lived at Greenham and believed that their experience of feeling 'outsiders' was inevitable, given that they were not taking part in the daily life of the community.

I think there was always a big division between women who actually lived there and women who didn't, and women who lived there had so much on their plate that I actually understood why they didn't want to be particularly welcoming to visitors. It was a chore to entertain people and talk to them. I never felt very much part of the camp, really. I felt connected to it. I didn't feel part of it really. I mean I think the camp itself was a particular community which I wasn't part of. And I never wanted to try to think that I was. There were so many things that women at the camp had to work through about living together that I never had to do ... there was so much that I didn't have to worry about. I could just come in and do my little thing and get great strength out of the fact that Greenham was there, and imbibe its spirit and go home.

*Clare Hudson*

There was an understanding that you were there for the same reasons, there was an understanding between you, and you didn't feel an outsider. I mean, even as an outsider I didn't really feel an outsider.

SASHA: *You did to some extent though?*

Well, at one level, yes. I felt I had a right to be there, but on the other hand when you see the people there who've been living there in such hardship, you feel that they have more right to belong than you. I didn't go up and say, I was on the first march. They would have said, bully for you. I was always interested in what was going on but I always felt slightly an intruder because I didn't really want to pry into what they were doing because it might be almost private to them.

*Margery Lewis*

Many women who lived at the camp were aware of the problem of the insider/outsider hierarchy as it related to those who were not living at the camp, and there was considerable debate both about how to make all women feel welcomed and involved, and about the extent to which Greenham should be the focus for women's peace actions.[14]

I think there were conflicts over who was a real Greenham woman. It was conflict between women who were living there at the time, between those who would belittle women who'd just come down to give something or just come down for the weekend, and those who would defend them. Women who've just popped down to give something have always felt quite intimidated and unrecognized really. And I think there was quite a bit of conflict between visitors and women who were living there, but also between women that were living there as to how and whether they welcomed them or not. There was a lot more conflict in the hierarchy than there was between straight and lesbian women. Probably because there weren't a lot of straight women, not after they'd been there a few weeks. Not many of them survived and came out straight [laughter]. I tried to be welcoming to women, partly because I didn't feel that I fitted in with the big shots anyway.

*Jenny Heron*

## Conflict over Resources

There were lots of times when I was so upset and angry and cross about the money and the things that happened, like the misuse of donated vehicles. But that's human failings, living on a day-to-day basis.

*Carola Addington*

Sometimes there were women who were determined to get whatever they could out of the camp, and thought that if there was money there it should be spent, and why shouldn't it be spent on them?

Sometimes women were too greedy. Some people said it came down to class, and basically middle-class women and perhaps women who were better educated were able to clearly categorize the terms of where the money should go, and that middle-class women were more concerned about spending money sensibly, whereas working-class women were much more into the here and now.

*Carmel Cadden*

Sometimes I got really cross about the way money got allocated. I can remember specific incidents that annoyed me. Somebody wanted a camera replacing because it got broken in an eviction. And my thought was, hang on I don't think that's right. If you've brought an expensive camera with you, then it's your look out ... There was a very angry money meeting about somebody wanting to go away on holiday. And they didn't want to just go away and get away from the camp, they wanted to go abroad on holiday. Like we all would have wanted to do those things, but I never felt that was justifiable with the money we had. I think we used the money very badly, 'cause there was a hell of a lot of it, for a while. That's why I think the miners' strike did a lot for Greenham because we started sharing it. A lot of that money then got channelled to other things. And that I really liked. And part of it for me, part of being at the camp, was to give up your worldly goods, and have nothing, and live in a bender, that you built from practically nothing, with things everybody would throw away. And it didn't matter then when it got torn down by the bailiffs. Because I've always been quite into things, and I've had my own things, and they were important to me, and they are again now.

*Jinny List*

I was horrified a lot of times. I thought it stank. And it stank for me because I lived on income support and I hitched to Greenham. I baked cakes and took them with me, shared my tobacco with everybody in sight and had very little money. I didn't draw camp dole. I never took anything out. I spent half my working life fundraising for this money, and then I saw what was happening to it, and I was appalled at some of the things that happened. That disenchanted me a lot in terms of individuals, not about the camp as a whole. The vast majority of women weren't doing that. But I thought it really insulting to women who were not at camp all the time, but were stood on street corners in the pouring rain, who were being just as vilified, and that wasn't recognized. There was all this nonsense about you're not a proper Greenham woman if you didn't live here all the time. I've never gone for that.

So I was shocked by some of it, some of the things that I saw happening. I thought women who lived at camp should have camp dole. That wasn't an issue. That was what we were raising the money for. What I didn't think it should be going on was what to me seemed to be really unjustifiable expenses that women weren't raising money for. That's partly why I didn't go to many money meetings. Blue Gate used to trot up, get their dole, get the petrol for the car, and that was it. And other gates would go away with like a thousand quid from the money meeting. And you'd think, what's going on here? Do you know how long it takes to raise a thousand pounds out on the streets of Nottingham? Obviously Greenham wasn't a place where you had auditors, but we'd have been shut down had there been any accountability on that. The credibility of the camp would have been really damaged. That upset me. I could see so many women really putting so much into that and doing such incredible things and yet there were freeloaders. I used to feel quite between two stools. I used to spend a lot of time here, very involved with this local situation, and a fairly equal amount of time at camp.

*Pat Paris*

As these interview extracts suggest, another major area of conflict concerned the distribution and consumption of resources. Against the backdrop of a commitment to collective consumption and communality, there were often vigorous differences of opinion about how money should be spent and about the rather fuzzy line which sometimes existed between personal and collective resources. In general, each woman's personal resources were respected as such and considered her business alone, although individual's cars would sometimes come to be considered 'camp vehicles', at times against the owner's wishes. However, the use of the collective resources of the camp to provide for individual women often generated conflict. Requests for money from the camp to replace damaged, stolen or evicted possessions such as boots, rucksacks and sleeping-bags were rarely contested. What did generate disagreement were demands for money for purposes which some women considered unessential, extravagant and an improper use of camp money. Such requests included money to  replace a camera damaged during an eviction, to go on a two-week rest holiday and to pay the large telephone bills which had been run up by women from the camp at a local supporter's house. Controversy arose when the same small group of women made repeated demands for money and became particularly intense when issues of internal hierarchy (particularly between Yellow Gate and the other gates) and about class were raised in relation to money.

Conflict about the use of money began early in the camp's history. During the first year and a half there was no clear system for collective decision-making about money. There were a number of different bank accounts in the name of the camp, each with different authorized signatories. Money was deposited in these accounts fairly haphazardly. Problems arose when it became apparent that the account with the largest balance could only be accessed by women who no longer lived at Greenham, and who were therefore able to exercise a veto over expenditure. These women were asked to hand over control of the account to women living at Greenham, but refused. They refused also to withdraw money to pay for equipment (such as Citadel locks) which women wanted for an action at the base, arguing that the proposed action was violent and against the Greenham ethos.

These events brought the issue of the control of money to a head, and a meeting was held at Greenham to discuss the matter.[15] The outcome of the meeting was the establishment of regular money meetings at which requests for money from individuals and for camp expenses (such as petrol and equipment for actions) could be discussed openly. Each week one woman offered to be 'money woman' and took charge of paying donations into a single camp account; she would also make one withdrawal, after the money meeting, to meet the agreed expenditure. In order to prevent a concentration of power in one woman's hands, this role was to circulate each week and there were to be several signatories to the new account, so that vetoes could not be exercised by individuals over collective decisions.

The system of weekly money meetings clarified to some extent the process by which money was handled at Greenham, but it did not eliminate conflict. During 1984 money meetings became the site of considerable disputation, often expressed with reference to hierarchies which were perceived to exist within the camp and between gates. Early in 1984 it was decided, after pressure from the other gates, that the weekly money meetings should not always be held at Yellow Gate, but should rotate. This was an attempt to deal with a perceived aggregation of power at Yellow Gate, particularly amongst women who had been at the camp for a long time. A small number of women from Yellow Gate were requesting and receiving considerably more money for personal use than anyone else. Sometimes these women offered no justification for their requests and others felt unable to challenge them. When women from other gates spoke out, often diffidently at first, against requests which they regarded as unwarranted, money meetings sometimes erupted into shouting matches. Women asking for money saw that they were being blocked, and accused those questioning them of being puritanical and middle-class in their attitudes to money. Meanwhile, many of the women who were reluctant to agree to the money being spent were in fact working-class and saw the issue as one of power and hierarchy, not class. They believed that it was the women who had been at the camp longest and who were the most self-confident who tended to ask for money.

Other women who were unhappy about camp money being spent on what they considered luxuries were those who were financially dependent on the camp; these were women who received 'camp dole' because they were ineligible for state benefits, usually because they were not UK residents. These women argued that their continued involvement with Greenham was threatened by the misuse of resources and that money should be saved to ensure camp dole could be paid in the future. Yet another group of women who entered the fray were concerned about accountability to those who donated money to Greenham and believed that money should only be spent on collective resources to support the needs of the camp. A further group argued that money should be redistributed to other campaigns, particularly in the Third World, once the basic needs of the camp had been met.

> We asked for the big open money meetings to talk about money. It came from us [at Blue Gate]. I don't know if it came from other people as well. Because we were finding we were going round there and people were insuring their cars, going to the dentist and taking taxis at Yellow Gate, and most of the women at Blue

hitched home and hitched back because they didn't have the money and most of us had lost our boots, because your feet used to be so cold you'd put them near the fire and somebody would say, your boots are on fire, your feet are on fire. And you'd lose another pair of boots. And women were borrowing wellies off each other because they hadn't got ten quid for a new pair of Docs. And there were people at Yellow Gate having their caps redone [dental work]. This really wasn't on, and that's when we said we'll all go en masse from Blue Gate to these meetings. And I just remember that meeting at Green Gate – you were there, weren't you? It was so terrible. And we were all there and there were six women who spoke continually, five of whom were from Yellow Gate, and they talked and everybody else just sat around. And they talked about themselves. And then somebody said, I remember it was a visitor, a woman who had visited Blue Gate and who was some union rep, she was quite a young woman but she was obviously politically quite sussed and articulate, and she said, I don't like to say anything, but this is a pretty odd meeting when there's only, there's like a hundred people here and there's only six people talking. And somebody said, OK, we'll have ten minutes where people who haven't spoken say things. Right everybody, you've got three seconds. Then somebody said, we'll go round the circle then. And so we went round and people said odd things, and we got to the big line of Blue Gate on the other side and nobody really said very much and people just said pass, and we got to me and I waffled ... And then an ice-cream van arrived and these six people stood up, started yelling, who wants a vanilla and who wants chopped nuts and ran off to the ice-cream van and came back and were going, slurp. And what I basically said was, I think it's appalling that you've completely hogged the meeting, you talk about you, you, you and everything that's going on, everyone's completely intimidated into not saying anything, like it always is, and when you feel like it, you stand up screaming and run off to the ice-cream van, completely without any regard for the other people that are speaking in this meeting at all. So that was it then. They were hysterical. Oh my god, you can't even go to the bloody ice-cream van without ... Then, I can't remember her name now but I can see her, says don't blame me, I've taken a long time to get to the point where I can talk about things, don't lay all that fucking working-class wimp trip on me. I didn't say another word. It had all come out wrong, what I'd said. Then there were all the Green Gate women who were next, who were sat there, who were actually much more articulate and said all the things that Blue Gate wanted to say but couldn't manage to get it out. I remember that being one of the worst days I ever had at camp. I just remember sitting there thinking, I mustn't cry, I mustn't cry, as this woman was yelling at me. And that just confirmed it all again. That there were these dreadful middle-class white women at Yellow Gate who thought they were our leaders.

*Penny Gulliver*


It was very difficult. There were all sorts of accusations flying backwards and forwards about class and how if a woman wanted money and she asks for it and she's working-class she should be given it. It just seemed a huge divide really, and I think if anything could have split the camp up to that point it would have been money. So I think that actually to divide it up amongst the gates was the best thing to do. But it still seemed to be a huge problem, because so much was coming in. And it was during the miners' strike. And at Orange Gate we had a meeting about money and decided that we were going to have a fund, that it was going to go out to different groups. We worked out that we would only keep a percentage of the money for things that were necessary and for emergencies, like if a woman didn't want to go to prison and her fine was due. And there was enough for camp dole, but there weren't that many women at Orange Gate that needed camp dole. It was small enough and equal enough – it felt more equal than some of the gates – that women could ask for it. It didn't feel that there was any power struggle going on. I think there was a bit, but it was all very friendly.

SASHA: *Do you think that the argument about money was about class?*
No. Well, I suppose it was about class, but I don't think it was middle-class women telling working-class women how to behave. I think it was women finding new ways, and I think that was all very difficult, because you do have different values about money. But I also think that there were women that very definitely exploited that. In that sense, it became a power struggle, and there were

women there who were claiming to be working-class but actually weren't. I think it was all very difficult.

*Penni Bestic*

Wider debates about class, power and hierarchy aside, conflict about money coalesced basically around four specific questions: whether individual women's requests were legitimate, that is, over the definition of 'needs'; whether individual or collective needs should come first; whether money should be spent as and when it was available, or whether there should be forward planning and saving of money for periods when donations were more scarce; whether the camp should be accountable for how donations were spent, or whether the ethos of autonomy meant that however women there chose to use it was legitimate. The issue of money exemplified the tension which existed between the principle of communality and the ethic of respect for differences among women. It also provided the occasion for the expression of conflict about hierarchies which existed despite Greenham's commitment to oppose them, and demonstrated disagreements in political analysis and priorities.

The eventual outcome of a series of heated money meetings in 1984 was the devolution of control of money to the gates. Each week money was distributed to a representative from each gate, roughly on the basis of the number of women living there plus camp dole for those who claimed it. Each gate was then left to decide how to spend its our money. This meant that decisions about expenditure could be taken in smaller groups, amongst women who knew each other well and were therefore more likely to trust each other and feel mutually accountable in their requests. As a result of this decision, the distinctive character, interests and concerns of the women living at each gate could be reflected in spending decisions. For instance, women at Orange Gate, who had been particularly disturbed by what they perceived as wastefulness and extravagance at Greenham, decided to redistribute much of their weekly income to other women's projects and campaigns in Britain and around the world which they believed were not receiving as much financial support as Greenham. Eventually the whole problem of money faded away. As the camp became smaller and donations fell off there was less to argue about.

## The Politics of Race and the King's Cross Affair

One of Greenham's major weaknesses was about the people who were involved there and the fact that it was largely a white middle-class movement that involved women who had in their upbringing quite a lot that gave them confidence and encouraged them. And that actually it didn't reach black women and poor women. Part of that is about networking, and if your networks don't touch any of those groups then you're not going to draw them in. I think if you're going to combat either classism or racism, you have to have a very positive policy or positive attitude that actually works to specifically attract and consider the situation of women who are poor and women who are black, and there was none of that. Individual good will is not enough. I think one of the structural problems with it was its anarchy and the fact that it wasn't thought-through anarchy, it was just anarchy. And so it didn't compensate for the people who were more powerful having more power. And so the people who heavied others got away with it, except in exceptional circumstances, because nobody knew quite how to combat that.

*Katrina Allen*

At the end of '83 a bunch of people wrote a statement about connecting with the struggles of other people and that was very important to me. I personally don't think that the camp did enough to address issues of racism. There was a lot of stuff about the Pacific and the use of the Pacific as this nuclear dumping and testing ground, and I think that was really important. But I really think there was a sort of cultural illiteracy in the camp about racism. And I'm sad about that, and likewise about class. I don't think that that was really part of the discourse there and I think that that's really unfortunate. I think there were a lot of reasons. I think a lot of it had to do with being white middle-class. I think that it's sometimes hard to make the argument that you want the elimination of nuclear weapons and again at the same time to say if you didn't use this money on nuclear weapons you could use it on this and the other thing, for human needs, as if there was some kind of bargain that you could strike. And I think that a lot of the tactics that we used were not necessarily the tactics that other people would use. I mean I think it's a privilege to get arrested by a cop, and when white people get arrested by cops they get much better treatment and so I think there are probably a lot of people who looked at us and thought, are you morons? Who would never put themselves in the same situation because they know that they would get different treatment. So I think that there's ways that we could have dealt with that better at the camp which is not to say that I think that we shouldn't have done those things, but I think that there was a way that they could have been addressed differently. We could have talked about it. We could have done other stuff to involve people in different ways and not so much in the getting arrested kind of thing. I think also that the whole King's Cross/Wages For Housework thing made it really difficult to discuss racism.

*Liz Galst*

It was white, predominantly, in my experience. But I lived at a gate that was predominantly working-class, to a woman, and very proud of it, all of them. But I don't know that Greenham was particularly middle-class. I think it would have been true to say that of a lot of organizations that were around at the time, be they trade unions or women's or what have you, they were all predominantly white. I think black women were doing quite a lot of other things with their own time and it was not necessarily a priority. I think women who face survival issues daily on the streets, you haven't necessarily got the time to face nuclear weapons ... I do think that there's things that would have made it more accessible, but again I think those processes were being worked through not just in Greenham but within a lot of other situations. I can't quite imagine how it could have been different. Somebody gets up and goes off and does something. Who gets involved gets involved. There was national publicity. It wasn't targeted at white middle-class women. We handed out handouts to anybody and everybody on the street. I think there was an element of choice for loads of women about whether or not they got involved. And I think black women would have found it harder to get involved anyway, and I also think they have other things on their minds. Anything and everything got discussed at Greenham, loads of work was done. You'd get women turning up at camp saying what seemed to you to be unbelievably naïve things, and it was the first time they'd set foot outside their house in twenty years or something. You haven't got the right to have those expectations of everything being perfect. People were at such different levels and paces the whole time … Beyond that there was just so much diversity. It was never a homogenous thing, and you couldn't criticize it as a homogenous thing.

*Pat Paris*

As in the wider women's movement in Britain in the 1980s, there was considerable concern at Greenham about issues of race and racism, particularly focusing on the fact that there were few black women involved with the camp and the women's peace movement. For several years this concern tended to find expression in informal discussions around the fire and occasional camp meetings to explore the question more systematically. Over time, and through reading the growing feminist literature on anti-imperialist, post-colonialist struggles, a collective analysis emerged which involved making connections between racism, imperialism and militarism around the world. The generally accepted view, in part derived from the writings of black feminists about the peace movement, was that most black women in Britain were occupied by issues of more immediate concern to them, such as racism and poverty, than the nuclear threat, and that taking non-violent direct action against the state involved more risk for black women. Greenham women developed an analysis of the connections between the struggle against Cruise missiles and that of oppressed peoples around the world who were fighting US imperialism, militarism, uranium mining and nuclear testing. Direct links were made with women in Nicaragua, with visits in both directions, and with women in South Africa, and in Aboriginal communities in Australia and the Pacific. This global consciousness was the major (and indirect) way in which women at Greenham dealt with their political anxieties about the relevance of their actions to issues of race and racism. However, at Greenham, as in the wider women's movement, there remained considerable white guilt about the absence of black women.

It wasn't until 1987, when the camp was well past its peak of mobilization (and the INF [Intermediate Nuclear Forces] treaty was about to be signed) that the race issue really exploded and rocked Greenham to its core. Working in a Leninist entryist style, women from the King's Cross Women's Centre/Wages for Housework Campaign in London gradually took over Yellow Gate by a two-pronged process of sending their own women to Greenham and targeting women they perceived as powerful and convincing them that they should accept direction from Wilmette Brown, one of the leaders of the Wages for Housework Campaign.[16] The way they did this was by mobilizing the discourse of anti-racism to divide the camp into 'racists' and 'anti-racists'.[17]

The King's Cross Women's Centre offered to solve the 'problem' of the lack of involvement of black women in Greenham by proffering the leadership of a black woman, Wilmette Brown, who, unlike many black feminists in Britain, appeared to believe that Greenham was an important site of struggle.[18] If Greenham women accepted her leadership (delegated in her absence to two of the long-standing campers who had joined the King's Cross project), they were not racist. If they refused it – on whatever grounds – they were.

> I think how Wages for Housework worked was that for middle-class women it guilt-tripped them, particularly on issues like racism. They used guilt as a way of controlling women. Both [x] and [y] [two Greenham women who joined Wages for Housework/King's Cross] were middle-class and vulnerable and nice and caring, and they saw this group who seemed to be doing something really strong. You can't really describe it. It's like, why do people join the Moonies? You get brainwashed. They'd spend less and less time at Greenham, but come back and talk about it. But at Orange Gate there were quite a lot of old lags who knew about Wages for Housework, and just wouldn't get involved in it. But it was guilt, all guilt. If you're white and middle-class, the last thing in the world you want is somebody accusing you of being racist, especially a black woman.
>
> *Penni Bestic*

The ways of working employed by the King's Cross women were in direct contrast to the Greenham ethos. They believed in the importance of leadership. Open participation in meetings was not encouraged, with the floor being dominated by their key personnel. They argued that only those living permanently at Greenham could speak about what should happen there (thereby excluding stayers and visitors – the wider Greenham network). Video- and tape-recorders and notebooks were used to record everything that was said in meetings. Meetings were structured around a closed agenda in which dissenting voices were silenced and where a single 'line' was expounded by the leaders. Meetings held at camp were also often patrolled by a number of 'guards' with dogs and cameras which many Greenham women found intimidating and physically threatening. A number of women who were identified as key figures at Greenham were targeted by the King's Cross women for particular vilification. They were repeatedly accused of racism in such a way that they came close to nervous breakdowns. Above all, the King's Cross women attempted to impose their brand of materialist feminism on Greenham, a project which was contrary to the theoretical openness and political autonomy which characterized the movement.[19]

Given the structure of Greenham it was impossible for the King's Cross women to be excluded or removed. Indeed many women for a long time held on to the belief that Greenham should be open to all and were reluctant to criticize the King's Cross women because they firmly believed that they had to take seriously the issue of racism, particularly as expressed by a black woman. However, as the women who did not join the King's Cross group left Yellow Gate and moved to one of the four other camps, they began to spread the news about what had happened around the Greenham network and through the peace movement. This galvanized thousands of women into action, many of whom had previously lived at Greenham, and in the winter of 1987 at large gatherings at all the other gates the problem was widely discussed. Effectively, the dozen women at Yellow Gate were isolated. They retained control over the water supply and refused women from the other gates access to the mail and hence to donations of money. But the other gates by-passed these problems by fetching water from elsewhere, and publicizing Blue Gate as the new postal address for Greenham.

The King's Cross affair did not cause a fundamental split within Greenham. Greenham's fluidity and flexibility enabled it to survive as an autonomous movement committed to anti-hierarchical, open and participatory forms of organization. Ultimately this attempt to take over and destroy the camp served to illustrate many of the strengths of Greenham's flexible, fluid structure(lessness).[20]

## Conclusion

> Perhaps a lot of us were terribly idealistic about women. I've said a lot of the idealistic things which were true to some extent but very much wanting not to recognize that women are also very destructive

to each other. You know, it's easy to project men as the Other, and all the things we don't like about humanity being part of what men are about. And of course that's not true and a lot of us have, you know, been very involved in Greenham and in women's groups and perhaps also if you were a lesbian you actually have to confront that in the most intimate relationships - you have to start facing that we can be pretty shitty as well. Sometimes I think because we're women and, because of the kind of oppression we've suffered, there is more circumspection about our shittiness, but it's still pretty nasty and maybe some women weren't prepared for what the King's Cross women could be like. I mean I would have thought after a few years at the camp most camp women must have been pretty clear about just how shitty we could all be to each other, because they'd seen a lot of it, but maybe it took some women by surprise.

*Clare Hudson*

Involvement with Greenham brought with it for everyone the often painful realization of the difficulties inherent in constructing a political project around the identity of 'woman'. However exciting and liberating women experienced Greenham to be they also soon faced the necessity of confronting the differences which exist between women. Debates and conflicts were not irritations or diversions from the real business of Greenham rather they were at the heart of what Greenham was about. Accepting that there was no final closure, no way of ultimately resolving all conflict and that to end debate would be to end Greenham, meant that women at Greenham were able to find ways, imperfect though they may have been, to live with difference.

There were a lot of contradictions, not necessarily always becoming conflicts. And they moved us. In spite of everything, in spite of all those contradictions and complexities and paradoxes, it did succeed. Maybe it succeeded because nobody was making rules.

*Penni Bestic*

I'm sure there's lots of things we could have done better. But then we didn't think along those lines. That would have been making rules about how to do things, wouldn't it? Instead of being spontaneous, and letting something happen and talking about how it worked out. I don't know how we could have done it better. At times it was awful, but if you're going to let everybody have a say about what they feel about it, I don't know how you could do it better, without making some rule about it.

*Leah Thalmann*

## Notes

1. There is a much longer history of concern with the particularizing and deconstructing of the category of 'woman' within feminism, dating back perhaps to the beginnings of the women's movement. It is certainly dangerous to assume that feminists only began to think about differences of race and class in the 1980s. See Hill Collins (1990), Riley (1988) and Butler and Scott (1992).
2. See Liddington (1989: 230).
3. See Harford and Hopkins (1984: 32).
4. Except at Green Gate, which when it was established made a policy of being women-only all the time. No men were allowed to visit Green Gate at all and signs to this effect were erected at the top of the track leading to the camp from the road.
5. Faslane is a naval base in Scotland where (British) Trident submarines are housed; Burghfield is a Royal Ordnance Factory where nuclear weapons are manufactured; USAF Molesworth was the second UK location for Cruise missiles; USAF Alconbury (Cambridgeshire) and USAF Upper Heyford were further sites involved in US/NATO nuclear militarism.
6. To my knowledge, there was no debate at Greenham about exactly where the boundary between man and woman lay; the implicit assumption was that sex was a biological fixity, and, it being several years before debates about transsexualism and transgendering reached Britain, the question of whether to allow the participation of male to female transsexuals (which has recently been much debated at the Michigan Women's Music Festival and the Sydney Lesbian Space Project) was not an issue. Imagining the arguments and how they would have developed at Greenham had the issue arisen has occupied many a spare hour for me in recent times. Ultimately, in the spirit of Greenham's strong streak of anarchism and believing that this would have been far more influential than radical feminist arguments, I think that a decision would have been reached that anyone who chose to call herself a woman should be treated as such. I also think it likely that there would have developed a clustering of transsexuals and those who supported them at a 'trannie gate'. I am open to debate about this.
7. This story contrasts with Margery Lewis's recollections of what she felt was men's respectful behaviour on the original walk to Greenham:
   > There were men. But men would not take the banners unless we were right out in the country and the women were tired. They would push the babies, quite deliberately, to release the women. They were caring at all times. And they would never take the banner in the front when we were getting to a town.
   
   However, she did go on to describe violent incidents in which men were involved at the camp in the run-up to the women-only decision.

8. Spivak (1987) both critiques and endorses the use of 'strategic essentialism' by subaltern groups, which Fuss also considers a '"risk" worth taking' (1989: 32).

9. Men were allowed to visit Emerald, but not Green, Gate.

10. CND (1983: 23).

11. The Skulls lived in a house opposite Blue Gate. They were publicly hostile to the camp and actively harassed the women who lived there.

12. There was little evidence of the 'sex wars' between lesbian/radical feminists and libertarian feminists over issues such as sadomasochism at Greenham. There were occasional discussions of these issues, but they did not ever develop into conflicts as they did in the late 1980s in London (see Green, 1997). On one occasion a woman living at Greenham pulled a knife on another and attempted to force her to have sex with her; this woman was considered to be mentally unstable and was taken to the police station where she was sectioned.

13. *Daily Express*, 9 April 1984.

14. Tension also existed in the opposite direction: for a time there was some suspicion and hostility amongst the women who lived at the camp towards the women who had set up and were running the Greenham office in London. A group of women in London applied to Islington Council for premises from which to run an office and a support house for Greenham, and were granted, on short-life tenancies, first a house in Petherton Road, Highbury, and later a house in Caledonian Road, near King's Cross. The idea was to have a London base for the camp, from which telephone enquiries from the media and from visitors and supporters could be fielded, actions in London organized and women in Holloway Prison supported. The houses were partly devoted to office space and partly to living space, with a kitchen, living-room, bathroom and bedrooms.

15. This money meeting is documented on the film *Carry Greenham Home* (made by Beeban Kidron and Amanda Richardson).

16. The King's Cross version of the history of Greenham has been written by Beth Junor (1996).

17. Readers will note a relative absence of direct quotations from interviews in this section. Such was the intimidation practised by the King's Cross Women's Centre women that most of my interviewees requested that they not be directly quoted on this subject. I therefore decided to write this section in my own voice, while still drawing extensively on the interview material. The views expressed here are not mine alone, although I accept full responsibility for them.

18. Compare Brown (1984) with Amos and Parmar (1984).

19. The International Wages for Housework Campaign is derived from the Marxist economism of dalla Costa and James (1972), and argues that women's oppression should be tackled by paying wages for housework. This position has been rejected by every other feminist group in Britain: see Segal (1987). There is also a history of attempts at 'infiltration' and disruption of feminist campaigns around Britain by Wages for Housework.

20. The media, however, has focused extensively on the split between the King's Cross/Yellow Gate women and the rest of the camp, as recently as 4 February 1999 (*Guardian*). The three women still living at Greenham in 1999 are all King's Cross/Yellow Gate women.

# Chapter 8
# Action Stories

Greenham began as a protest against Cruise missiles and over the years tens of thousands of women made their own personal statement of opposition to nuclear militarism by taking part in actions there. These actions took a great variety of forms ranging from the individual and solitary to the mass collective action of over fifty thousand women, from the carefully planned to the completely spontaneous, from the secret to the utterly overt. Some actions stayed within the law, but many consciously broke it. Some were over in a matter of minutes, others lasted hours, days or weeks. Some were designed to be purely symbolic, others to directly disrupt and sabotage the workings of the base. Some went as planned, others went awry. Some led to bruises and broken bones, others to hysterical laughter. Some led to court and prison, others to a hasty escape and a hot drink back at the campfire.

To write anything like a complete history of actions at Greenham would be an impossible task. For several years there were dozens of actions taking place each night but no written log was kept. Even the women who did the actions do not necessarily remember every one in which they took part. This chapter does not, therefore, attempt to narrate a comprehensive history of Greenham actions. And whilst it is important to recognize the significance to the camp's history of the mass actions which brought tens of thousands of women to Greenham, such as the December gatherings of 1982 and 1983, it does not focus exclusively on these. Nor does it just concentrate on those actions which entered camp legend - turning-point actions such as the occupation of the sentry box, which was the first incursion into the base; big, flamboyant actions, which captured the interest of the world, like the silos action; the smaller actions which amused and cheered the women living at the camp when times were hard, such as the Teddy Bears' Picnic. Rather, the chapter seeks to give the reader a flavour of the variety of actions which women did at Greenham and a sense of what they meant to the women who did them. Through this a picture of Greenham's particular form of queer feminist direct action emerges: a brave, confrontational, brash, parodic, spectacular and humorous yet passionately committed mode of doing politics.

## The Meanings of Actions

Every Greenham woman has her own biography of actions, a set of stories of those actions which, for a range of reasons, were important to her. Some of these were 'big' actions, which made a special impression, others were 'smaller' actions, which were particularly significant in an individual's history of being at the camp, or were particularly politically important to her, or were simply exciting, dramatic or fun. Just as there was an enormous range of actions taken at Greenham, so these actions had a multiplicity of meanings to the women involved. For some women doing actions was central to their experience of living at Greenham, and they took part in actions regularly. For others actions were less important than just the fact of being at the camp.

For Penny Gulliver, who did her first action on her second night at Greenham, actions were a vital part of living at the camp.

> We did loads and loads of actions that winter. And they all went wrong. I think I never took part in an action that went right. But I loved it. It was really exciting. My mate Trina says, everyone gets this amount of excitement in their life, and we had all ours in one year, and it's all downhill now. Most people spread it out over 45 years. It made you feel strong and confident.
>
> *Penny Gulliver*

To Leah Thalmann and Barbara Rawson, the actions which they did together at Greenham were a personal challenge and a great achievement. They were also enormous fun.

> People like me didn't do things like that [cutting the fence]. I mean, it was alright for those young and really strong women, but

people like me didn't do it ... I knew I'd got to do it for my own peace of mind. I'd got to do it.

SASHA: *Did you feel pleased with yourself when you first did?*

Yes, exhilarated. Awful, over-the-top singing, shouting, and things like that. Which was also stuff that I'd not done. I'm ever such a quiet little woman ... I was always very glad when we'd done it. How great that was, especially if you'd done it in the night, and you came back and crawled into your sleeping-bag – it was lovely.

*Barbara Rawson*

SASHA: *Was being involved in actions an important part of being there for you?*

Oh yes. I was really playing out a lot of childhood adventures. I used to like playing in woods when I was a child. I used to like stories about Robin Hood because they lived in the woods. And I think I always had a vision of how lovely that would be, to just live in the woods among the trees. And I think that was a lot of what I was doing. Living in the woods, with a group of people and doing things. I loved cutting the fence and doing actions.

I think there was always that frightening feeling just before you did something, not really frightened, just, would I get in before they found me? Come on women, get on with it. Barbara and I talked about that a lot, and tried to get over that feeling. Is it that we're defying authority, that we minded being caught? We minded the idea of being caught and feeling like bad children who've been caught. And we were trying to get past that and it was quite difficult to do. I think perhaps in the end I did.

*Leah Thalmann*

Liz Galst felt that the most significant action she did at Greenham was occupying the air traffic control tower within the base, an action which received international media coverage and proved a serious embarrassment to the government. She decided that she wanted to do that particular action because:

I felt like this whole thing was based on air power ... And it was this time that Michael Heseltine was saying all this stuff about how Greenham women may be able to get into the base but they can't get into any sensitive areas ... The actions that I liked were about finding out what was going on in the base that we weren't being told about.

But actions weren't the be-all-and-end-all for Liz.

> They weren't that important to me. I mean the media stuff that we did, the *Newsletter* and just talking with people, that was much more important to me, and just living life there. I thought we were creating a model of how people could live differently in society, and that was very important to me, much more important than the actions.
>
> *Liz Galst*

For Clare Hudson, what was important about actions at Greenham was their integrity - the fact that they had meaning to the women who did them and that they were not constructed purely to attract the attention of the media.

> I always used to get very annoyed when people talked about the amazing things that Greenham women would do for publicity, because I actually don't think we did. I think that was one thing that we actually sorted out really early on - all of us, throughout the camp and outside it. That when you did something, you did it because it made sense to you. And the publicity was a very secondary consideration. You didn't do anything as a publicity stunt, and if you did, it was going to be a very empty and futile action.
>
> *Clare Hudson*

## (Dis)Organized Spontaneity and Secret Openness

> All those wonderful actions that are going to go down in our collective history were someone's little idea that they had, and actually became these major actions that were splashed in the papers and resulted in prison sentences, and which would have upset some organization with grand plans.
>
> *Carola Addington*

There was no overall strategy or grand plan for actions at Greenham. The openness of Greenham to spontaneity and individual creativity, and to constant change, meant that ideas for actions emerged in different ways. Some were the product of intense, focused discussion around the campfire or in a meeting; others were the property of individual women, musing as they chopped wood or walked around the base. The sorts of actions which women did changed over time, as circumstances changed and as priorities and ideas about what was appropriate or effective shifted. Broadly speaking, there was a movement from actions outside the base to actions which breached the boundaries and entered the base; from demonstrations to direct, confrontational actions; from legal to illegal actions; from the use of women's bodies as tools of protest to the use of mechanical tools, such as bolt-cutters. Whilst all of Greenham's actions were symbolic, there was an increasing tendency for actions to have a direct impact as well as a symbolic impact, for them to involve physical interventions in the work of the base, or sabotage and damage to fixtures and fittings, buildings, vehicles and equipment.

At the moments at which new types of action were being considered, such as entering the base or cutting the fence, there was much discussion of what such an action would mean, both in terms of its relationship to the ethos of the camp and the likely consequences for the women involved, in terms of arrest, charges and imprisonment. The first time new actions were done, and on a number of occasions afterwards, a considerable amount of collective thought went into planning. But over time, as particular types of action became commonplace in the Greenham repertoire, and as individual women became familiar with breaking the law, being arrested and working together, the amount of planning and discussion tended to diminish. Actions became more spontaneous, but paradoxically, sometimes also more routinized. Cutting the fence to enter the base became the most common action.

> The organized actions started to fade out. It became very much more anarchic and individual after women started cutting the fence. I suppose that once you had bolt-cutters, actions didn't need to be planned. Unlike the Sentry Box and the Silos and things like that. For a start you had to buy the ladders; there was a lot of organization involved. Once you could come back from the

pub drunk and snip your way in and paint a few planes, you
didn't need to plan in the same way.

*Rowan Gwedhen*

Carmel Cadden recollected how the lack of rigid central planning of
big actions at Greenham meant that it was initially difficult for women
to know what to do.

At the beginning there was this feeling of confusion often with big
events at Greenham. Everyone would mill around, going, 'What's
going on? I don't know. Aren't we supposed to be doing this major
action?' [laughs]. And then somehow it all just gets together, and
you get to feel that you have to go through this period of hanging
around looking confused for a bit, and then somehow you'll know,
it'll all just come clear. And that's what happened quite a few times.
So when things are like that, I always think it's a good thing.
Something will happen, and it's almost like everybody's letting it
happen, just judging the right moment, rather than jumping in
with a very clear plan. So they do the unexpected brilliant thing,
which they wouldn't have been able to plan beforehand.

*Carmel Cadden*

She believed that it was a question of balance between organization
and spontaneity.

You've got to have good organizing skills, up to a point, and
you've got to let things happen, up to a point, and it's that
balancing of things. Sometimes you can be too laid back and not
organized enough, the right newspapers aren't contacted, so you
don't get the maximum benefit. And then other times, it's too
tightly controlled. There's always criticism, whichever side it goes
to. Sometimes I've felt that women have no concept of personal
safety in actions, and yet they've pulled it off. I suppose because I'd
done the NVDA [non-violent direct action] training and thought
you had to be very together before you attempted anything illegal,
and suddenly you'd find all these women who've been at camp
much longer, or were just naturally more daring, would just be
having a party and someone would have an idea or something,
and they'd go rushing off and get some bolt-cutters. And I'd think,

I don't believe this is serious, they really are going to go in. And they would too, and be quite happy the whole way through. And I really admired that too. And later on when I got more involved I could enjoy that too. Once I saw that it worked and I realized that you have certain rules to help you when you have no idea what to do, but once you have some experience and you know what you're dealing with, then you don't need the rules because you can suss it out yourself.

*Carmel Cadden*

The first mass fence-cutting, which took place on 29 October 1983, the Saturday closest to Hallowe'en and just weeks before the first Cruise missiles were flown in, illustrated the (dis)organized spontaneity which characterized Greenham actions. The idea for the action originated at the camp and was spread by word of mouth through the Greenham network across Britain and beyond. It struck a chord among the network, in which many women were by then ready to do more than just protest outside the base. Without any central direction or instruction, thousands of women arrived at the camp and, finding their own places, spread out along the nine-mile perimeter fence, began, sometime after 4 p.m., to cut the fence. Over four miles of fence were brought down that afternoon.

Katrina Allen, who had been involved in discussing the initial idea at Greenham, reflected on how letting the action take its own course was vital to its success, and made it much harder for the authorities to intervene.

The classic was what we did on Hallowe'en when we cut down the fence, and we decided to do it at fourish, which could have been a code, or it could have simply been what it was, which was quite simply around about four, when you felt like it ...

The whole thing of talking about it, planning for it, thinking about it, and just making up our minds that that was how we were going to do it, and the discussion about whether it was the right thing to do or whether we should do it differently – it was a very, very interesting thing. And I felt that it was a good action in that it was quite coherent and quite active without being so organized that it would be sabotagable. I think that if it had been more organized it probably would have been able to be fucked up. But the fact was, it was small groups of women coming to the camp, having picnics, then heading for the bolt-cutters. And each woman did her own thing, which actually worked very well …

I think the police knew that there was going to be an action, but they certainly weren't prepared for what happened, because they had more police on the inside than on the outside, and if they were actually going to arrest people and stop them from doing it, then they needed police on the outside. And they didn't have enough police.

*Katrina Allen*

Some actions were planned to be carried out in secret to avoid detection until the goal had been achieved. For instance, women often wanted to cut through or climb over the fence in order to reach a particular place inside the base. However, the secrecy was far from military and there was a fundamental openness about the fact that the law was regularly being broken.

What I used to think is that most of what the women are doing here, they're dead open about anyway. I mean, if you actually were going to plan to go into the base you wouldn't particularly want to let the MoD know at that particular moment in time that that's what you were planning, but I mean there wasn't any great secret going on. We were doing something very subversive but it was actually very open. We were very open about what it was about and what we were doing.

*Vee Wright*

Carol Harwood's recollection of the planning of the Silos Action was a clear example of Greenham's secret openness.

I remember us all sitting round the fire and sort of planning it. I don't know where it came from. It's like these ideas, they sort of you know molecularly spring from somewhere. I don't know where it came from. And I remember us discussing whether we should wear really dark clothes and I was very much against that. I remember that's the first time I spoke at the meeting. I felt very strongly that I didn't want to wear dark clothes and go in secretly. And that we should wear really bright clothes and we had to sort of oppose those forces with the opposite all the time. You know, that we weren't the camouflage and balaclava people, you know that we should go as women, and sort of looking how we felt.

SASHA: *And was that accepted, was that what you decided to do?*

It was, actually, yes. Yes. Yes, it was accepted. That we go very openly, I mean not, you know we were very, very secretive. But when we actually go over the fence, we go in a blaze of colour and badges and ribbons. And I think that's the way it should always be, really.

*Carol Harwood*

## Greenham Gatherings

The first action to take place at Greenham was a gathering, the gathering of those who had walked from Cardiff to the base together with local anti-nuclear campaigners in September 1981. Over the years there were many gatherings of different sizes, focused on different activities: the Equinox Festival in March 1982, Embrace the Base in December 1982, the Rainbow Dragon Festival in June 1983, the Ten Million Women gathering in September 1984, annual gatherings to commemorate the  December date of the decision to site Cruise missiles at Greenham, and monthly Common Women's Days from 1984. Some of these gatherings were organized with the intention of bringing large numbers of new women to Greenham, others were smaller gatherings, not so widely publicized, designed to celebrate or mark a particular event.

Greenham gatherings were unstructured with no platform and no programme of speeches. There were no stewards or organizers to direct the proceedings or to police the event for the authorities. Indeed, gatherings at Greenham were *initiated* rather than organized. The idea would usually originate from the camp and would be spread through the Greenham network by chain letter and word of mouth. Local groups would then hire coaches and minibuses and publicize the event in their area in order to bring women to Greenham. Rather than the placards and banners of the organizations which they represented, women would bring musical instruments, candles and torches, and sometimes symbols of personal significance, such as paintings and photographs. (At the Embrace the Base demonstration, the maternalist high point of Greenham, these were often of their children.) Women at the camp usually sought to spread information about what should be brought (food, warm clothing, candles and so on), and sometimes produced leaflets suggesting the theme of the day, but they did not tell anyone what to do. It was up to those attending to perform the action, to create their own demonstration, by singing, dancing, keening, chanting and talking to each other. Gatherings at Greenham were expressive and emotional, harnessing the creativity of those attending to draw sharp contrasts with the cold, supposedly rational military world behind the fence.

## EMBRACE THE BASE

The first mass demonstration at Greenham, 'Embrace the Base' on 12 December 1982, was an important moment in the history of the camp.[1] It was the occasion which first drew large-scale media attention to Greenham and was the entry-point for hundreds of women who later went to live at the camp and for thousands who became regular stayers or visitors. The idea to try to mobilize enough women to assemble at Greenham to encircle the entire perimeter of the base arose several months earlier during a conversation about what 'dream' actions they would most like to see happen at the camp. Initially cautious that the ten thousand or more women needed might not come, no figure was quoted in the leaflets inviting women to Greenham. Everyone was encouraged to bring scarves to hold between them, in case there were not enough women to surround the base holding hands. In fact over 35,000 women gathered at Greenham that day, establishing a distinctive Greenham protest style and galvanizing the movement into action.

The Embrace the Base demonstration was a liminal experience in the lives of the women who came to Greenham that day.[2] Outside the structures and routines not just of everyday life, but also of 'normal' protest and political action, it was a moment of de-differentiation, when individuals experienced a collective effervescence, an extra-ordinary sense of solidarity, excitement and strength.[3] This feeling of collective energy and the breaking down of barriers and differences had a particularly gendered significance. Unlike men, whose sporting events occupy large areas of towns and cities every weekend, women rarely gather together in any number to take up public space and to feel the power of the crowd. Seeing and being part of large throngs of women who were coming together as women was exhilarating and women were deeply moved.

> You never saw so many women in such a big group before. I remember when we turned up that weekend, and we started looking out of windows when we knew we were nearly there and we started seeing coachloads of women, more and more. It was incredible. So many ...
>
> *Ann Armstrong*

> I was elated, absolutely elated, I really was. It was just very thrilling. I was happy being on my own because it was so crowded, so many women. I enjoyed this feeling of keeping on walking and being in this atmosphere, and feeling, where have I been all this time?
>
> *Carola Addington*

Unlike any other event before or since Embrace the Base saw an unleashing of individual and collective emotion about the nuclear situation. Tens of thousands of women responded to the camp's suggestion that they bring symbols of their hopes and fears to decorate the fence and within hours the nine-mile perimeter fence was transformed into a giant art installation. Photographs of children, parents, friends, family, lovers, were pinned to it; ribbons and flowers were woven into it; paintings, poems and messages were hung on it; intimate possessions, clothing, nappies, tampons were displayed. The messages and symbols took a huge variety of forms: many were expressions of emotion welling up from women's experiences as mothers; others were consciously feminist, others passionately inter-nationalist. Around the base of the fence, as dusk fell, thousands of candles and torches were lit, and women sang and danced together. This unstructured, unplanned expression of women's creativity and life in the face of the preparations for nuclear war captured imaginations around the world. The fence which divided the Common, separating the people from the nuclear base, was symbolically reclaimed and humanized. Those on the base were reminded of the people outside and the reality of the lives threatened by the arms race.

One of the evenings suddenly there was a circle dance, only it wasn't formal. Somehow we just danced, and it was so exciting. There were all these women, and it was like a snake dance. It was all very spontaneous, and it was so exciting when I looked around. There were women of all ages in that dance, and all having such a good time. Everyone looked so pleased to be there and doing that. It was really magical.

*Carmel Cadden*

It was really strange coming up to Blue Gate, the first thing I could hear was a Welsh hymn being sung. So I immediately felt at home, 'cause you were feeling a bit scared and lost. And all of a sudden the first thing you hear is Welsh being sung. So I immediately went and found this gang and slotted in somehow. And it was a mixture of being enormously excited that this enormous crowd had got together, mixed with horrible feelings about actually seeing the place. You hadn't imagined in your mind's eye what it was like.

I spent the day plodding around the perimeter, being amazed at how big it all was. And I just remember the candles in the evening, when the candles started lighting up all around, just being very, very moved by it, the symbolism of the power of individual women gathered together. Whatever was in there [the base], it could be stopped. And I couldn't just go home then. I wanted to stay and do a bit more.

*Sian Edwards*

Simone Wilkinson had been in prison for taking part in the Sentry Box Action in the run-up to the Embrace the Base gathering, and was overwhelmed by the sheer number of women who arrived at Greenham.

I think 12th December was just such an incredible experience. We'd not long been out of prison and we went straight down to the camp. And women were two and three deep, you know. No scarves needed. And what I felt about that day was that incredible kind of crossover of women from all classes, all age groups, all different backgrounds, you know. And there was such a sharing. And the decorating the fence was spontaneous. They just wanted women to come and surround the base but women just spontaneously put photographs of their kids or their child's first shoes or a picture of their granny or whatever. Just walking round that fence afterwards was an incredible experience of that kind of spontaneous creative response that came out of women at that time.

And I remember we were stood at the fence, it was around Green Gate, and there was a vehicle that went along, a military vehicle, and like right down this line of women there was this incredible kind of noise started up in response and it was like ... it was like some kind of primitive crying or wailing that came up. And we all took part in it, it was like something that we all remembered. It was a very powerful experience and I remember thinking that day that for me, what I felt what was happening at that fence was that women weren't waiting for somebody to do it for them, they weren't relying on the peace movement to do something or governments to do something, or anybody to do anything, but it felt to me like each individual woman was making a commitment that I personally am not going to allow this to happen. I personally am going to stop these missiles. And I think that was what was going on. I think that a very personal commitment was taken by thousands of women and it changed their lives. I actually think that day changed the lives of thousands of women. It's funny, because when we were in North Allerton a few months ago, we were getting fish and chips and this woman came up to us and she said oh I remember you she said, I was at Greenham on December 12th. And, she said, it's so nice to see you because that day was the changing point in my life.

*Simone Wilkinson*

## DECEMBER GATHERINGS

Over the years many more gatherings and demonstrations were held at Greenham. The second weekend in December became established as an annual mass protest, drawing over 50,000 women in 1983 and continuing to bring women to Greenham until after the missiles were finally removed. The December demonstrations were the occasions on which women who supported the camp but for whom nuclear weapons were not a personal or political priority could register their objection to nuclear militarism and draw strength from the largest women's gatherings to take place in Britain. Each year's event was given a slightly different theme. The 1983 theme was to symbolically reflect the base back on itself using mirrors. In 1985 it was 'Widening the Web' to direct attention to the connections between nuclear militarism and other struggles and to 'Celebrate Our Differences'. In 1986, it was 'Reclaiming Our Lives', focusing on all forms of violence. By 1987, the year of the Intermediate Nuclear Forces Treaty which provided for the removal of Cruise, the theme was 'reweaving the web' and 'celebrating the birth of a post-nuclear age'.

The gathering in December 1983 was particularly significant, taking place as it did only weeks after the first missiles had been flown into the base. It was the largest single gathering ever to take place at Greenham and the atmosphere was distinctively different from the year before. There was a new anger, urgency and intensity amongst the women there and, without any advance planning, thousands of women started pulling at the fence, rocking and swaying in unison, bringing large sections down, concrete posts and all, with their bare hands.

> People were like pushing their non-violence to the limit that day. The cops were being real shits and people were really angry at them. They were really angry about the base and they were really angry and they were really frustrated because they had done all this stuff for so many years and it hadn't worked as far as they could tell at that point.
>
> Liz Galst

> Heseltine had said anybody who goes into the base would be shot and I think we had good reason to feel that worried about the future of the planet at that time, but there was a great sense of drama which does kind of also carry you along and make you say and do things which are sort of above or beyond what you'd normally do, you know. And you sort of don't get any sleep and, I mean, I was amazed that the first time I was pulling down the fence just the amount of physical strength in my hands. I couldn't believe it. I mean I actually felt I could fly. I can remember feeling it. You know, just feeling that there was nothing that could stop me and there was this fence and there were all these soldiers and I felt invincible and I mean ... it is a very intoxicating feeling.

So there were all these very intense feelings of kind of a great sort of immense passion, excitement, exhilaration and fear and terror you know, it's a very sort of heady cocktail, isn't it?

*Clare Hudson*

THE DRAGON FESTIVAL

Other gatherings tended to be smaller (thousands rather than tens of thousands) and to involve primarily those who were more centrally part of the Greenham network. There was, for instance, the Dragon Festival on the summer equinox in 1983, when 2000 women sewed a four-mile patchwork dragon, made from thousands of pieces of cloth sent by women from all around the world.[4] The Dragon Festival was Jenny Heron's first visit to Greenham:

> I thought it was marvellous. It was a really hot day and we were sewing this dragon thing together, with hardly any clothes on, and there was this freedom and fun. And the women who lived there came round and did a play which was all full of matriarchy and witches and all this stuff that was totally fascinating, and they had half their clothes on as well. And they were standing on each other's shoulders and juggling and things like that. I thought, wow, this is just something else. I've never seen anything like this before. And we all went home on a huge high. This sort of earth religion bit, you know, really appealed to me. And I couldn't wait to get back.
>
> *Jenny Heron*

New Year's Day in 1984 was celebrated by a thousand women weaving a giant web from wool on the clearing at Green Gate. Hundreds of helium-filled balloons carried the web over the fence and into the base. In May 1984 Saturday monthly gatherings were initiated, 'Common Women's Days', at which women were encouraged to 'make your own contribution, from simply being here, planting, picnicking, singing, sharing experiences, to non-violent direct actions'.[5]

## Blockades

Blockades were the first form of non-violent direct action to be undertaken at Greenham and they became a regular part of the repertoire of action for the first few years. There were two sorts: mass blockades, 'planned' in advance, in which women were invited to participate; and spontaneous blockades, which arose in direct response to unforeseen events in the base or at the camp. Mass blockades, such as the first major action at Greenham in March 1982, the 'Close the Base' blockade the day after Embrace the Base, and the week-long July blockades in 1983, involved several thousand women and caused serious disruption to the everyday work of the base and to the construction of the silos. In the latter two, every gate and gap around the base was blockaded and few of the dozens of bus loads of workers who normally entered the base were able to do so. The smaller scale, more spontaneous blockades were often even more effective because the lack of warning meant that the authorities tended not to have sufficient police immediately available to move women away. Spontaneous blockades were often provoked by unexpected visits of senior politicians or military personnel or by the arrival of particularly significant military equipment and aircraft. Women would also blockade police vans which were attempting to drive away women who had been arrested and bailiffs carrying out evictions.

CLOSE THE BASE

Many women found taking part in blockades an empowering and exhilarating experience. The Close the Base blockade in December 1982 was particularly memorable for Kim Smith and Carmel Cadden.

> It was a real buzz. It was a real adrenalin buzz, being there, doing something like that with such a big group of women. There was lots of music going on, food being brought round, women looking after each other. It was an incredible atmosphere, and whatever they did to you, you'd sort of bounce back out of the ditch and carry on. It was great.
>
> *Kim Smith*

> I'd done illegal things before, but never like that. Nothing as dramatic and premeditated as that. And that was quite frightening. We knew what we were supposed to do, and it was all dark when we took up our positions outside the gate. We had our song

sheets. It was all an unknown thing. We didn't know what the reaction would be. I am afraid of violence. We just got pushed out of the way, but there was nothing worse than that. I got pulled out of the way and dumped, and then you'd think, well, maybe I'll go back. It was quite a game really, And then when you'd had enough, and you'd got thumped down a bit roughly, you'd just sit there for a bit longer before going back.

The freedom of it was good. You didn't feel that somehow because you'd said you'd blockade that you had to. In fact, there was a lot of emphasis by women saying that you don't have to stay there until the bitter end. I did need to be told, you don't have to do it. You can change your mind. You don't have to be super brave. It was up to you.

*Carmel Cadden*

Blockades at Greenham had a powerful symbolism and there was widespread media coverage of the mass blockades of 1982 and 1983. In a cultural context which constructs women's bodies as more fragile than men's, and which still regards men as women's natural protectors, for women en masse to lie down in roads, to place their bodies in front of lorries and bulldozers outside a military base, and then for them to be confronted by serried ranks of policemen in riot gear, many on horses, produced potent images of the gendered contest at stake. As women were picked up by policemen and thrown in ditches or carried away to police vans under arrest, a symbolic enactment of women's refusal of nuclear policies decided by men was played out. The fiction of women's protection by male military and social chivalry was exposed. Through this women's bodies were refigured as disruptive and dangerous to the state and to the military.[6]

After the initial police confusion in 1982 about how to deal with blockades (they sometimes just waited for the action to finish) and as the date for the deployment of Cruise approached, the police became more violent in their handling of women and developed new techniques for policing blockades.[7] Although hundreds of women were arrested for obstruction, it was impossible, even with processing stations set up at Newbury racecourse, to arrest everyone. Thus the repetitious performance was established of policemen picking a woman up under the arms, dragging her away from the blockade and dropping her at the side of the road, whereupon, having taken a brief break, she would return to the action. Individual policemen differed in the degree of force they used, but most women would sustain bruises and scratches, and often had their shirts pulled off. A smaller number of women were badly hurt, suffering broken limbs, concussion, torn ears and severe friction burns as their bare skin was scraped along the surface of the road. Certain women were targeted for rough treatment, particularly black women and women from the camp thought to be leaders, often big, powerful-looking women, women who were obvious lesbians. The July blockades in 1983 saw the police practising techniques which were later employed during the miners' strike. They organized into wedge formations, marched along the road towards the blockades, rhythmically slapping their thighs, and charged at the women lying in the road, while policemen on horses also rode at them.[8]

## THE CITADEL LOCKS ACTION

While many women continued to believe in the power of blockades as a form of protest, others began to question the wisdom and utility of actions which were resulting in more and more injuries. The principle of non-violence meant that women did not lash out physically if hurt by policemen during blockades. But some women suggested that deliberately entering a situation in which women would be on the receiving end of men's violence was a form of masochism, women martyring themselves and offering up their bodies for a greater cause. Increasingly women began to turn their attention to other ways of taking action against the base. One result of this was a 'blockading' action in April 1983 which did not involve women placing their bodies in the line of policemen's boots. The Citadel Locks Action involved simultaneously locking each of the gates around the base with a solid reinforced metal U-lock. So impenetrable are these locks that policemen trying to remove the lock from the Main Gate with five-foot-long bolt-cutters actually pulled the gate off its hinges.[9]

> A series of blockades had been going on, and an awful lot of women were getting thrown around and getting hurt, and it seemed at that time to be quite an inefficient way of trying to stop stuff getting in and out of the base. And Nicky and I were talking about it when we were in Comiso. We were standing in this court

or something in Sicily, and one of us said, what about a Citadel lock? And it grew from that, because they are very good locks. So we pondered around the idea for a while and thought it would be really good to try and be able to lock every gate at the base simultaneously, early in the morning before the shift change, and just bung Citadel locks on them, and sit back and watch them try and get people in and out, instead of being thrown around and arrested or whatever, just see the trouble they'd get in with them.

So we came back, and we had a fair bit of problem organizing the money to buy the locks. There was a lot of money in the Greenham bank account, but at that stage a group of women in London, who were living in London, were the signatories for the account ... It was a group of women who'd originally been on the original walk, and started the camp up, and I think Helen and ShuShu were still the signatories.

It ended up with Nicky meeting Helen in the Hampstead Tearooms - Helen chose the spot - [laughter] to get some money for this action, and it was really strange because it was a case of going and saying, this is what we want to do, we've talked about it at the camp, women think it's a good idea, and we need the money for the locks, can you do us a cheque? And Helen said, no, I'm not releasing the money for that ...

So we got back to Barbara's house, and Rowan was sitting around, and I was absolutely fuming and mouthing off about what had been going on, and Rowan said, well, I've got a cheque here from, I can't remember which peace group, one of the peace groups, for £300. I think it was actually somebody had willed it to the camp, somebody had died and it was part of somebody's will. Some very sweet story involved with that as well. But anyway, and it was actually made out to Rowan, and so she cashed it, and instead of it going into the bank account, it went towards the Citadel locks, and the rest went into a different account.

So we had the money to get the locks, and set up a date for doing it, and had a whole group of women ready and waiting to go off and lock different gates. Then we had a hell of a time trying to buy the locks - you wouldn't believe how difficult it is to buy nine Citadel locks, or however many we wanted. There weren't any in Newbury, so we went to Reading and got a couple, and there were no more to be had in Reading. So we thought, Oxford, bikes,

Oxford. Got to Oxford, got another couple, and that was it. It was absolutely fucking ridiculous, I mean Cryptonite and Citadel locks, we weren't even being specific about Citadel, and we ended up charging up to London, and at 5.30 in the evening just buying the last two bike locks when it was set to go off the next morning, which was slightly hysterical. But anyway, it was typical Greenham really. So badly organized that nobody could ever get a hint of what was going on.

So the next morning, bright and early, just before dawn, everybody hopped up, got into different cars and went off to different gates and locked the gates simultaneously. And they had a lot of trouble unlocking them, and it was quite hysterical watching them try and do it. That was a goody! It was a bit of light relief. It was an amusing action. It shows up on *Carry Greenham Home* so well. The only thing that doesn't come over on that film was the fact that it was every gate that was done, not just Main Gate. It actually worked beautifully that one. Every gate was locked, there were no arrests made, and they were the ones who ended up breaking the gates down.

*Kim Smith*

THE BEETLE ACTION

Other 'blockades' of the base involved sabotaging key services supplying the base. Leah Thalmann recalled one such unsuccessful but amusing attempt.

We had a lovely action around the time of the 10 Days [in 1984], when we tried to block up a drain that came out just beyond Green. There was this big drain pipe comes out and we felt it was a bit mysterious because there was a soldier who came out of the base every week and went and inspected this drain and went away again. We thought there was something fishy going on there.

And we decided to block it up, with concrete, so that all the water coming out would back up into the base. And we spent nights humping bags of sand and concrete, mixing it. I remember mixing all this quick-setting concrete. I was bagging it up into little paper bags, greaseproof bags, it was like making up Cornish pasties or something. I'd be slapping these to the next woman and she'd be passing them to the next. And we tried to block this drain up. We spent nights on this. We put wooden batons across. Jenny was organizing it. We eventually got most of it blocked up, but there was a bit that we couldn't.

We went the next morning and the concrete had all burst out again. So we decided instead to put a fake dead body coming out of this drainpipe and we made this body and stuffed it with rags and old clothes, and then had this hand, this rubber hand, and we shoved this thing into the drainpipe, with this hand coming out and hung about to see what the soldier would do, and it was a bit disappointing because he just came and ignored it or laughed or something. And we never found out what they were doing. It was all rather a waste of time but it was great fun.

We called it the Beetle Action, because we used to go to this big sandpit which was near Blue Gate, somewhere there was a great works and we used to get sand from them, and we'd fill our haversacks with sand, put them on our backs and get up from a squatting position, and we'd all fall over on our backs with our legs waving in the air because they were so heavy. It was the silliest thing imaginable, but it was great fun.

*Leah Thalmann*

## Breaking and Entering

THE SENTRY BOX ACTION

The first time that women entered the base was a momentous occasion. It marked the beginning of Greenham's distinctively disobedient, irreverent and humorous form of direct action. In August 1982 eighteen women walked through the unguarded Main Gate, and occupied the Ministry of Defence sentry box.

Greenham was a place where I allowed sides of me to come into being, sides of me that I think I had always suppressed and kept under because they were unacceptable. The sense of humour and the fun, it was just amazing there. And that kind of creativity, the ability to almost be a child again and allow that to come up in yourself. It was like all the things that you've read about in books about girls' boarding schools. I missed all that. I never had all that when I was a kid. So it was wonderful to start having it in my thirties, late thirties, and you know, to allow that side of yourself, that sense of fun and craziness. I think for me personally there is a spontaneous side of my nature which I had always, always repressed, for all kinds of reasons.

The best example was when we were in the sentry box, which was a really up-beat action. We went through this big discussion about whether we should do it and we were trying to encourage women to come into the sentry box and Lynn Jones was telling them they might get fourteen years in prison and, and it was like, oh God. And she was being cautious I suppose but at the time it felt like you know, let's take Lynn Jones out and bury her quickly before we lose everybody. Anyway so we ended up with this group of women running through the main gate and into the sentry box and it was like a big serious action because it was a big step actually. I mean it's like now of course it doesn't seem like it but at that time to take the step of going inside the fence - it hadn't been done before and it was a big thing. It was an unknown quantity.

And I remember as we ran into the sentry box this guard had come out as had been predicted that he would you know. And like in rugby, he had gone for Helen because he recognized her. And Helen's quite small, and as I ran past this guard had Helen by the scruff of the neck with her toes dangling above the ground. And he was saying, 'Now come along, Mrs John. Don't be stupid.' And she was saying, 'Put me down. I want to be stupid.' You know, and this was supposed to be dead serious this action, there was this woman grinning from ear to ear and playing a goon you know.

And then when we got inside the sentry box there was a moment when we all pushed the table against the door to keep the guard out. They came and said, are you coming out? And we were all crowded against the back wall like this and said, no. And the minute he disappeared to go and get help we blocked the door with the table. And at that point the phone rang. And everybody was absolutely terrified when this phone rang. And Susan Lamb said to me, go on, she said, you answer it, you're good on phones. So I picked this phone up and I said, 'Hello can I help you?' And this voice said, 'Oh ahm, ah, oh do I have the wrong number?' And

I said, 'This is the Women's Peace Camp, actually.' And he said, 'Oh, I didn't know you all had a telephone.' I said, 'We do, and it's yours. Have a nice day now.' And put the phone down.

*Simone Wilkinson*

THE SILOS ACTION

After the occupation of the sentry box, which took the police completely by surprise, the guarding of the main gate was stepped up and actions remained largely focused outside the base until the Silos Action on 1 January 1983. The Silos Action, in which women climbed over the fence at dawn and danced on the (as yet empty) missile silos, established the project of invading the base in order to demonstrate its insecurity as the most frequently undertaken form of action at Greenham.[10]

The Silos Action was the first mass incursion into the base, and as a result of careful liaison with the press, it achieved worldwide media coverage.

> We slept at Barbara's house the night before. It was all tactics. Some of the women who were going to do it did sleep at the camp and overslept, and didn't get there. Most of us were sleeping all over the house. I think we were all, well, I was quite nervous. And I remember Skeeter putting her arm round me and saying, are you nervous? I suppose she must have been nervous as well. And we arrived in this furniture van, I think it was, in the early hours of the morning, and yet I just remember thinking, there's no way they can't know this.
>
> And all the hotels were full of cameramen, there were camera crews all over the place. They'd all been contacted, all the newspapers had been informed, but to keep it quiet. And they'd all been told it was all embargoed. But you'd think, surely somebody, and the fact that all these camera people had booked in, I mean somebody in the base is going to twig on this. But they didn't. They certainly didn't know. And we planned it all really carefully, and we planned to go over as dawn broke on New Year's Day. And we did it to the second. It was about 7.45 – I can't quite remember the exact time, but I know it was absolutely spot on, and we got out the great clunking ladders and bits of carpet, and over we went ...

And we suddenly realized that we had been spotted because a police car drove round and its headlights were full on us, all clambering over this fence and there we were in the spotlight. And we started running. The clay was very, very heavy up to the silos, because it was where they were working. And the policeman, two policemen and a dog, started to run after us, and we all linked hands and ran. I remember writing a poem about it in prison after, because it was almost as though the clay was sucking the policemen with their big boots back, but not us. We were just running on top of it. It was really funny. I mean we were running really fast on this sucky, heavy clay, and suddenly we were right there, up on the top of the silo and dawn was coming up and it was really something. And going round in a big anticlockwise circle on the top of this awful place.

Yeah. That was a really powerful moment, because you knew that whatever, you'd put your mark on it. You'd put a touch on there which would weaken it. It couldn't ever quite be the same again. And then we all got arrested [laughter]. It started to rain, and it was broad daylight when we got arrested, so it could have been minutes or it could have been an hour. I will never know actually. And then they had to drag us off the top of the silo, one by one, which was a long way down a slippery, muddy thing. It was still muddy, and they had those wire frameworks into which they are going to pour the concrete. And I remember we wrote notes and dropped them into the silo, and they must still be there concreted in. They said things like, 'Greenham women say don't build the silos', and 'Stop it now', and 'It's not a good idea, chaps' [laughter], and that sort of thing. Just messages like that and symbols. It's funny because they've presumably been concreted in. It's like being at the bottom of a pyramid, leaving a message for the people who might chop off the top sometime.

I remember the headlines, 'Women invade the Base', and all that sort of thing. But the coverage of the trial was remarkable. It was extraordinary. And when we got sent to prison, it made headline news all over the world, and that was a surprise, because you could send 400 women into the base now and you'd be lucky if you got a paragraph, which isn't just the press choosing to ignore it, it's that women have made it normal to break into a high-security area and dance here and graffiti there. We've made it normal to breach the most serious security in Britain. It's now normal, so why should they headline it?

*Carol Harwood*

The Silos Action went down in Greenham's collective memory as a 'top action', and those who missed it regretted it sorely.

The Silos Action is one of the most painful memories of my life. I didn't make it to the silos. I got caught before, I got caught and then the police decided to give up arresting. A few women who came over the fence later got caught. But I was with the first group over, and they got me and shoved me in the back of an American police car. And then realized that there were too many women and they couldn't do anything about it. So I watched the women climbing up the silos and dancing on top of the silos, for two hours, sitting in the back of an American police car, with this woman American cop and me banging my head on the rail, saying, 'why me? why me?'... But I still did prison for it.

*Rowan Gwedhen*

SNAKES AND LADDERS

During the first half of 1983 women entered the base on several occasions, playing a game they called 'snakes and ladders' – sometimes over the fence using ladders, at other times, unbolting sections of fence, to 'snake through'. On 1 April, partly in response to the pompous earnestness of CND, which was organizing a mixed human chain from Greenham to the Atomic Weapons Research Establishment at Aldermaston against the wishes of many of the women at the camp, two hundred women climbed into the base dressed as furry animals, with a court jester in accompaniment, to have a Teddy Bears' Picnic. The women involved in the Silos Action were charged with the civil offence of 'breach of the peace', which led to a high-profile court case, but other women entering the base were bussed out without charge; they were an embarrassment to the government and had not technically committed any crime.

CUTTING THE FENCE

During the planning of the Silos Action there had been much discussion about the means by which women should enter the base. Some women suggested cutting the fence with bolt-cutters so that everyone could just walk in, but consensus could not be reached about whether or not fence-cutting was a violent act which contravened Greenham's ethos of non-violence. By July 1983, however, after many more injuries from blockading and with incursions into the base an established form of action, there was a group of women who remained committed to cutting the fence even though not everyone agreed with it. They argued that damage to property did not constitute violence, that damaging the fence around a nuclear base was a legitimate and transformative action, and that age and disability meant that not everyone could climb over the fence, whereas more women would be able to walk through.[11] The principle of personal responsibility to decide what is right ultimately overrode that of collectivity and during the week of the July blockades a group of women cut the fence to enter the base. This action served to shift the debate about non-violence, and before long fence-cutting was accepted as a key form of action. Cutting the fence became both the usual way that women entered the base and an action in itself, a form of sabotage which cost the state millions of pounds in repair and maintenance.

HALLOWE'EN

The Hallowe'en Action on 29 October 1983 was many women's first experience of committing criminal damage at Greenham. It was just before Cruise was to arrive and over two thousand women, many dressed as witches, stood on each other's shoulders to cut down more than four miles of fence. This mass criminal damage took the soldiers and police completely by surprise. Many women were badly beaten with sticks and truncheons, resulting in broken fingers, arms and dislocated shoulders. One hundred and eighty-seven women were arrested and charged with criminal damage.

We were doing the section right by the silos. It was really funny because afterwards we heard all these reports of women who were saying they were cutting the fence and the soldiers were just watching them. And they went for us. They went for us with truncheons on fingers on the wire and they dragged us all in through the gap. They just went for us. What happened to me was that I was actually wandering away, and a policeman came out through the hole. They came out after us. It was soldiers actually. They went crazy. Sticks on hands, knuckles and things. I wasn't actually cutting, you see, because of my thing about cutting, and they came down after me. Because I thought it was just as important to get away and tell people what was going on up there. And he grabbed me and twisted my arm behind me and started walking me back, and pushing behind, and I was going 'ahh', and there was this snap. And I went 'aahh'. But he hadn't actually broken my wrist. I don't know what it was. I thought he had broken my wrist. Newbury Hospital said a couple of small bones of the hand had gone. We were taken and put in this compound which they had obviously got ready, this open compound just inside the fence. We got herded into this compound and left there. It was fucking freezing. We got water sprayed over us at one point. We were kept for hours in this compound. But then they let us out without charge

*Rowan Gwedhen*

Carol Harwood was also injured that day, but remembered the occasion more positively.

I ended up in hospital actually. I cut the fence and there was a US soldier on the other side and he said, 'If that bitch puts her hand through the fence again', I just had my hands like that through the wire, and he karate-chopped it and it went through, straight through to the bone ... I wasn't alone. There were quite a few injuries, in fact there were a lot of injuries that day. And the soldiers got pretty heavy with the women cutting the wire, because we were taking whole pieces of fence down.

And there had been all the debate before it as well. I remember driving down with the Porth women and we were still discussing whether it was violent to cut the wire.
SASHA: *And what did you think about that?*
I thought it might have been. I thought it might be the escalating

thing. I was quite unsure about it. I wasn't certain until I got the wirecutters in my hands. And then [laughter]. It probably just goes to prove my point that it was escalatory. I loved it. I thought it was wonderful. You see the wire coming down, and suddenly you can see what was the Common and you see the line starting to blur between the woods and the concrete. And you see the possibilities. That was lovely. At the end there were metres and metres of wire flat, and that was a really good sight.

*Carol Harwood*

Carol Harwood was not the only woman to describe fence-cutting as 'addictive':

I was there the Hallowe'en when we cut the fence down. I went down there, and because I'd got a car I took down three young girls from Weybridge. And I said, I'm just going to help you, I'll drive you back, I'm not going to get involved [laughter]. I'll take you, you can sit on my shoulders and all this [laughter].

And of course as soon as we started, I was, let me have the bolt-cutters, let me have them. I want to do it, I want to do it. And it was so wonderful. When the fence came down then you just felt, we can do anything now. We can stop it. I just felt so powerful. I was so high after that. It was amazing. I just thought that if that number of women could cut the fence down, more women, if we all got together, we could do anything.

SASHA: *You'd been arrested before, you'd sat in front of gates, you'd got arrested in London on obstruction charges, why did you feel that you couldn't do criminal damage?*

It did seem a bigger step. I suppose it seemed a little bit violent also, about damaging property [laughter]. I've done a lot of cutting since then. It's dreadful. In lots of ways you can see how addictive it is. I've often got to the stage where I've thought, I'm just enjoying this so much, and not quite sure whether that was right.

*Ann Armstrong*

Shortly after the Hallowe'en action, in order to deal with the increasing number of incursions and breaches of base security, large numbers of British soldiers were brought to Greenham to guard the perimeter, leaving the US military to protect the missile silos. Soldiers were stationed every few hundred yards around the base, searchlights were installed, watch towers built, and extra fences and rolls of razor wire placed inside the fence. In November 1983, when Cruise arrived, the Secretary of State for Defence Michael Heseltine announced that women entering the base might be shot, and that any soldier who fired shots in the base in order 'to protect lives or property' would be immune from prosecution.

None of this prevented women breaking into the base, indeed incursions reached an all-time peak in 1984 and 1985, and continued until 1994. For a considerable period there were frequent incursions into the base day and night by many thousands of women. Once inside women did a wide range of actions. These ranged from small acts of defiant criminal damage, such as the painting of 'Greenham Women Are Everywhere' on base buildings, to the 2.5 million pound damage done to a Blackbird spy plane by women who painted peace and women's symbols on it.[12] On other occasions women sabotaged lighting systems and generators. Many actions involving breaking into the base were designed to test its security and to directly challenge Heseltine's threat to shoot. One group of women actually camped inside the base for two weeks without being found and many hundreds were only apprehended when they gave themselves up.

OCCUPYING THE AIR TRAFFIC CONTROL TOWER

The occupation of the air traffic control tower was an action which achieved widespread publicity for its breach of base security.

> It was just like a B-movie. We sussed it out and staked it out for a few days. And we wore dark clothes – we wore black pants and black shoes, black jackets – and we went in just when we thought it was the darkest. And we made a run for it and we got up there. It was not very far from the Violet Gate at all. I think we had a little decoy kind of thing going on at the Violet Gate, and we just cut this little hole in the fence and we crawled in and we ran and we got there and there was nobody there.
>
> Then we were on top of the tower and we had to decide how we were going to get in. Eventually we did break in and get into the actual tower, and we read some documents but meanwhile we'd been there for three hours and we thought, I don't want to

spend the whole night in this fucking air control tower, you know. So then there was this guard who was clearly climbing up on top of the air control tower to spy on the Violet Gate so we thought, OK it's time to attract a little attention here, and we also felt like we had to do a little criminal damage that could be directly attributed to us. So that they would have to charge us with something and that they would have to prove that we were there and that would have to disprove what Michael Heseltine had said which was that people can't get into these areas which are sensitive to the base. So we scribbled on a few slogans and things like that and then we started to try and flash lights in the tower. And we eventually attracted his attention and he was really freaked as you can imagine if you think that you, that you're there by yourself and you're spying on Violet Gate, and so this guy, he was pretty freaked out and he sort of pushed Spider downstairs and a bunch of MoD police threw us in a van and they took us to the interrogation centre.

*Liz Galst*

## THE WENDY HOUSE ACTION

Less ambitious than the air traffic control tower action, but also designed to demonstrate the insecurity of the base in spite of government protestations about its impenetrability, were the many hundreds of successful and unsuccessful attempts to reach the runway. Leah Thalmann remembered one such action.

I did the Wendy House Action. The Wendy House was near Blue Gate. It was this funny little concrete and sandbag mountain along near Indigo and we called it a Wendy House. We all went in through the fence, and we decided if we dived over this Wendy House and slid down the other side we could get straight onto the runway and paint on it. And of a whole lot of people who got in, nearly everybody managed to get over the sandbag mound and onto the runway. But I and someone else were the last two and we got caught. Which troops were they? I forget. But they were laughing as much as we were. And they threw us out and we got in again, and they kept trying rugby tackles to catch us but couldn't and I just streaked along the edge of the base because I couldn't get onto the runway and I shot up one of the watchtowers and I had some green paint so I painted something inside the watchtower and the policeman came up after me, and I was arrested. That was fun.

*Leah Thalmann*

TAKING AND DRIVING AWAY

For many women the ultimate aim of entering the base was to reach the missile silos – this would represent the most serious violation of US military security. After knowledge about the routines of the soldiers had accumulated over the course of many actions, and with techniques for cutting razor-wire honed, several women actually got through the many layers of fencing and razor-wire to the last fence and into the ultra-high security area around the silos before being arrested. Dozens more managed to enter military buildings deep within the base, wandering around freely for considerable lengths of time and even listening in on briefings being given to US servicemen about the missile convoy. Carola Addington was one of a group of women who got very close to the silos.

> Twenty-one of us took a bus from inside the base and drove around inside the base ... A couple of women had gone down a couple of days previously to test them out. You can fiddle it. They were very clever women, who had a way with machines, and managed to get a bus started. They were very easy to start apparently ...
>
> What was so funny was the meeting-point. We arranged to meet at midnight, on the runway, next to the second generator [laughter]. This was the classic thing. There were originally about forty women who were prepared to do it, but only one half made it. One half took off and disappeared and tried to get to the silos. Once again it was so funny. We got in, and we just lay in wait, literally lying low next to the second generator, and nothing happened. And the bus came along, and we started to run out, and then we realized it was the police. So we kept lying low [laughter] and then eventually the bus came along but we were so scared to run out, it just went straight past us.
>
> So we ran out onto the runway and tried to do this [waves her arms above her head]. And it was so cold and their windows were

all misty and steamy. We didn't know whether they'd seen us. They went the whole length of the runway, and eventually we saw them turn round at the end. We didn't know whether they'd even got the bus or whether it had been stopped. It was all iffy. And we were getting colder and colder. The bus turned around eventually and came crawling up towards us. And we went running along and we jumped on it.

And the plan was to all lie low but of course we were so excited our heads kept popping up. Then there were two police cars ahead of us and we were just convinced they knew what was happening. But we just kept on driving. And these two policemen were just talking to each other on either side of the road. It was amazing. We drove straight through them. We went on and on and on, and past vehicles and got right up to the silos. And as we were approaching the silos, we realized that either a van or car was following; it was going as slowly as we were [laughter]. And we got there, and just started chopping the fence. One of the soldiers was just totally freaked out. We had to keep telling him to calm down - he was quite hysterical.

SASHA: *How much fencing was there now between you and the silos?* Three layers. We got through two, so there was one left ... I think again there was fear because we really did think at this stage, because they were so reinforced, and they were armed, we knew that. Heseltine made it perfectly clear. So there was that worry. And they did have guns with them. But when we were doing it it was fine. I didn't feel scared at all.

*Carola Addington*

To begin with, women were charged with criminal damage for cutting the fence and thousands of cases were processed by Newbury magistrates' court over the years. In almost all cases the amount of criminal damage with which women were charged was less than that allowing trial by jury in the Crown Court ('criminal damage not exceeding £200'). As the amounts seemed to be completely random and to bear no relation to how much damage an individual woman had actually done, it appeared that the Department of Public Prosecutions was deliberately choosing to keep cases within the summary system and to remove the possibility of acquittal by a sympathetic jury.[13] Later, with Newbury Magistrates' Court clogged by women defending themselves in lengthy trials which consumed considerable police, military and court time, a new policy of non-charging was adopted. Increasingly women were ejected from the base without charge (usually deliberately at the gate furthest from that at which they lived) and had their bolt-cutters confiscated.

Then in 1985 the Defence Secretary, Michael Heseltine, instituted new by-laws to deal with the problem of women's incursions into the base. The by-laws (RAF Greenham Common By-Laws 1985, SI 1985 No.485) were made under the Military Lands Act 1892 and made it an offence of trespass for anyone without authority to 'enter, pass through or over or remain in or over' the parts of Greenham Common occupied by the base. Thereafter thousands of women were charged with trespass for entering the base, and charges of criminal damage, which were much harder to prove, became less frequent.

MASS TRESPASS

The trespass action was a direct challenge to the new by-laws.

> It was when they brought in the by-law, and it was lovely. We had this hilarious time. It was a Monday that it was coming in, so at midnight on Sunday it began. It was a weekend in which the base was sort of opened up. Well, it wasn't opened up - they didn't think it was opened up, but we thought it was. And so everybody was in and out. We were vying for records of how many times we could go in and out. The idea was to get in and be discovered fairly quickly so you could have another go. So this happened all of Sunday, and I reckon there would have been at least two hundred, three hundred women, all of whom would have probably gone in once or twice, if not five or six times. Everybody was in like rabbits. And it was very good fun, and they were quite good natured about it too. Towards the end of it they were getting a bit pissed off and dropping people at gates opposite the ones that they lived at and stuff like that, but they didn't seem too bothered.
>
> And then at night, it began in earnest, the breaking in to be charged. And we went in as the Violet Gate Amateur Dramatics Society, in which we were pretending to be sandbags on the

runway to see how far up the runway we could get as sandbags. And so we'd walk along the runway and whenever a car came along, we'd all lie about, like sandbags. And we actually got an incredibly long way up the runway [laughter]. It was just really funny, it was so absurd. There were about eight of us, and we were one of the last groups to get caught at about four o'clock in the morning, which meant we went into a transporter rather than one of the huts, which was rather cold.

*Katrina Allen*

Two women, Georgina Ashworth and Jean Hutchinson, later challenged the legality of the by-laws, taking the case as far as the House of Lords. They were eventually declared *ultra vires* and all convictions under the by-laws were therefore invalid. Only a fraction of the women convicted have applied to have their convictions squashed and for financial redress.[14]

## Greenham Away from Home

'Greenham women are everywhere' was a slogan coined early in the life of the camp to suggest that Greenham actions took place beyond that one corner of Berkshire and were not confined to women who lived at Greenham. Whilst there was, at various times, considerable tension about the label 'Greenham woman' and over the centrifugal pull of the camp, women's peace actions inspired by Greenham and conducted by women who identified as 'Greenham women' took place all over Britain. Some of these were the actions of campers playing away from home, but most were those of stayers and visitors, women whose primary commitment was to working in their home communities. It was particularly in taking action beyond Greenham that the project was pursued of 'making connections' between nuclear weapons, women's oppression and other forms of injustice. Greenham actions away from home were of two varieties: those that related directly to Greenham, but which took place away from the camp and women's peace actions in the style of Greenham, but not concerned primarily with Greenham.

The first group of actions was directed mainly at raising the profile of Greenham or taking the protest about Cruise to other locations. Examples of such actions were the occupation of the lobby of the

House of Commons in January 1983 to demand that the issue of Cruise be debated, and the dumping of a vanload of Greenham fence outside the Ministry of Defence in 1984 to highlight the amount of damage women were doing which was not being reported in the press and for which women were not being charged. To protest against Cruise and raise awareness about Greenham, local women's peace groups throughout Britain held demonstrations in town squares, set up peace camps on roundabouts and outside other US military bases and engaged in dramatic street theatre, particularly on 24 May each year, International Women's Day for Disarmament.

In 1984 the USAF started to take convoys of Cruise missiles out of the base on exercise around southern England, practising making them 'blend into the countryside'. Greenham women immediately began to take action to draw attention to and disrupt these war games.[15] Demonstrations were held at roundabouts as the convoy passed, roads were barricaded by cars and human blockades were held in London and other cities. Then in summer 1985 a large group of Greenham women set off on a walk to 'reclaim Salisbury plain', the most heavily used firing range in the country and the main area where convoys were exercised. En route the walk visited ancient religious sites such as Avebury and Stonehenge.

Women also took the campaign against Cruise abroad, to Geneva and to New York.

THE GENEVA TRIP

In late summer 1983 a group of women from Greenham travelled to Geneva to make their presence felt during the arms limitation talks at the United Nations. Carola Addington was one of the women.

> Geneva was amazing. God it was mad [laughter]. Again, such fun as well. But also terrifying. It was just extraordinary. There we were about fifty women descending on Geneva, and it was classic. The morning of the action I was driving the van, and we had to pick up a ladder from some supporters on the other side of Geneva, and it was 8 o'clock in the morning, not knowing Geneva, driving round the place to pick up this ladder. The ladder didn't fit in the van. It stuck out of the back [laughter]. So we all piled into this van. We

hired a van from Reading, Winchester, or somewhere, we thought, we mustn't let them know where we're going; I don't think we told them we were driving over the Channel.

So we were going round Geneva in this hired van, with the name of the British hire firm on the side, ladder sticking out, about twenty women squashed inside [laughter], pretending we were just tourists [laughter]. It was a joke. And we got lost. We were meant to be meeting behind the embassy, the Russian or, I don't know, the American Embassy. But because we got lost, we ended up driving towards it, towards the main entrance. And there were these guards at the main entrance. So I had to do a loop around. And we were convinced we were being followed. Then we did an enormous detour around the whole town again, and eventually met up. We actually made it by some crazy way. A whole load of women got in at the back of the Russian Embassy, climbed up this wall and there was electric fencing at the top. And we thought, what are we going to do about this. And I can't remember her name now, this wonderful, beautiful woman who was at Green Gate for ages, tall thin woman with long red curly hair. She just went and climbed up and touched it. And it wasn't on. So that was fine. We all scrambled over and got in. And then there were other women who had joined the mixed peace group. There had been a mixed peace group from West Germany who'd marched down to Geneva.

So they were protesting at the front, doing sit-downs, blockading the gate. They were the distraction. It actually worked very well, because we'd gone to Geneva and were cross because we were supposed to be meeting the women's peace march from Germany, and there was supposed to be an alternative peace conference taking place. And of course they were men. That aroused a lot of anger. And we took that over and we sorted that one out [laughter]. The men kept introducing the women, so we all got on the stage and just linked hands across and said this isn't how the conference should be. I think we all broke up and had workshops outside. I remember lots of groups of women outside.

We set up a peace camp in the park in Geneva. We got offered nuclear bunkers to stay in from the municipality. The West German contingency had prearranged accommodation. We didn't know what we were going to do when we got there. We took over the women's centre, which they were a bit cross about. And then we set up a peace camp in Geneva square. They were terrified. They really thought we were going to cause a stir. Because there were all sorts of official protest peace groups there, including various women from England ... We got evicted the next morning, which was fine. We'd made a point ...

The plan was to scale the back walls. It was pretty high. And we thought, what sort of reception are we going to get? It's all very well in England in American bases, they seem to know how to treat us, to a certain extent. They know the rules. We were quite frightened by it. So we scaled them. And Russian guards chased us. They couldn't believe seeing us. And they chased us. That was the very first time I'd been physically roughed up, not roughed up, but very roughly held and kicked out. They were so frightened they treated us very roughly in their fear. But because of our numbers about four women actually got in. Not to the room where the talks were, but right up to the front, and presented our statements. And somebody from the talks came out and accepted our statements and promised to read them inside. And it got TV coverage in West Germany, it was on the main news and so on. And there was nothing here. I think there was a blackout, because we spoke to Reuters, who were interested, and did a long interview with them.

*Carola Addington*

THE US COURT CASE

Perhaps the most ambitious action away from Greenham was the court case brought in the New York Supreme Court by thirteen Greenham women and their seventeen children, a larger group called Greenham Women against Cruise, and two US Congressmen against Ronald Reagan, Defense Secretary Caspar Weinberger and US military chiefs of staff. The aim was to get an injunction against the deployment of Cruise at Greenham using international law and the US Constitution to argue that deployment was illegal.[16] The case caused considerable dissension within the camp. Many women argued that the huge amount of money being spent should be directed to the basic needs of the camp. Others objected to working so closely with men and with lawyers in a manner which they believed deradicalized Greenham and incorporated it into the system. Nonetheless, the case attracted widespread support from the wider Greenham network and from the mixed peace movement, and for twenty-four hours on 9 November 1983 camps were set up at all 102 US bases in Britain in support of the case.

The second group of 'Greenham away from home' actions was inspired by the distinctive ethos and style of protest of Greenham but went beyond the issue of Cruise, often aiming to draw attention to the connections between nuclear militarism and other issues. For instance, on the occasion of President Reagan's visit to London (7 June 1982) women from the camp and from the wider Greenham network performed a symbolic die-in outside the Stock Exchange to highlight the huge profits made by the international arms trade. In February 1983 women camped outside Holloway Prison to protest about the treatment of women prisoners, and six women were arrested for climbing into the prison. In March 1984 women demonstrated in central London outside a seminar and sales conference for missile systems and technology; they threw red paint at the building in which it was held. There was a women's camp at Porton Down (the chemical and biological weapons research establishment) making links between militarism, the exploitation of animals in research and women's oppression.[17] To highlight the use of uranium mined in Namibia in the production of warheads for Trident nuclear submarines, a women's action was held at the British Nuclear Fuels plant at Springfields. Greenham women, working with Women against Pit Closure groups also organized a series of women's walks from mining villages in south Wales to the Hinckley Point nuclear power station, to demonstrate the relationship between the closing of the mines, the expansion of nuclear power and the manufacture of nuclear weapons. The other major form of action in this category was the establishment of women's peace camps at other nuclear bases. Inspired by Greenham, there were, at different times, camps at military installations at Menwith Hill, Waddington, Morwemstow, Rosyth, Capenhurst, Fylingdales and Brawdy (amongst others). Blockades, fence-cutting and incursions took place at these and other bases.[18]

Speaking about the camp at meetings, conferences and demonstrations was the other facet of Greenham's roving public face. Over the years Greenham women were invited to thousands of such events, ranging from CND and other peace groups, student unions and Labour Party branches, to the Women's Institute, Housewives' Register and Townswomen's Guild. Greenham women were also asked to take part in delegations to Nicaragua, to give lectures at peace conferences all over Europe and the US, and to speak at miners' rallies and galas during the 1984-85 miners' strike. Without ever appointing spokes-women, most of these requests for speakers were met. To a large extent the women who did 'speaks' were self-selected; a list of requests was read out after the weekly money meeting and volunteers called for. Many groups asked for particular women, usually one of the four or five whom the media had designated as Greenham's leaders, and were often disappointed to find an unknown woman arrive to speak to them. Most women found themselves fielding questions about Greenham's women-only policy, and meetings often divided between those who thought the camp was a diversion from the real business of opposing nuclear weapons ('a lesbian feminist separatist' plot and a 'bourgeois deviation') and those who constructed the camp as the apotheosis of heroic martyrdom in the cause of peace. 'Doing speaks', as Greenham women referred to it, was often a tiring form of action, but one which many women believed to be very important. Not only did it inform the peace movement about what was happening at Greenham and raise money for the camp, it also encouraged the use of non-violent direct action by others, initiated discussions about feminism and women's autonomy in mixed groups, and provided a link to Greenham for women who might otherwise have felt the camp too remote an ideal for them to join. In addition, doing speaks was an empowering experience for many women who had never before spoken in public.

> One of the wonderful things that Greenham did for me personally was that I always lacked a kind of self-confidence ... During that time at Greenham I found that I had particular gifts that I never knew that I had before and I never would have found out. And I might never use them again, but I know they're there ... I could go and talk to an audience of a thousand plus people and touch their hearts in a way that I knew changed their lives ... And that's a wonderful thing to find out about yourself.
>
> *Simone Wilkinson*

## Conclusion

Greenham's distinctive style of protest – an emotional, anarchic, irreverent, disorderly and queer way of doing politics – was not just the public face of challenge offered by the camp and the movement to the threat of nuclear militarism. It was also the glue that bound Greenham together. The pleasures and excitements of actions energized the women who took part and were part of the process by which women reinvented themselves. They threw off many of the trappings of their gender-as-normal, of traditional feminine behaviour, and experienced themselves as wild and rebellious in ways beyond the imagination of childhood adventure tales. Greenham women became the stars in their own action stories, their own and each others' heroines. They gave up hoping for the good guys to save the world and instead took their futures into their own hands.

## Notes

1. This date was chosen because it was the anniversary of the NATO decision to deploy Cruise.
2. Rothenbuhler (1988) draws on Turner's (1977) concept of liminality, which refers to a ritual 'time-out' when everyday structures and rules are swept aside.
3. The process of de-differentiation at the societal level involves a transformation of consciousness, one in which the relatively distinct individual consciousness of everyday life becomes sentient with others in a common situation and common enterprise. This transformation is characterized by a high level of energy, for the individual and for the aggregate (Tiryakian, 1988: 45).
4. The symbol of the dragon, or rainbow serpent, drew upon Chinese, North American Indian and Australian Aboriginal mythology, and represented women's demand for life and peace (Harford and Hopkins, 1984: 153).
5. Leaflet entitled 'Common Women's Day'.
6. On women's physical embodiment see Iris Marion Young (1990).
7. For a discussion of the policing of Greenham, see Johnson (1989).
8. However, the level of police violence at Greenham did not match that at Orgreave. See Coulter et al. (1984), Lloyd (1985) and Scraton (1985). In part, at least, this has to be explained by the fact that, unlike some miners, Greenham women did not use violence in response to police violence.
9. This amusing incident is captured on Beeban Kidron and Amanda Richardson's film Carry Greenham Home and is described by Kim Smith in Harford and Hopkins (1984: 139-40).
10. For another description of the Silos Action see Harford and Hopkins (1984: 97-101).

11. For an exposition of the case for fence-cutting as a non-violent action, see Rebecca Johnson in Harford and Hopkins (1984: 40-41).

12. This was such a major breach of security involving a top-secret aeroplane that charges against the women were dropped. See Tracy Hammond in Harford and Hopkins (1984: 154-6).

13. Those cases which went to Crown Court generally did result in conviction (e.g. the women who cut the fence in July 1983). The most severe sentence given to a Greenham woman was that imposed on Ann Francis; she received two one-year sentences to run concurrently, which were reduced to six months on appeal.

14. Late in the camp's history Newbury residents began a campaign to retain their 'commoners' rights', against the by-laws. With much of the base now having been returned to common land, under the charge of English Nature, Greenham women and local residents achieved much of what they argued for.

15. In this Greenham women were joined by Cruisewatch, a mixed network of peace activists, which women at the camp activated by means of a telephone tree whenever the missiles were brought out of the base. Greenham women and Cruisewatch successfully tracked and disrupted many dozens of exercises.

16. The case was eventually dismissed in 1985. See Center for Constitutional Rights (1984), Hickman (1986) and Young (1990) for a more detailed discussion.

17. For a discussion of the connections between animal liberation and women's liberation see Adams (1990).

18. There were also women's peace camps inspired by Greenham at the Cruise missile base at Comiso, Italy, and in the Netherlands, Denmark, Germany, the USA, Australia and Canada.

# Chapter 9
# Que(e)rying Authority

One of the most distinctive aspects of Greenham's queer feminism was its uncompromising and irreverent attitude towards authority. When confronted by the forces of the state most protesters will eventually, albeit rather reluctantly, obey the orders of the police and courts. Most, having made their statement in their chosen way, will disperse and head for home, fearing that if they do not they will face forcible removal, arrest and imprisonment. But Greenham was different. It refused to grant power to those who sought to control and curb its activities. Women at Greenham simply would not do as they were told or behave as they were expected to by the British state.

Greenham que(e)ried the conventions which govern political protest. It resisted the traditional acceptance of the police's right to police and the government's right to govern. It asserted its own presence and actions as right, although Greenham women often stepped outside the law. The strand of anarchism which ran through Greenham's politics rejected the authority of a state engaged in preparation for nuclear war and derived legitimation instead from the moral conscience and ethics which were developed at Greenham. Women at Greenham engaged in a continual dance around the authorities, side-stepping them, working around and behind them, cheating them and laughing at them. And as they continued to live where they were told they could not and repeatedly disobeyed the police and the courts, they became outlaws, developing new and critical ways of thinking about power and authority.

This que(e)rying of authority had a distinctively feminist flavour. In entering so directly into conflict with the state, in enacting their opposition to American, NATO and British military power and to the global organization of geopolitics, women at Greenham were explicitly challenging the delineation of politics as men's business. Although, since women's achievement of the right to vote, women's exclusion from politics was not *de jure*, their absence from the arenas of geopolitical decision-making rendered Greenham's claiming of a voice for women on these issues profoundly feminist. Greenham women confronted an array of state actors charged with controlling them who were almost exclusively male. This fact underlined the gender politics which were at stake at Greenham. It was impossible to ignore that, with few exceptions, it was male bailiffs who evicted, male soldiers who patrolled, male police officers who arrested and male magistrates who convicted Greenham women. These men were not acting explicitly as *men* in carrying out their work as state employees, but by seeking to silence and close Greenham they were *in effect* re-enacting what Carol Pateman calls the 'fraternal social contract' which specifies that government and politics are the domain of men.[1] Men were seeking to extinguish the major visible expression of women's collective voice on matters of military policy, to re-establish the situation where decisions about nuclear weapons were taken by small, secret groups of military men and politicians. That the military men and the politicians failed to remove and silence Greenham is testament to the relentless disobedience of Greenham women.

This chapter explores the queer feminist challenge to authority posed by Greenham. It tells stories of Greenham women's encounters with the personnel of the state – bailiffs, police, and soldiers – and with the institutions of the state – the legal system, the courts and prison. It explores how women understood these experiences and how their consciousness was often transformed.

## Evading Eviction

When the Commander of the base said to the people who had arrived at Greenham at the end of their walk from Cardiff that they could stay as long as they liked, he could have had no idea that there would be a camp outside the base for the next twelve-and-a-half years. No one anticipated that battle was about to be enjoined over the right of a group of women to live on the land outside the base.

Greenham's most important action was undoubtedly just the simple fact of being there. The camp's public presence outside the base constituted its most powerful statement of resistance to nuclear weapons and ensured that the installation of Cruise missiles could not be kept quiet. From the earliest days of British involvement in the development of nuclear weapons, secrecy has been the government watchword and every day the camp was there defence policy was highlighted and called into question. This continuous insult to geo-political privacy combined with the traditional hostility of house-holders and local authorities to unauthorized camping by 'undesir-ables' (as long experienced by Gypsies and Travellers) provoked a response from the state: the camp must be removed.

Attempts to evict the camp began in January 1982 with a formal letter from Newbury District Council requesting the removal of the camp within fourteen days and threatening court proceedings to secure eviction if the camp did not disband.[2] By then, the camp had been in existence for four months. This might have seemed to represent a lengthy protest and the local authority might reasonably had expected that the campers would accept that the time had come to pack up and go home. By the 'normal' rules of extra-parliamentary political action, this indeed would have happened. But Greenham did not play by the rules. It refused to move. A letter was sent to Newbury District Councillors in reply, pointing out that the law was not neutral and independent and that there had been times in the past when laws had had to be broken; if there was a law which allowed the council to destroy the camp it was an unjust law and the councillors were asked to ignore it. The camp remained where it was and Newbury District Council went to court.

The first eviction took place on 27 May 1982. Bailiffs, backed up by one hundred policemen and bulldozers, arrived to remove the camp. However, the women refused to leave; two climbed up into the tree house and were pulled down by bailiffs and policemen. Other women started weaving webs around the bulldozers and lying down in front of them, and one woman climbed into the cab to prevent damage to a tree.[3] The bailiffs and police used considerable force to move women out of the way of the bulldozers so that they could pull down the camp shelters and a number of women sustained minor injuries and bruises; many were also the target of verbal sexual harassment. In all, five women were arrested for breaching the peace and the next day, refusing to agree to be bound over to 'keep the peace' (except under their definition of 'keeping the peace'), four were sent to prison for a week.

All this did not, however, mean that an eviction was secured. The women who had been living at Greenham did not leave; instead they moved onto a piece of land owned by the Ministry of Transport right next to the common land from which they had been evicted. The publicity following the first imprisonments served only to draw more women and more support to the camp. The local council's attempted eviction from the common land having failed, national government stepped in and the Ministry of Transport obtained a High Court Order to remove the camp. The second eviction, on 29 September 1982, involved the confiscation of all the camp's caravans and the dumping of lorryloads of boulders on the MoT land in order to prevent women moving back there. But women just moved back onto the common land where they had been before the first eviction.

> The second eviction was when they took the caravans away and actually left us with almost nothing, 'cause I remember that night we went out gathering bracken and someone had managed to hold on to a bit of polythene. They took things away and impounded them, so you could go and get things from them. But I remember that night it was just all wiped out, and we went and gathered bracken and we just all slept together under this bit of polythene by the fire and there wasn't anything.
>
> *Rowan Gwedhen*

Many women had now been living at Greenham for several months and considered the camp home. With a general election approaching, twenty-one women decided to register to vote with the camp as their permanent address. It was then that the opposition of local residents began to surface. A local resident lodged an objection to the entry of the women's names in the electoral register on the grounds that they were not British subjects and  that they did not have a residential qualification. At the hearing at Newbury District Council Offices on 22 December 1982, however, the objection was overruled.

> We all went along and they asked us questions. It was really silly. They were questions like, 'Have you got belongings anywhere else? Is this your only address? Where are your possessions?', and all that sort of thing. And we all said, 'This is our home.' And we

got it. Probably lots of people did wonderful things, but Aggie rushed off to Barbara's and got hold of this whopping great dictionary and started reading out definitions of 'home', and nowhere in the dictionary did it mention anything about a house. 'Home' was about your emotions and feelings. And we got it.

*Rowan Gwedhen*

Whilst this victory indicated that liberal democratic principles could be mobilized to protect the right to live at Greenham, other arms of the state continued to act, increasingly in concert, against the camp. Particularly significant was the meeting, in camera, of a small group of councillors on a special working party which revoked the common land by-laws which related to the parts of Greenham Common which were not covered by the base, thereby taking for Newbury District Council (NDC) the rights of private landlords. This enabled NDC to issue a High Court writ against the twenty-one women listed on the electoral register who were seen as the leaders of the protest. The writ was the most draconian use of the law to be attempted against Greenham women and with solicitor Jane Hickman they fought it at the High Court on 9 March 1983. The first charge, 'conspiracy to trespass', was found in favour of the Council. An injunction was granted by the Court requiring the named women to vacate Greenham Common and 'be perpetually restrained thereafter' from setting foot on Greenham or Crookham Commons, and from conspiring with anyone else to trespass on the Commons. The penalty for so doing would be up to two years' imprisonment. The second charge of 'conspiracy to incite others to trespass' was successfully challenged. It would have made possible the imprisonment for up to two years of any of the women for no more than mentioning Greenham in public.

But even being banned for life from Greenham Common under threat of two years in prison did not prevent those women from returning to Main Gate. Taking the ruling literally, they moved the camp off the common land back onto the narrow strip of Ministry of Transport land from which it had been evicted in September 1982; the MoT land was not covered by the injunction. It was, however, impossible to live at Greenham without violating the injunction because the MoT land was so small. The named women lived with the threat of imprisonment hanging over them. Rowan Gwedhen was one of them:

I remember being quite terrified, going back. 'Cause you know what bastards they are, and you didn't know if you were going to get out of the car and a policeman was going to say, 'Right, you're nicked' ... There was quite a bit of wondering about whether policemen were going to jump out of the bushes when you went to the shitpit.

*Rowan Gwedhen*

The injunctions were never invoked, although there was every opportunity to arrest women in the act of defying them. Perhaps they were only ever intended to intimidate and threaten, it being anticipated that the women would obey them for fear of two years in prison. Or perhaps the huge publicity which had surrounded the imprisonment in 1962 of six anti-nuclear activists for up to eighteen months under the Official Secrets Act warned the state against taking this action against a group which had at this time huge support and intense media interest.[4] Since the Embrace the Base and Close the Base actions in December 1982 and the silos action of 1 January 1983, media coverage had been heavy and it was clear that Greenham could mobilize not just the 35,000 women who had come to Greenham but also large parts of the increasingly vociferous mixed peace movement.

In March 1983 NDC secured another eviction order for the common land and carried out the third eviction. This time bailiffs impounded eight vehicles which would not be returned unless £3000, the cost of the eviction, was paid to the Council. Women blockaded the bailiffs as they seized the cars and were violently handled out of the way. Again, the unintended consequence of the eviction was to swell the numbers of women at the camp and to increase the financial and other support being given. From then until the beginning of 1984 there were no more evictions. The peace movement was at its height, the camp was growing every week and NDC backed away from confrontation for a while.

In November 1983, the month when the first missiles were flown into the base and which saw thousands of arrests of peace campaigners protesting both at Greenham and in London, preparations were made for what was hoped would be the final push against the camp. Prime Minister Margaret Thatcher pledged herself to get rid of the camp once and for all. New by-laws were enacted which forbade the erection of tents or other structures and the lighting of fires on the Common, and gave NDC the power to remove such structures and extinguish fires. The Council, however, shelved plans to enact them in November because of the huge number of women who were staying at Greenham.

But early in 1984 NDC appointed two full-time bailiffs solely to enforce the new by-laws and a number of evictions of Blue, Indigo, Violet and Red Gates were carried out. The bailiffs and police also began appearing at all times of the day and night to extinguish campfires at all the gates. They filled the fire pits with water or foam, making the relighting of the fires extremely difficult. At the end of February Berkshire County Council appointed NDC as its agent so that they could act together against the camps which were sited on roadside land controlled by the County Council. Then, in the clearest evidence that local government and the central state were working together, the Department of Transport joined the informal consortium and requested that Berkshire act for it in securing the eviction of Yellow [Main] Gate from the land in its control.

In March 1984 Newbury District Council, Berkshire County Council, the Department of Transport and the police began to work together systematically. In the week beginning 5 March the camps on the north side, whether on common land or roadside land, were evicted regularly, sometimes several times a day. The first few of these evictions were relatively gentle affairs, with women given time to take down tents and pack up communal property. However, by Wednesday of that week anything not carried away within minutes of the bailiffs' arrival would be thrown into the 'muncher' [the refuse lorry]. Dozens of women lost all of their personal possessions, together with food, cooking pots and firewood. The bailiffs became increasingly violent and struggled to snatch things out of women's hands, often hitting women in the face and pushing them roughly to the ground. Invariably the police stood by while this happened, though they sometimes stepped in to arrest women. During the early hours of 9 March it became apparent why this concerted effort to evict the northside gates had been made. Cruise missile launchers were brought out of the base on exercise for the first time.

Shortly after this, the Department of Transport announced its plans to permanently evict the camp at Yellow Gate; the access road to the base was to be widened, and the women were given until 2 April to leave. As ever, they did not go. The DoT was granted a possession order over the land it controlled and there was a blaze of publicity about the threatened eviction. The eviction of Yellow Gate, as the oldest camp and the one where Greenham's 'leaders' were thought to live, became the focus of the state's attention. Hundreds of women from around Britain came to the camp for 2 April and NDC was forced to postpone the eviction at Yellow, though it went ahead at Green and Orange. When it eventually happened, two days after the deadline, 400 police and twenty-four bailiffs were used and a two-mile stretch of the A339 was closed to traffic. The reason given on local radio was an overturned lorry. Thirty women were arrested during the course of the eviction and fences were erected around the DoT land to keep the women off. As ever, however, the women simply used their knowledge of the ownership of the land around the base to set up camp back on the common land close to Yellow Gate.

Newspaper headlines proclaimed triumphantly that the camps were gone: 'Peace Camp Cleared Out' (*Standard*, 4 April 1984); 'Flaming Goodbye to Greenham' (*Sun*, 5 April 1984); 'Dawn Raid by Bailiffs Ousts Camp' (*Newbury Weekly News*, 5 April 1984); 'Goodbye and Good Riddance!' (*Daily Express*, 5 April 1984). None of these papers reported that evictions at Greenham were never permanent, nor that there were more women at Greenham after the evictions of 4 April than before. From this moment on the tabloids fell silent about Greenham, implying that it had indeed been closed for good.

From April 1984 onwards, evictions of all the gates except Yellow were a regular part of life at Greenham. Their frequency was exhausting and served to wear down the spirits of women living at the camp. The uncertainty about when the bailiffs would come meant that it was difficult to do anything but wait for them. For more than one or two women to go into Newbury to shop, wash or sign on was a risk. Vehicles always had to be available (with a driver) to load with possessions.

> We were being evicted three or four times a day during the spring. It did all our heads in because all you could do was hang about and wait for the muncher. I really loved the winter at camp, and it was really, really busy and there were a thousand things to do. And then when the spring days came and the days were longer and the muncher was coming four times a day my time span shortened, and it was so boring. You had to stay there and wait because anytime the muncher could come and drag everything off.
> *Penny Gulliver*

Over the months, the bailiffs became more aggressive and increasingly violent, and women were often injured trying to save things from being thrown in the muncher. Pat Paris, who lived through months of regular evictions at Blue Gate, remembered how the evictions heated up and recalled the effect that had on the women at the camp.

Initially they weren't too bad, because they weren't that regular, but it did get very wearing and tedious. In the early days we used to get away with murder. You'd put a pair of boots outside a tent and say somebody was ill, and they would leave the tent, and there wasn't anybody in it. There was one time when I'd just boiled the kettle one morning and I'd just made a cup of coffee when they appeared, and I said, 'Can I drink my coffee?', and they waited for me to drink my coffee. They would quite often say, well just let your tents down. As it got increasingly heavy it became an increasing irritant - I hate getting up in the morning at the best of times, without getting up and being evicted. If they came later on in the day, I didn't used to mind so much. But when they came at a quarter to seven on a cold winter's morning and you had to leap out of bed and run around like a lunatic trying to save things.

It was quite a way on before they got really violent, the bailiffs. I watched Sharples in particular and Willis. Sharples I watched from being quite a young sprog, and I remember a couple of years on, round at Green Gate in an eviction, watching him go around, I hadn't seen him for quite a long time - for about six months - and he had this really set face, really grey lines. And I actually thought, this bloke once let me drink my coffee, waited for me to drink my coffee, and once when somebody was ill at Blue Gate, he brought them fags up. This was in the early days. Because they used to stop and talk to us. And I remember saying to him this day at Green Gate when he was being really heavy, snatching things out of women's hands and deliberately knocking them over while he was doing it, I actually went up to him and said, 'I remember you when you were a human being.' And he just walked off.

SASHA: *Why did this change take place?*

I think they just got pissed off. I mean we got pissed off with it and I think they must have got pissed off with it. They went out every day, sometimes two or three times a day, with the intention of evicting us, and it never worked ... I think they just got very bitter.

It must have been a soul-destroying job. I've got no sympathy for them, but doing the same thing, day in, day out, and getting absolutely nowhere.

I think they thought women would be ground down very quickly. And it was very tedious and I think it did have an effect. I think women didn't last as long as they had done previously because it was so tiring. It was also very expensive to keep losing your equipment. I lost tents and bedding. Books were lost. Really important papers were lost over the years. At one point Blue Gate had a brilliant song book; it was eventually munched. And records that women wrote. A lot of that stuff has been destroyed. It did have a wearing-down effect, but it didn't achieve what they wanted it to achieve. By the time you'd been evicted twice a day for three or four days, you were tired. If you were got up regularly at six in the morning and you'd had the MoD up at night, or you'd had prowlers, or you'd had vigilantes, or you'd had yobs shouting at you, or you'd just had a party, and then you'd get hit by the bailiffs in the wee small hours. It was freezing, you couldn't get a drink because they'd evicted the kettle and they'd put the fire out and they'd taken the water. And as it wore on you hadn't seen a visitor for weeks, and there was nothing to evict anyway – those were the desperate days. But I think it did make women determined to stick it out. It had the opposite effect to what they'd determined. But it also made it harder for people individually to be there for any length of time.

They got worse. They definitely got more bitter and more hardened and less concerned about their behaviour and more prepared to do it in public than they ever were in the early days. Willis once tried to smash Chris against the back of the muncher; he had hold of quite a large piece of wood, a plank, and she had hold of the other end, and there was no way she was going to win, obviously because of the size of him and he was swinging it and swinging it, and I could see that she was getting nearer and nearer to the back of this muncher, and it was obvious what his intention was, that he was going to keep swinging until he hit her on the muncher and she would fall off it. And I could see what he was doing and I was saying to Chris, it isn't worth it – it's only a piece of wood, it isn't worth being hurt for, let him have it.

*Pat Paris*

However, women devised ways of coping with the evictions, ranging from humour and teasing and hexing the bailiffs, to treating it as a refuse collection service for which they saved up their rubbish. Possessions were pared down to an absolute minimum, with most sleeping in Gore-Tex survival bags rather than tents or benders, and systems were developed for packing up quickly. The numerous attempts of Newbury District Council to eradicate, or at least displace, Blue Gate by erecting fences around the triangle of land it occupied were foiled when women took axes to them and used them for firewood. In all, evictions became something of a routine 'cat and mouse' game, a regular form of harassment, and although they may have shortened the length of time individual women were able to live at Greenham, they never achieved the goal of eradicating the camp.

## Soldiers, Sexism and Subversion

While the local state was attempting to dislodge Greenham women from outside the base, the forces of nation states were busy trying to keep them from breaking into the base. The base as a whole was under the control of the United States Air Force and the security of its contents – from the runway and air traffic control tower, to aeroplanes and nuclear missiles – was the responsibility of the USAF. However, as Greenham and the wider peace movement began to provoke public debate about the question of 'whose finger was on the button', the involvement of the British military in NATO nuclear policy began to be emphasized by the British and American governments, fearful that a nationalist anti-Americanism might turn against Cruise missiles. As more and more people visited Greenham Common and saw for themselves how the base was controlled by the Americans, and as news coverage became more extensive, a decision was made to bring in British troops to guard the perimeter of the base. From the time of the July blockades in 1983 British soldiers became the first line of defence against Greenham women, leaving the US military to patrol deeper inside the base and to guard the missile silos.

For several years a number of different regiments were stationed in rotation at Greenham for short tours. Women living at the camp soon became familiar with the peculiarities of the different regiments and learnt that some were considerably more hostile and violent than others. The worst were the Paratroopers, who were first brought to Greenham when the missiles were flown in. Levels of harassment also differed according to the officers in charge; some clearly encouraged their men to make life unpleasant for the women whenever they could, whereas others did not. For instance, there were periods when officers commanded their men to blow horns or bang oil drums every quarter of an hour throughout the night. Others did drill calls at first light and brought brass instrument players to the fence to play through the night. This sort of low-level harassment was stressful and disturbing.

> I couldn't talk to them after a while. I did initially. Then I couldn't. I was amazed at women who did. But I just got exhausted and drained and found myself repeating myself all the time ... I found that after the missiles arrived, there were all these Paratroopers there who were horrendous, and I just hated men for a period. I just couldn't talk to any. I just couldn't stand them. Because our benders were right next to the fence and they would just stand all night long chucking abuse or hurling stuff or whatever.
> SASHA: *What, actually throwing things at you?*
> Mmm. They got to the point of doing that. And one morning at about 5 or 6 o'clock – they have their drill calls at 5 or 6 o'clock in the morning – one morning they arrived with a full brass band at 6 one morning. Just started thumping three feet away. It was so horrible, so horrible. There are hundreds of stories like that. But women kept on complaining and issuing formal complaints and so on, inside the base. I was always amazed at that. I always thought, what a dead loss [laughter]. There was always the woman who would issue a formal complaint and things would actually happen.
>    I couldn't get out of my bender, because I thought that that was just what they wanted. I just stayed in my bender and pretended to be asleep [laughter].
>
> *Carola Addington*

Women who had lived at the camps close to the fence recalled being subject at times to bouts of prolonged verbal sexual abuse from individual soldiers.

> They basically were young men who had been brutalized by a process deliberately intended to do that, and they were quite nice

enough as individuals, but I had no illusions. They'd been trained to follow orders and it didn't matter what those orders were. It was the Ruperts that made any difference; it was the officers.

Because Violet Gate was so close to the gate, we used to get to know the soldiers quite well, and always found this particular officer was just unbelievably rude. And that's a very polite word for it. He was an extremely foul-mouthed hideous person, who would just stand and shout abuse at us, of the most unbelievable stuff. Things like, you smell so bad you must eat the, now what did he call it? The sticky stuff that's on your pants, 'cause you wear them all week. He obviously meant vaginal discharge, but he said, it wasn't as polite as sticky stuff. It was absolutely ... And he would just run down anybody who was in his sight, absolutely foully, to a degree that I found astonishing. That somebody would just stand and shout that sort of thing at you, and could do it with complete impunity, and was obviously used to doing that sort of thing. He was just a particularly horrible individual. And the other soldiers would just stand around, and they certainly weren't going to say anything, and they didn't seem at all astonished by it. It made me realize that that's probably what they talk about all the time.

SASHA: *Was a lot of it very sexist then?*

Oh, absolutely. Sexist and sexually based. A lot of it was about us being women. The funny part was Veronica took him on one morning. He kept it up for about two weeks, he kept shouting at us in the middle of the night, just basically slagging us off, and slagging in a really foul, horrible, disgusting fashion. And Veronica one morning had enough, and went up to him and just really went to town on him. Hers was not as foul, but a lot more cutting, and very personal, and it was incredibly funny [laughter]. I must say I was totally admiring.

SASHA: *Had you all held off from responding until then?*

Oh no. Every now and then someone would shout, 'Shut up', or something like that. But there wasn't really that much you could say. It was just so foul and so over the top, and involved whole nights of tooting horns and shouting and making a noise and all the rest of it. I mean we were so close to the soldiers that they could disrupt us, if they chose to. He was exceptional in that he was loud about it. He stands out in my memory as somebody who was particularly awful. I'm quite sure that that sort of thing wouldn't be below any of them. I would think that that was quite possibly how they talked, but they didn't talk to us directly like that, because they couldn't stand the flack, and he could get away with it because he only ever came, I mean he gave his men orders to toot and make noise, but they didn't actually shout abuse. But every now and then he would come across and start shouting abuse at us, regularly for a half-hour at a time, probably six or seven times a day. I don't want to give you the image that it was just every now and then. But it wasn't 24 hours of it. And as soon as he went the men wouldn't say anything. But they would toot their horns and all the rest of it, because that's what he'd ordered them to do.

It was basically just to disrupt our situation. I suppose the aim of it was to make us sick of it all that we'd go away, which of course it didn't, and they couldn't keep it up. It's sort of ludicrous to even imagine that something like that would put us off after daily evictions. It wasn't in the same sort of league at all.

*Katrina Allen*

More dangerous than the verbal abuse was the violence of some of the soldiers. This ranged from throwing skinned rabbits and buckets of cold water over the fence at women sitting around the fire, lobbing rocks and stones both during the day and at the tents and benders at night, and heating metal rods in their braziers and poking them into tents and benders.

At Orange Gate one night there was a maniac sergeant in charge of the men who was just exciting the men, all the time, and using filthy language, and calling us everything. And they started throwing clods on to the bender and suddenly they got hold of a big spike, part of the fence, and just rammed it through the side of the bender. I suddenly felt this thing hitting my arm. And I just went out and screamed at them. And they were shouting 'Lesbian slags, you fuck them whatever way you can.'

*Sian Edwards*

We had a spate of very nasty soldiers at Violet. I had a burning poker put through my bender beside the fence. It was awful because I was in the fucking bender at the time, lying on the bed, and smoke started. Obviously from outside he couldn't see where I was. Fucking burning straight through the plastic, straight through the blankets. And they started shouting; they all thought it was such fun, ha, ha, ha, ha. I was so angry. It was bloody scary. My head could have been there. I think we did complain against that lot and I think they were removed – this may or may not be true, but somewhere in my brain, I think there was one lot that we actually got removed.

*Rowan Gwedhen*

It was this sort of unofficial state harassment that was particularly hard to deal with and it was this, rather than the officially sanctioned threat to shoot anyone who approached the missile silos, which constituted the immediate danger to women at Greenham.

I never thought that anyone was in danger from being shot. I think where women *were* in danger was being harassed by soldiers. I remember one night when we had the benders up against the fence, there were some squaddies who were lobbing lumps of concrete onto the benders. And Mary got hit. And metal stakes that they were shoving through. But that was their extra-curricular activity.

*Penni Bestic*

Women developed a range of strategies to deal with the problem of the soldiers. These ranged from the purely practical – such as moving tents and benders away from the fence – to attempting to reason and converse with them in order to convey a sense of shared humanity and to try to undermine the process of 'othering' in which the soldiers were engaged. Through talking and thinking with each other about the organization of the military and reading about the brutalizing and profoundly misogynist training regimes which operate in the army, women developed feminist analyses of their experiences which helped to make sense of them.[5] Whilst they held individual soldiers responsible for their behaviour and did not seek to excuse it, many women believed that soldiers were themselves victims of the military system. For working-class men with few qualifications during the period of high unemployment in the early 1980s, the army was one of few routes to a job. Many women had brothers who were soldiers and understood the reasons why men joined up. Others came to understand through talking to the soldiers themselves.

> I used to think, they don't have to be in the army. But if you get to talk to them, you find out that they didn't have that many options. It was a place where they could get some training, get some self-respect in their own eyes. They didn't have a lot of choices. And most of them were very disillusioned.
>
> *Carmel Cadden*

> It was really important for me to deal with the soldiers because I think that there are humungous issues of economic justice that come into play when you're talking about the peace movement. I don't think that most people go into the army because they want to go into the army. I mean I feel like I come from a very privileged background. I have a lot of choices about the information that I can get and I have a lot of access to that and have access to people who knew about that, but a lot of people don't. And I was not going to be a person in the peace movement who saw the people in the army as my enemy.
>
> *Liz Galst*

Carol Harwood's commitment to talking to soldiers was rooted in her belief in their common humanity and she saw herself as sewing seeds of disaffection.

> I've always had a strong commitment to actually talking to them ... When you're talking to somebody and you ask them what it's like in Northern Ireland and what does their mother think about it, you're home and dry. Because their mothers don't think it's a good idea. Whose mother would think it a good idea? And they talk to you about their girlfriends. They really are only human beings in uniform. And I know that they have the capacity to kill and maim, but so do we. We all have that capacity. Some of us have been trained, and some of us have it at a more highly developed level. But we all have that capacity, and they have that capacity not to kill, and not to maim, and if you're going to write them off, then you may as well go home anyhow.
>
> I remember Pat Arrowsmith being sent to prison for a long time

for disaffecting the troops. There's nothing worse than disaffecting the troops. Right through history that's been the terror of governments, whether they were radical so-called, governments, like Cromwell, or more conventional sorts. But disaffecting the troops ... well we should be busy at that.

*Carol Harwood*

Women at Violet Gate in particular, after the period of sustained verbal harassment described by Katrina Allen, developed cordial and even friendly relations with certain groups of soldiers.

At Violet Gate, because the camp was so close to the fence, we'd pass cups of tea through to them, especially when it was very, very cold. And they'd grumble to us about being on the base with the Americans - they've got everything and we've got nothing. The Americans had marvellous facilities, and the British hadn't, and they'd moan to us about it. And we'd say, never mind, have another cup of tea. And then they'd say, do you want any coal? Because they had a little coal brazier up at their hut. So they'd give us coal. It was great, because I suppose they shouldn't be fraternizing with the enemy. I guess sometimes they felt they had more in common with us because we were both sitting out in the cold, and the Americans were safe on the inner circles.

*Carmel Cadden*

It was at Violet Gate that women most consistently engaged with the soldiers. This was partly because it was at Violet that women lived in closest proximity to the fence, but it was also perhaps because it was the least separatist gate. Women there were more open to social interchange with the soldiers and more interested in the project of subversion.[6] Katrina Allen described some of the ways in which women's interactions with the soldiers produced subversive and insubordinate actions by the soldiers.

They were quite dependent on us for coffee and biscuits and conversation, and it was a very different relationship at Violet Gate because they were so close. They were only about six or eight feet away, and they used to be quite happy to have coffee and all the rest of it, but there were also some terribly funny incidents.

The classic being when three women went in for a barbecue; the soldiers had invited us in, and Donna and Criss and Sharon went in, and the soldiers actually cut them a hole in the fence, and they met them round the other side. They'd agreed where to meet them, and they went off and they actually ended up staying the night because it was too difficult for them to get out, because the watch changed. One group of soldiers would take 12 hours, and another group of soldiers would take 12 hours. They went into the base before 7 p.m., which was when the first group of soldiers came off duty and had a barbecue. So they went to the barbecue, and then they went to stay the night in the barracks. The reason why all this happened was that the chap that was their immediate commander, he was only a sergeant or whatever, but he was their immediate officer, was very, very friendly, and pissed off, getting out of the army, and just couldn't be bothered with it all. And he had invited them anyway.

I was just about to go down to Newbury nick, 'cause I was just thinking, shit, they've got caught, and I was just deciding to do that, and they all drove up, and he said, 'Look, you know where you dropped them yesterday - go round there and pick them up.' So I went round there, and sure enough, that's where they were, and the soldiers had actually cut them a hole in the fence so they could get out. In fact it was absolutely hilarious that week; these blokes were on their last week of duty, they couldn't give a shit, and so we used to go in. And it was terribly funny. We had a large hole cut in the gate, so we could get in easily, and we'd go in and play skipping with them, and dance, and Jane went in, and inside the soldiers' little hut, while the others were playing skipping, she painted 'Subversion Begins With Tea' [laughter]. And that was actually inside their little shelter. And then that day they came round outside, and offered Criss a lift into the base, so she jumped in the back of their van. It was really funny because there were actually visitors there at the time, and they were just open-mouthed. So she jumped into the van, and about ten minutes later came back around the other side of the fence, had a cup of tea with them, and then got through the fence - in broad daylight.

And then the next day, there was this bloke, Barry, who used to run a sort of supply service to the soldiers, selling them Mars bars and stuff like that, a real wide boy [laughter]. But he'd struck up a real friendship with Donna, and he used to sell us Mars bars and stuff like that, so we'd use him as a canteen too. And he came round. And Donna said, 'Look, something we'd really like would be to have a key to the padlock to the gate. Could you organize that?' And he said, 'Oh yes, I think I could.' And so he turned up the next day with this pair of bolt-cutters a good four foot long, passed them. This is terribly funny. I was at the fire with some visitors, and Barry turned up in his truck, and Donna went over to him to say hello. And he pulled out this massive pair of bolt-cutters, and said, 'Here, if you cut the lock off, because you can do it from your side.' And so Donna cut the lock off, and he passed through another army lock with two keys, gave her one key, and kept the other key. And they were supposedly defending the outer borders against this invasive enemy – us. And this was only a couple of months after the bastard I was telling you about earlier. And so it was very, very variable.

*Katrina Allen*

Carmel Cadden was one of the women who held out hope that soldiers might reflect upon their actions and change. She saw this belief as part of her philosophy of non-violence.

It must have been two or three years later, one of the guys who had been responsible for the violence and abuse at Violet, his regiment was back at Greenham. And he was talking to one of the women, and he said, 'Yes, I've changed my views a lot since last time I was here.' And he said, 'I was very bad last time I was here.' And he described this incident. And he'd changed his mind. So if you're talking about non-violence and you're talking about communicating with people and hoping that they will change their mind, it did happen.

*Carmel Cadden*

Many women were asked by soldiers for information about how they might leave the army and the telephone number of 'At Ease', a counselling organization for military personnel wanting to leave, was regularly passed through the fence. One Greenham woman, several years later met a number of ex-soldiers who had been stationed at Greenham, on a training course for Greenpeace activists. These men spoke of how the experience of talking to Greenham women had sparked off a process of transformation in their ways of thinking.[7]

Clearly these small-scale rapprochements between soldiers and Greenham women were never going to bring down the military industrial complex or even lead to a mass exit from the army. But at the level of individuals, in some cases, change was enacted and within the terms of Greenham's politics individual change mattered. Being offered the opportunity to engage in everyday humane interactions with Greenham women opened the door to a destabilization of the 'us/them' 'friend/foe' mode of thinking which grounds the operation of militarism in general and which was fundamental to the Cold War.

### Encounters with the Police

While bailiffs and soldiers were important to the state's campaign against Greenham, it was the police force which was the day-to-day front line. Thames Valley Police, the local force, had ongoing responsibility for policing the camp. Police officers from Newbury were the first to be called out to make arrests at impromptu blockades and it was at 'Newbury nick', the local police station, that women were held and charged with offences which took place outside the base. The local police engaged in routine surveillance of the camp, making regular visits to count numbers of heads, to record vehicle registration numbers of visitors, and – sometimes armed with warrants, sometimes not – to make both random and systematic searches to confiscate bolt-cutters; on 11 December 1983, for example, over 100 pairs were confiscated. For a period of five months, from after the first Cruise missiles were flown into the base, there was a 24-hour-a-day police presence close to each gate. The police also accompanied the bailiffs on their regular evictions, frequently arresting women who sought to reclaim their possessions from the bailiffs' clutches, and they patrolled the Common extinguishing campfires.

As the April 1984 *Green and Common Newsletter* described it:

> The police put out our fires to prevent us cooking and keeping warm at night, try to prevent us putting up tents and structures, stand at our fireplaces to harass and intimidate, follow women into

the bushes when they go the toilet, prevent us parking our vehicles and intimidate visitors by saying they cannot park their cars along the road. This outrageous behaviour by the authorities is meant to force us to end our campaign and leave Greenham Common

*Jane*

When women entered the base, they passed into the jurisdiction of Ministry of Defence police who opened a detention centre within the base in which to interrogate, detain and charge Greenham women. On occasions of large demonstrations the local police force and the MoD police were backed up by thousands of reinforcements bussed in from all over the country. When hundreds of women were being arrested for blockading or cutting the fence, temporary detention centres were opened at Newbury Racecourse and police stations up to fifty miles away were used to hold women, often overnight, until they could be brought before Newbury Magistrates' Court.

Prior to getting involved with Greenham, most women had had very little personal contact with the police and, like the majority of the British population, they tended broadly to trust the integrity of the police and the criminal justice system.

I was relatively neutral about the police. I'd never been a great fan of policemen, but I certainly hadn't got the anti-feeling by that time because I hadn't had much experience of their operating.

*Katrina Allen*

This was long before the public exposure of police lying, deception, invention of evidence and violence which accompanied the over-turning of convictions in the cases of the Guildford Four and the Birmingham Six, among others.

Breaking the law, confronting the police and facing arrest were frightening acts for women brought up to respect the law. Like most people being arrested, women tended on their first arrest to cooperate and to do as they were told.

I was brought up with a respect for authority, and at first I did find it very difficult to outwardly defy. Like the first time I got arrested to do with camp wasn't at camp, it was at the keening at the House of Commons, which was in between the first time I went down and moving there. I was still living in London. And we did this action of marching and keening to Parliament. And two vans full of police just came out of nowhere, grabbed us and threw us into the back of the van, because we were in Parliament Square, where I don't think you're supposed to be. We were kept in separate cells at Bow Street nick or whatever it was. That was the first time I'd been arrested. And when I got called in I told them everything. I filled out their form, they took my photograph and my fingerprints. Now I'm not clear whether someone had told me that I didn't have to do that or not. I think I would have found it really difficult not to. I hadn't moved to Greenham then, and there was this policeman asking me questions, and I answered him. It didn't occur to me to say no. I don't think that possibility entered my head ... I had that sort of authority thing. If someone in authority asks you a question, if they say, 'Right we're going to take your fingerprints now', I didn't have any of that, 'No, I'm not going to let you.' I was totally amiable to them.

*Rowan Gwedhen*

Rowan's cooperation with the police on her first arrest was not at all unusual. Women's attitudes to the police changed as they experienced repeated arrests, harassment and violence, and as they heard police lying in court. Experiences such as the ones described by Pat Paris and Sarah Benham contributed to the development of a highly critical attitude towards the police and the legal system.

The police were very bad over the fires. You remember when they used to put the fires out – they actually aimed a fire extinguisher once when I had Rowan there. She was about two-and-a-half, and they aimed a fire extinguisher straight at her. That was the nearest I ever came to assaulting a policeman. The only thing that stopped me from going at the policeman was that I scooped her up first to get her out of the way. That was deliberate. That used to drive me insane, emptying tons of water into the fire. Then we devised a system of putting it in a bucket and carrying it off, a tin bucket with holes in it, and then we'd carry the bucket off and then they'd be trying to arrest women for being on the Common with a fire.

I mean there weren't supposed to be missiles on the Common either, but they didn't enforce that by-law. It actually says so, on

the noticeboards scattered round the Common. If you look at
them, it says, thou shalt not discharge missiles on the Common.

*Pat Paris*

There was a time when I was being arrested and put in a van, the
police were taking everyone to be photographed, and I refused to
move, and they had to drag me. And when they were dragging me
my T-shirt came up exposing my breasts, and there were a load of
police officers, off-duty, shouting out horrible comments, and that
was just so horrible. And they were dragging me along the ground
and the gravel, and my back was getting torn up, and gunged up,
and they were shouting out insults about my tits. It was awful.

*Sarah Benham*

It was through talking about and reflecting on incidents such as these,
drawing on critical ideas about the state from within anarchist and civil
libertarian thought, that Greenham's defiant attitude to the police
developed. Women stopped cooperating with the police and granted
them less and less of the automatic, unquestioning obedience which
was expected. They would refuse to cease blockading the road or
cutting the fence when told to do so by a police officer, and often had to
be dragged or carried into vans on arrest. If the police were seen to be
targeting one individual rather than arresting everyone engaged in an
action, women would blockade the police vans to prevent them taking
the single woman away and to force them to arrest everyone. If they saw
a policeman injuring someone, they would intervene, pointing out what
was being done loudly to his colleagues, noting his identification
number and asking for his name (often to no avail, because the police
frequently removed their numbers and refused to give their names). Or
they would attempt to make citizen's arrests on policemen, accusing
them of assault or of breaching international law on genocide.

Greenham's characteristic refusal of the power of the police was
exemplified on the Reclaim the Plain walk across the army training
ground on Salisbury Plain in 1985. Ann Armstrong recalled how
empowering this disobedience felt:

They wanted us to be a march, but of course we weren't a march,
we were these women straggling across the plain. But there were a
lot of us. There must have been a couple of hundred or so, or

more than that. When we actually went across this part where they were firing they really got very, very upset about it, and kept telling us to stop. Then after they'd stopped the firing they attempted to escort us across that bit, and of course we had to keep stopping, and saying no, babies wanted feeding, or nappies wanted changing and we all had to sit down. It was totally disorganized, as far as what they wanted to do. And of course we just kept singing all the time which they found incredibly threatening. They'd come at us with dogs and great forces of police, and we'd just sing at them or dance around them.

Every day we'd start the walk and the police would say, 'It would be better if you would go this way.' And we'd say, 'No, we're going this way, we're going across the plain.' And they'd say, 'No, you can't do that because they're shooting today on the plain and it's dangerous.' 'No, we're going this way.' And every day they'd line up and link arms and try to get in front of us, and we'd just walk through. And they'd do it over and over again. And they actually stopped the firing on this range that day. That was amazing. And there were women with babies in arms, and they got these dogs out, but they couldn't do anything against us. We just felt all-powerful. It was about 5 days, we camped each night, and we walked across the plain. It took me a long time to come back down to earth after that because I thought then that we could do anything. We could just do anything we wanted to do. We were just so powerful. And they couldn't do anything about it at all. At the end of it all they suddenly got really nasty, and started dragging women off to prison, and it was a terrible shock to think, well, perhaps you couldn't do everything [*laughter*].

*Ann Armstrong*

Having been arrested women would often refuse to answer questions, or would answer with lengthy explanations of the moral justification of their actions. Or they turned the tables on their accusers, and fired questions at the police, asking them to account for their role in defending the nuclear state. Women made it deliberately difficult for the police to predict how they would respond to questioning, sometimes confessing everything, at other times denying that they had done anything wrong. Sometimes they would spin elaborate stories about how they had entered the base by trapeze, or as human cannonballs, ridiculing the ritual questioning process and on occasion provoking amusement amongst even the most hostile police officers.

Relations with the police, however, were characterized by fewer instances of boundary crossing and human exchange than those with soldiers. Generally women had less sympathy for the police, who did not share the experience of long, cold nights outdoors and who were not tied into the military system in the way that young working-class soldiers were. The police were not systematically violent to Greenham women, but the many hundreds of incidents in which women were manhandled, pushed, hit, kicked and thrown around by policemen tended to be seen as more worrying than violence from the soldiers. It was more frightening because the police were outside the base and because if the police were against you, it felt as though there was no one in authority there to protect you. Police violence undermined faith in the state as protector.

> I found the police much more worrying than the soldiers because they were on the outside and could sneak up on you. I also have even less time for the police than I do for the army in the sense that although I don't agree that it's right, I can see that working-class lads who can't get a job do join the army. They get treated like shit, but they are still part of the army. But they don't join the police force because they can't get a job. It is a different sort of people who join the army. Same sort of ignorance, but I think the police are worse. You got cut and bruised and hit and slung about by the police.
>
> *Penny Gulliver*

> I must say my own personal experience of violence from soldiers was that I found the police more violent. I found the soldiers on the whole, once they'd got you, that was their job done, and they would just convey you to where you were supposed to go, whereas the police were more often angry about it, and more likely to push you into the back of the van with the others, or grab women and actually put holds on them, when it was absolutely obvious that the woman wasn't going to do anything.
>
> *Katrina Allen*

The way the police responded to Greenham changed over time, varying particularly with the level of media attention focused on the camp and the public pronouncements of politicians. When the government wished to see firm action taken against the camp, such as in the run-up to the installation of Cruise, there were many thousands of arrests, most of which resulted in charges and cases being brought to court. It was at times like these that women were treated, in Carol Harwood's words, 'like terrorists'.

> There was that whole business of being shoved in the riot vans when we were taken to Holloway after the [Silos] trial. The meat wagons with the tiny little cages. One might complain that they were treating us like terrorists; but so they should, in a sense. You're threatening the biggest financial deals ever made anywhere in the world. And the fact that they do treat you in that way is, I don't really think one can complain, because, yes, you are challenging the government, you are challenging the arms dealers, and you're challenging billions and billions of pounds and dollars … I think they employed methods used with terrorists initially. And I think they were right to. I'm not saying it was pleasant, and I'm not saying they should have done, in humanitarian terms, but in their terms, yes, they should have done.
>
> *Carol Harwood*

At other times, the police were more hands off. After the much publicized eviction of Yellow Gate in April 1984 (designed to remove the camp once and for all) and with the courts still full of cases from the run-up to the installation of the missiles, the police became much less ready to charge women, although more were being arrested than ever before. Instead of charging women who broke into the base, they drove them to the gate furthest away from the one where they lived, or even miles from the camp, and just let them out. The women, however, quickly began to subvert these new techniques.

> They'd arrest us, and instead of charging us and giving us a court appearance, or holding us over night, they'd just drive us to the other side of the M4 and drop us off, and we'd have to walk back … That happened two or three times to me. Or maybe not that direction. They'd drive us down to near Crookham Common … It was like a game to them too, because we were from Blue Gate. We sometimes used to say we were from Yellow Gate, and then they'd

drop us off at Blue Gate, because then they'd think it would be annoying for us. It was all about who could win.

*Jinny List*

We used to want to go and see somebody at Yellow Gate and it was big long walk. And so we used to just cut the fence so they'd arrest you. They never took you to the police station, but they used to drop you off at the furthest gate away, so you'd have to walk back. So most of the time, I'd cut the fence to get a lift over to Yellow Gate.

*Linda*

## Courtroom Dramas

Over the years thousands of women were arrested at Greenham, many of them numerous times each, and as a consequence Newbury Magistrates' Court, and to a lesser extent, Reading Crown Court, became outposts of action for the camp.[8] Women were charged primarily with the offences of 'criminal damage' (for cutting the fence and painting symbols and slogans), 'obstructing the highway' or 'obstructing a police officer in the course of his duty' (for blockading) and 'trespass' (for incursions). There were also charges of 'breach of the peace' (a civil offence) in the first two years, and of 'taking and driving away', when women drove around the base in a military bus.

Greenham women queered the trial process, transforming the court rooms in Newbury by refusing to play the conventional role of the accused. Although individual women tended to be nervous on their first appearance in court, because they were supported by others and filled with a passionate sense of injustice they enacted a collective defiance of the rules and protocols of the criminal justice system. Women would be neither victim nor supplicant, humble nor repentant. If they confessed to the actions with which they were accused, they did so proudly, never with remorse. If they refuted the accusation because they believed their actions to be legitimate protest against the evil of nuclear weapons, their refutation was bold and accusative, never defensive. And if they refuted the accusation because they had not done what they were accused of, they were not afraid to expose inconsistencies, fabrications and lies in police evidence.

Whatever the case, the trial process was turned on its head as women sought to hold the state accountable for its actions. Most of all, it was impossible for the prosecution to predict what each woman would do in court: whether she would plead guilty or not guilty; whether she would focus on the big issues of nuclear weapons policy, or the small details of the prosecution case, whether she would say so little that the case would be over in half an hour or call so many expert witnesses that it would last days.

The disruption wrought on the smooth operations of Newbury Magistrates' Court, on the schedules of the police officers and soldiers who had to set aside days to attend court, and on the organization of the prosecution service is hard to overstate. The administration of 'justice' in Newbury was profoundly disorganized by Greenham for many years. The court became the site of political theatre. Instead of sitting nervously in the corridors on the edge of their seats, dressed in their smartest clothes, women sprawled in huge numbers, often on the floor, unpeeling layers of clothing in the centrally-heated building and singing and talking loudly as they waited. Once inside the courtroom, those on trial and their supporters would refuse to stand when the magistrates entered the room, an action that would be considered contempt of court in most courtrooms but which was so routine at Newbury that it was impossible to punish. Most women would then refuse to swear on the Bible, often offering to swear on the goddess instead. The public gallery would usually be packed with other women who would sometimes intervene in the proceedings by humming loudly when policemen were lying or by singing when women were convicted. This sometimes resulted in women being sent to prison for 'contempt of court'.

In the early trials, and at Crown Court, women were generally represented by feminist barristers and solicitors who were sympathetic to Greenham and who worked with the women to construct cases which would allow the maximum opportunity to raise the political issues at stake. In many of these cases the defence centred on arguing that the women's actions were legitimated by the duty to prevent the greater crime of genocide, and citing international law developed since the Second World War.

At the Silos Trial in 1983, for instance, at which forty-four women were accused of 'breach of the peace', a series of women expert witnesses was called to testify about nuclear proliferation, the effects of radiation and the connections between uranium mining, nuclear weaponry and the oppression of black people in Namibia.[9] Then each woman made her own statement to the court, explaining her participation in a highly personal way.

> Rarely do you encounter a trial like that. It really was anarchic … It was a magnificent thing, because everybody spoke, and everybody had something really different to say, and you watched the policemen, big tough policemen, leaving the court rubbing their eyes. There was more than one policeman in tears who went out. One policewoman was sitting there with her hands really gripped, and her knuckles were all white. We had Rosalie Bertell, who is a scientist from America, talking about the effects of low-level radiation on children. I knew the facts, and I cried. It just cracked you up. The expert witnesses were very, very moving. They weren't expert in the cold sense of the word. And then each of these forty-four women stood up, some of whom had never spoken in public before, and said why they had done it. And it was really moving. And I remember when we came back, the magistrates had gone out to consider their verdict, there was a policeman for every woman, so there were forty-four policemen ranged round the room. And yet we hadn't been found guilty. So we all stood on the chairs and turned our backs on the court. And the magistrate sent all the police out. So that was quite a victory. There was a lot of throwing flowers around and general misbehaviour. And then they gave us fourteen days …
>
> In my speech I took a historian's view and talked about the magistrates and juries in the eighteenth century when there were a lot of trials of radicals and dissenters, during the White Terror in Britain after the French Revolution, and how they did find people not guilty. They did, they flew in the face of government opinion and did do this, so there was a precedent, so they ought not be afraid to find us not guilty. They could go ahead; there were good legal and historical precedents. And I think then I spoke about my own personal feelings about nuclear weapons, and why I'd done it, and my particular interest in children. I think listening to the stuff on low-level radiation, the fact that children being born at that time, in global terms and for lots of

other reasons, not just low-level radiation, reasons like hunger, which is also mixed with the spending on nuclear weapons, but children being born at that moment had less likelihood of living to eighteen than a child being born at the time of the plague in the fourteenth century, and that's a very odd thing. If that's progress, it seemed a bit odd really. And that they really ought to listen to what each of these women was saying, because it was important and it affected them, and they were foolish if they didn't listen. And they did listen. You knew that they were listening. It wasn't that they were sitting there coldly; they were listening.

SASHA: *How could you tell?*

'Cause you can tell when somebody's going through emotional trauma. And they might give you fourteen days at the end of it, but you know just by looking at them whether they're listening to you or not. And I think they were.

*Carol Harwood*

Each woman was asked by the magistrates if she agreed to be bound over 'to keep the peace', provoking many to interrogate the meaning of this promise and producing a range of responses from the women who were charged.

I said something about wanting them to show me the peace that they were talking about, that they wanted me to keep. And how could they talk about peace, when there were actually wars going on all round the world, every minute of the day. If they could show me this peace, then I'd keep it. But what was this peace that they were on about, that they wanted me to keep?

The best bit in the trial was the Brighton women; they didn't want to go to prison because they were setting up the Brighton women's peace camp the next day or something. They had no intention of going to prison. But the first of these Brighton women was about number 26 on this list, and we'd already gone through about five hours of these political statements and songs – it was sort of like a women's cabaret – we got to number 26, and they said such and such a name, do you agree to be bound over to keep the peace. 'Yes.' They couldn't believe it. They looked at each other. And they said, 'Do you understand the question?' They looked at each other, mumble, mumble. OK, you are free to go. And we all went 'whay!' Talk about dramatic effect. They'd been sitting there for hours.

*Rowan Gwedhen*

So powerful were women's statements at the Silos Trial that Clare Hudson confessed:

I think I felt sometimes competitive about having to kind of do more or say more wonderfully original things about what the bomb meant to me. I did sometimes think standing up in court sometimes in a large trial with a lot of women was a competitive process about who could be more moving than anybody else! You know, who could make a policeman cry? Who could really have the most impact and be the most stunning? There were some of the aspects of a beauty contest to it, wasn't there? And who can do the most daring and adventurous things, in court and in the base.

*Clare Hudson*

At later trials the vast majority of women defended themselves. This was partly because legal aid applications began to be regularly refused, but more importantly women discovered that there was more opportunity for them to explain their actions and to seize control of the proceedings if no lawyer was present. Bound by their professional codes of conduct and knowledge of court procedure, it was very difficult for the lawyers to let women have the floor in court to the extent that most wanted.[10] Many women became well versed in court procedure, having sat through dozens of friends' cases. They became skilful at cross-questioning prosecution witnesses and at conducting their own defence.

If I was represented in court, it was only once, 'cause I used to love it all, the asking questions. I really liked all that, and all the refusing to stand up in court, which I never did after I left camp – you stood up and did what you were told.

SASHA: *And you liked doing it?*

It was a game. I did really enjoy it. I love thrillers and I love all that asking questions and trapping people and I used to say, 'I'll ask the questions.' And I'd get up and do all the 'But isn't it true that ...?', 'Are there a lot of cars at Blue Gate?' And the officer would say 'Yes, there are.' And I'd say, 'Even though there are a lot of cars at Blue Gate at night, you still think you had a completely unblocked view of the fence? This is what you spend your time doing? What duties are you supposed to be doing?'

We·got off sometimes, like cutting the council fence, which I'd actually done, to get firewood, when most of the other things I got charged with I hadn't actually done.

*Penny Gulliver*


I've never had a solicitor, and I've always cross-examined the witnesses. You got very well up on it, and one got all the proper legal reasons, and would be able to quote from the Genocide Act and the Geneva Convention, which actually does specifically say that it is a crime to prepare for nuclear war. I always pleaded not guilty on the grounds that I had a lawful excuse. They never took any notice - legally. They listened, they always listened. And maybe every now and then I'd do something wrong, and they'd say, 'You can't say that.' 'PC Thingamebob is lying' - 'You're not allowed to say that.'

Before I got involved in it, I used to think the law had something to do with justice. I realized afterwards, once I'd been involved in it, the law is just the law. It doesn't actually have anything to do with morality at all. So you know what you're saying is morally right, but the law only wants to know whether you were in spot A and walked to spot B on that day. That's the only thing that's important and anything else is irrelevant. Why you walked there, why you did it, is not important, to them. And that was a bit of a shock.

*Ann Armstrong*


We got really clever with the legal system. You'd have someone sitting in the dock and then ask for a McKenzie friend, which nobody ever knew about. Sometimes people would get their lover in the dock with them and they'd just sit there holding hands or they'd have their arms round one another. And sometimes people would stand up and do absolutely brilliant speeches about nuclear weapons and the oppression of women in the world. Then other people would stand up and they would just abuse the judge: 'Who the fuck do you think you are? Don't you realize what's going on?'

*Linda*

When women were found guilty, which the vast majority were, they took the opportunity to explain their actions. Some statements were cool, detached and descriptive, arguing the case against Cruise and for disarmament, but more were intensely emotional and personal, sometimes involving recounting dreams, reading poems or singing songs. Many women drew explicit links between male domination and militarism, and made passionate speeches about violence, the threat of nuclear war and environmental destruction. Frequently women ended by declaring their contempt of the court and their refusal of its authority over them.

Over time trials became routinized. The court officials largely gave up trying to make women stand up or shut up, magistrates appeared to have decided verdicts before cases were heard, and women tended to shift from investing court appearances with great political and personal significance to treating them as everyday occurrences, rather like going to the dole office to sign on. As women clocked up lengthy criminal records (many went to prison repeatedly) some began to alter their approach to the criminal justice system. There was a gradual shift away from seeing the courtroom as an arena in which to contest militarism towards jamming the courts and the prisons as a form of protest which would bring about the collapse of the system. The thousands of court cases were slowly processed by stipendiary magistrates brought to Newbury for the purpose. Hundreds of women were sent to prison, causing severe overcrowding for short periods of time. The system groaned, but was able to cope and women became disillusioned with the legal system. Many women began to give false names when arrested (there were dozens of 'Bridget Evans' living at Greenham) and decided not to attend court.[11]

There was some controversy within the camp about the tactic of non-appearance. The argument was expressed that such action constituted a refusal to take responsibility for the consequences of one's actions and that each woman should be prepared to see her protest through to prison. Those who took this position tended also to argue that women should never pay fines, as this was a contribution to the state and a tacit admission of guilt. The riposte to this mobilized Greenham's principle of respect for diversity and individuality, suggesting that the material conditions of some women's lives (having children for instance) meant that they could not go to prison, or that prison was an easier option for middle-class women than working-class women, for whom the stigma was greater. Generally, however, it was the notion that women should act according to their own consciences and feelings, and that their choices should be respected, which guided discussions about the legal process.

> I got arrested loads of times but after my first time I never went to court. The first time I went to court I stood up and said it was for peace for the world and all that, but afterwards I got clever. The second time I went I denied it, and then after that I never went back.
>
> SASHA: *What made you change?*
>
> I'd seen women stand up and as soon as you turned round and said I did it, they didn't listen to what you said. There were that many women that had gone before me that had said this, that and the other. And times had changed from when people got sympathy for doing political things - I mean nobody cared any more. You were just arrested and put down. The stipendiary was putting women down for just giving their address as Blue Gate. You had to give another address, unless you paid your fine straight away.
>
> *Trina*

> Whenever I could avoid it, I avoided going to court. Initially I thought that the courts would actually listen to what was going on. I had this naïve belief that justice would prevail. And with the silos trial, and some of the evidence that came up at that was so glaringly obvious, some of the expert witnesses called there were absolutely brilliant, the way it was put over - Rosalie Bertell and that bunch, some brilliant stuff was brought up. And the statements the women were making as well were incredibly moving. And the magistrates just totally ignored everything. And that's when my belief that the British justice system would see us right just went straight out of the window.
>
> And I was in court once or twice after that, but the only times I would go to court was when I was held. If I was ever given bail or not held, then I wouldn't turn up in court. It just seemed a pointless exercise. Most of the time I gave false names. Occasionally I had to use my own name.
>
> *Kim Smith*

I've been to prison nine times, but I've probably been arrested much more than that. I did count at one point, but I've lost count. Until when we were breaking the by-laws I always went to court; at that point with all the hoo-ha about whether we were or weren't breaking the by-laws I didn't go to court once. I decided I didn't care any more. Up till that point I'd always gone to court and then I suddenly realized that I didn't have to do this anymore, I didn't have to bother. I didn't see why I should waste my time going to court. It felt like a waste of time. Before that I could never understand women not going to court.

*Leah Thalmann*

This anarchist attitude towards the legal system, which rejected its legitimacy, was fuelled by the new knowledge which women developed through their involvement with Greenham of the injustices which are routinely perpetrated in the British courts. Women who had grown up to believe in the integrity of the legal system came to question fundamentally the whole system as they experienced it first hand. For instance, the policeman who arrested Katrina Allen the first time she was arrested at Greenham caught himself up in a complex web of lies, which led her to begin to think more closely about the way in which the police and the courts operated.

The thing that struck me most was the way in which the police lied. And the thing that irritated me was that there was no need to lie. When I was in court they described something that didn't happen. And there was no need to because what they'd seen happening, under their own eyes, was perfectly adequate. And it wasn't as if it was difficult to recall. They were personally involved. I've thought about it. I thought maybe if they weren't personally involved they couldn't remember it in the detail that I could. But actually this is their business; their business is to remember exactly what happened, and to recall it exactly, and to record it exactly. It wasn't difficult. It wasn't as if the person who arrested me also arrested three other people. He had only arrested me. And yet he still managed to completely cock up what he described as happening, which made his evidence much more shaky, because actually he couldn't remember the sequences of things, because they had never happened.

And I also witnessed several times actions that I had been involved in where other women had been arrested, and exactly the same sort of things had happened. It seems to be such a basic thing that if you are going to arrest, you are much better off telling the truth, particularly in these sort of circumstances, where women aren't disguising what they're doing, they're actually defending it on the grounds of criminal damage in relation to a greater damage that could occur. It's not as if they were saying, I didn't do it. They're saying, I did it, but I did it because I want to defend myself against a nuclear holocaust. And their evidence was so often a lie, not what happened.

And I think in our situation that's not so much of a worry, because actually we're fighting on a completely different ground anyway, but the fact that this is obviously how they proceed in any situation, that they just lie, and it is completely acceptable. And I can see from their point of view they're trying to convict somebody who they think has done wrong, but the way to do that is not to lie. It makes a mockery of the whole situation, and I think it's very significant that recently politically motivated convictions, such as the ones that have just been released, the Guildford Four, and the football fans, both of those have actually fallen through, and they say it's because the police made up the stuff, and they say it as if that's a surprise, but obviously it's not. And they talk about the football fans police not being adequately supervised and being young but what that means is, that they're not sufficiently practised at doing it, and therefore they haven't stitched these blokes up adequately. And I just think, what is the point of trying to sort out any social dissonance if you actually employ means that are themselves dissonant. You're just going to end up actually creating a situation which a lot of people acknowledge exists, which is that the police just go ahead and stitch up people they think ought to be stitched up. Obviously this doesn't operate in a vacuum, because it is actually colluded with by everybody, and in some cases maybe they think they are justified because they wouldn't be able to get these people otherwise. But I think it then makes it impossible for them to tackle the real criminals ... And it might be a rather idealistic view of the police, but if you're going to obey society's laws, then you have to have some respect for the law enforcers, and if you don't, then you move outside of it. And you do destabilize society, and maybe that's appropriate.

It's always a bit of a shock to be involved in it yourself ... It's something I'd always suspected, but I'd never actually put my finger on.

*Katrina Allen*

Many other women experienced similar transformations in their attitudes to the legal system.

I never really understood why they bothered lying, considering we had climbed over the fence and danced on the missile silos, and nobody was denying that. And that for me was part of the whole point of Greenham ... The other thing [Greenham did], was the thing about the trials, the thing about the police lying ... The out-and-out lying of the police was just so unmistakeable. The way the justice system was shown up to be such a load of crap. Policemen *do* lie. And I think for hundreds of women that must have been quite a thing ... And seeing policemen break women's arms, and things like that ... I was brought up with a respect for authority.

*Rowan Gwedhen*

It's made me question things more, question what's going on. Like the way the judiciary works in this country, knowing all the shenanigans that goes on there and stuff. I guess it makes you a lot more cynical really. No longer wide-eyed and all believing. There's a lot of old cynical dykes wandering around thanks to Greenham.

*Kim Smith*

## Prison Education

For many thousands of women actions such as blockading or cutting the fence culminated in a period of imprisonment. Although in a small number of cases women were given custodial sentences, in most cases women actively 'chose' to go to prison, by refusing to pay fines imposed by the courts. Even if they could not themselves afford the fine, the camp or a support group would generally pay it for them, if they wished, so that those who did not pay were making a conscious decision to go to prison. Women explained this in a range of ways: not wishing to contribute funds to the state; not wishing to accept their guilt by complying with the court; wanting to carry their disruption of the legal system through into the prison system.

> I could have paid my fine. Basically I thought about going to prison in terms of cocking the system up really. I wasn't into giving myself the experience of going to prison. I had enough insight into it to know that it wasn't going to be my kettle of fish, quite possibly. Not that it would be anybody's. But I think that I also thought that paying a fine actually makes it very easy for them, and puts money in their coffers, whereas it would cost them a lot more to keep me two weeks in prison, to transport me out from Newbury and all the rest of it, than could possibly be matched by this piddling fine.
>
> *Katrina Allen*

> As a mother, I had terrible pangs about going to prison, because one of my kids was still very young, and the others and my mum – you know what it does to people close to you, and that's a painful thing. But then that's a choice that you have to make, because you know what nuclear weapons are going to do to them, and it's going to be on the whole more permanent. And I know not everyone agrees with this, but I know women who have notched up a thousand pounds on Cruisewatch fines, and then the peace movement's busy having jumble sales to raise the money to pay them. And that really pisses me off, because you're just pouring money into the pockets of the MoD. And I think unless there's a bloody good reason for it, you should either not bother in the first place, or you should actually follow that through to its logical conclusion. I think once you've taken that first step against the state, you've really got to force the state to follow its own logical route, right through to the conclusion of saying to somebody, alright, you might believe that what you're doing is right, we might believe what you're doing is right, but we're going to lock you up. And that's very important. And that you don't pay fines.
>
> *Carol Harwood*

Prison sentences for non-payment varied from one week to two or three months depending on the size of the fine, with the most common sentence being two weeks. Ann Francis's custodial sentence of a year was the longest received by any Greenham woman and obviously made her experience of prison very different from those who only spent a few weeks inside. Women's experiences differed also depending on whether there were other Greenham women inside with them or not, and on which prison they were sent to. Being one of a large group of Greenham women at Holloway, where the other prisoners had met Greenham women before, was very different from being the only Greenham woman on a wing at Bullwood Hall, a youth custody centre where very few Greenham women were ever sent.[12]

Many women were conscious that their experience of prison was very different from that of other prisoners, because they had chosen to engage in political actions which they knew carried the risk of imprisonment and because the support of other Greenham women (inside and outside prison) and the goodwill of the wider peace movement eased the isolation and dislocation of being in prison.

> Both times I was in prison with a group of lots of other Greenham women. So it wasn't 'prison'. It's totally impossible to compare it with actually being in prison. Being in prison for Greenham is a bit like calling Greenham evictions 'evictions' ... It's so totally incomparable with being a woman sent to prison for anything else. It's a whole different ball game. So I don't feel that I came out of my spells in prison with any knowledge at all about what being in prison is like. It was a doddle. Some Greenham women can talk about that because some women have been in for a few months on their own. I should think that that's a totally different ball game. That is being in prison. But when you're in with a bunch of your mates, for two weeks ...
>
> *Rowan Gwedhen*

> I felt very privileged in there because I was part of a Greenham group, and the idea of prison is to isolate women, and in fact what happens of course is that they end up having hierarchies of people who know each other usually not because they know anybody else, but because they've stayed there the longest and got to know people during the time that they were in prison. So when you first come in you're expected to be really mousey quiet. And of course when we first came in there were a whole lot of other people

who'd been there for a week or two before us, and so we'd meet them and we'd be off, and it'd be very different, and you'd sit by them at meals and stuff like that. It's not as if you were on your own. And so a lot of that was cushioned.

*Katrina Allen*

Fuelled by a sense of injustice at being sent to prison (while, paradoxically, also having chosen to be there), Greenham women engaged in a range of disruptive actions while inside. They sought to challenge the routine disciplinary regime which operates in prison, with its demand for unquestioning obedience to those in authority and its dehumanizing of the prisoners. Women refused to learn their prison numbers and would give their names rather than their numbers when asked. They refused to stand up as was required when in the presence of an assistant governor. They often refused to do prison work, particularly if it was the manufacture of military toys (as it often was). They would talk and sing when silence was expected, and would run and skip when they were told to walk. During exercise they would hold meetings. They demanded frequent appointments with the governor to complain about the treatment that they and other prisoners were receiving.

Carola Addington recalled being in Holloway after the Silos Trial:

We caused such a riot in break times. We'd go out and run, which you weren't allowed to do. And in the church, disrupting the service. We decided we'd take it over, because it was the one time everyone could get together. We obviously couldn't communicate very well, but somehow we'd all passed on the message to be in church on Sunday ... We were very quiet all the way through because we appreciated some women would be very upset if it was disrupted. Then right at the end we started singing Greenham songs, and we wouldn't leave.

*Carol Addington*

Simone Wilkinson's sentence in the open prison East Sutton Park offered even more opportunities for subversion.

They were going to stick me in a room on my own. And I really didn't want to be on my own. I mean I was really upset about this, but the assistant governor said she couldn't find anyone to move the beds. So the other women just went and picked a bed and moved it into their room. It was like, we'll organize the prison, you know. And then we had all this stuff about we wanted vegetarian food and the food was appalling, and so Susan and another woman took over the kitchen and organized the cooking. She cooked for the whole prison while we were there. And they had these sort of stupid rules like you know, you have to wash your own cup and plate and saucer. I mean there's nothing about prison life that teaches you to cooperate or come together. The idea is that sets you against each other, it certainly doesn't in any way really help to rehabilitate people. And so there was this thing about, you had to wash your own cup saucer and plate. So we disbanded that very quickly by having a few people washing up, a few people drying and the rest teaching the other women in prison Greenham songs and it was like they couldn't do anything about it, you know. These women singing these songs for hours and there was nothing they could do about it.

*Simone Wilkinson*

As more women from Greenham spent time in prison a body of knowledge was accumulated about how to ameliorate the experience and how to work the system. Women learnt that they should take six books with them to court when they expected to be sent down because six was the maximum number allowed to a prisoner; they learnt not to take any spare underwear because the prison had to provide it; and they learnt to make sure that they gave as their home address the place to which they wanted a travel warrant on their release. Women who had been to prison shared stories with those who had not about the journey to Holloway in 'meat wagons' and the processing system on arrival, with its disinfecting baths and strip searches. This helped to diminish the sense of shock and unfamiliarity of these distressing experiences. Perhaps most importantly, women learned knowledge about the rules relating to remission and release dates close to weekends and bank holidays, and when they should give themselves up to the police for their unpaid fines so as to maximize the amount of remission they would receive.

But however different from the experience of non-Greenham prisoners, and however tempered by the company of friends and knowledge about what to expect, prison had a profound effect on every Greenham woman who went there. Direct, first-hand experiential knowledge of what it is like to lose one's liberty and of the brutalizing, dehumanizing prison regime, provided a unique education in the mechanics of the penal system. Conversations with other prisoners about their lives before prison and about their offences opened up new knowledge about the reality of women's experiences of poverty, racism and male violence.

> Having led a very privileged life and being middle-class I'd never had that sort of confrontation with basically how vicious the state can be. And how people are prepared to carry out that kind of policy. There are some nice screws, I'm not saying they're all shits, but in the end it was a really abusive system. The pettiness of the punishments that they dished out. The rules. All that is very shocking when you hadn't realized quite how nasty it was. It's that very black-and-white kind of confrontation. It just seemed very stark, seeing things very starkly. And seeing how people who go through that system and are disenfranchised once they've been through the prison system. They then lose credibility as citizens and human beings and then they're kind of locked into it. And I can't seem to talk about it very articulately, but it's just that sudden realization that the state can be a very sinister and a very violent thing, even though I knew theoretically before what happens.
>
> *Clare Hudson*

It was horrible. I think it was just the most demeaning and degrading and awful place. It was also a lot of learning. And I certainly became aware that the vast majority of women who were there were in because of debt, you know, and some outstanding cases. We were waiting about eight hours in the receiving room at Holloway because they were taking their time processing everybody, and there was one woman there who was eight months pregnant who'd got six weeks for shoplifting around December. She had five other kids. This was her sixth. And in the same court, on the same morning was the man who said he'd been shoplifting while drunk and actually got off, and she'd been put in prison and her child would be born in prison. And it was so obvious that she'd been shoplifting around Christmas, and I don't care whether she'd been shoplifting for food or shoplifting for clothes or shoplifting for presents. I just felt that the system that would imprison her and let that bloke go free was completely wrong. And most of the people that we were in there with, there were a few in for drugs, and there were a few in for murder, but the vast majority were in for doing credit cards and for not paying fines. It was just the financial punishment for being poor. That was so clear, and it was so degrading and so awful. I don't think you can minimize what a horrific situation that is ... I found it a really shocking experience, and it confirmed for me the validity of breaking the law, actually. 'Cause I just thought, all these women are in here, and they've done nothing. Most of them have done nothing. Most of them are poor, or disorganized or both, and so they've ended up trying to cheat the system, and they've been caught. Tax evaders are among those who are judging them and they're not going to prison. I think the system stinks.

SASHA: *Was this a revelation?*

Yeah. Yeah it was. It clarified a whole lot of things in a very shocking fashion, in a way that really woke me up. I think actually it was really good for me, it was really useful in terms of making me understand more fully the way the world works and how it penalizes people who are poor. That's something I'd appreciated intellectually, I suppose, but never really had the guts of it pointed out to me.

*Katrina Allen*

I found being in prison itself very enlightening. The women I met in prison were amazing. None of them should have been there. They were all just victims of society or men. They were in for such petty things; men wouldn't have been put in for such things. Non-payment of fines, shoplifting. So many young black women who had got nothing else to look forward to in life ... I felt so fortunate in my life. And I knew I was going to come out and it wouldn't make any difference to my life. And I got so many letters and flowers and you know, it was a privilege to be there, you know. It was no hardship. I mean the food was lousy, but one could each day complain, and ask to see the governor, and we knew our rights. And they all hated us because we knew our rights. But the women, the prisoners, were so supportive.

*Ann Armstrong*

I felt really strongly that women were there that shouldn't be there. And the brutality of the regime disturbed me as well. And things just like getting strip-searched. That was like really unpleasant where you have to take all your clothes off and twirl round in the nuddy. I could make my mind work it so that didn't bother me that much, inasmuch as I'm not actually somebody who minds other women particularly looking at my body and therefore I wasn't that bothered about it. But I was aware of the power dynamic ... And every night people like had these slanging matches between different wings and windows and where they called each other dreadful names. And it was like the oppression of being incarcerated boiling over. There was that feeling of, God fucking hell, one of these days the lid's going to come off here and everything's going to bubble over the side. And there was this other thing where we all went into dinner one day and there were these prisoners helping the screws give out the oranges and I noticed that there were some rotten oranges in amongst the ones that were OK and, I thought, oh God, some poor bastard's going to get given deliberately, is going to get given, a rotten orange. And there was things like you were only allowed one spoonful of sugar for your tea, and there was other times when they made this tea and they put sugar in everybody's and gave it out, and it's like piddling petty. And the food was revolting. I mean I basically didn't eat anything for three days.

*Bridget Evans*

The woman in the next cell was having fits regularly all through the day. She was on her own. She was on heavy tranquillizers, and I don't think women who are having fits right through the day should be on tranquillizers. Towards the end I could hear when she was going to go into a fit, so I could ring the bell. Because she couldn't do anything. They'd taken her bed away and her mattress was on the floor and everything. And then there was a woman there who'd gone into the hospital wing pregnant with a letter from her doctor saying, this woman mustn't under any circumstances be examined internally. And this male doctor, who they had several names for, including the Angel of Death, actually said she must have an internal examination, and she miscarried when she was about six months pregnant.

So you saw it all. There was a woman there, a black woman, who'd come over from the West Indies carrying a parcel from her husband, you know, the usual story, and had been picked up at the airport for possessing drugs, and she had a son at home. She'd had a hysterectomy fourteen days before, and she was out there scrubbing floors. Her kid had nobody to look after him; there'd been no proper follow-up. I wouldn't have missed it for the world.

My first day in hospital [in prison], they came round and gave me this yellow sticky stuff, and said, drink this dear, it'll make you feel much better. Something I'd never do in normal circumstances, I'd want a chemical breakdown on it first, and I swallowed it and slept for about twenty four hours non-stop. And then I never took anything else after that; I wouldn't take an aspirin off them. But they used to come round and say, anybody want tranquillizers? It really was like Smarties, the way they'd hand them out. And that's the thing; the female prison population is tranquillized, and the day they withdraw those tranquillizers, the shit will hit the roof. It's a very serious form of oppression. And I had no idea about the way they dished out tranquillizers.

*Carol Harwood*

It was important to go to prison. I'm very glad I've been to prison. Because I'll never ever forget what it's like. You forget for months and months on end, but now and again you think about women in prison and it's important to know what it's like, to know the roundness of the whole system. I found that really important.

*Barbara Rawson*

I remember once in Pucklechurch I was listening to a woman banging her head in this isolation cell and screaming for valium. What I found most appalling about it was I was sitting there thinking, I understand that. Society actually institutes that – a society that creates bombs, that degrades the planet and all the rest of it. In one sense prison was really positive because it really is like seeing the weapons, seeing the mentality of the system. And I remember thinking, I haven't met any criminals yet. And that bothered me. And I can remember thinking, maybe if I met a real criminal I'll feel differently.

*Christine King*

Reflecting on their time in prison, some women felt that the experience was not only positive because of what they had learnt about how society operates but also because of the self-knowledge they gained. Prison challenged them to face fears about stepping outside the boundaries of socially acceptable behaviour and forced them to explore the limits of their willingness to be different, to take risks about their futures and to mark themselves as outlaws in ways which were more permanent than just breaking the law. Women who went to prison were testing their personal resources of strength, resilience and self-confidence.

> I was really glad I did it. It was a really positive experience. Because I mean the very first time I got arrested I was really frightened, and then it escalates - you think, well, I did that and that was alright. And then after you've been to prison, you think, they can't touch me any more. I can cope.
>
> *Ann Armstrong*

> It was horrible being locked up, and I certainly wouldn't want to have that again. But it was also a bit like winter at Greenham, you learnt you could survive it.
>
> *Katrina Allen*

> And to beat the fear was really important. For a working-class woman - well, for anybody to go - there's a lot of fear, but for a working-class woman it's like a great disgrace, or it feels like it. It's like the last place you feel you'll ever end up. The bottom of the pile. To go by choice helps, because you feel in charge.
>
> *Barbara Rawson*

There were other women, however, who found the experience of prison very distressing. They came to believe that choosing to go to prison was a pointless and even harmful activity, which smacked of masochism. Some felt that they had been rather unquestioningly doing what was expected of them at Greenham by going to prison and resolved, after one or two periods of imprisonment, to do everything they could to avoid it in future.

> It was horrendous. I wouldn't do it again if I had the choice. Everyone was doing it and I thought, 'I'm not going to pay my

fine.' It was the done thing to do. But I think it was absolutely crazy. The women I met in there just couldn't understand it at all. They would do anything rather than go to prison. They thought we were absolutely cracked to have the choice to pay your fine or go to prison, and there were people there with money in their hands saying, we'll pay your fine if you want us to. And there's all us middle-class feminists saying, no this is a matter of principle. I think it's absolutely nutty, looking back on it.

I was locked in a cell by myself. It was awful, dreadful. Because it went on and on and on. That was the thing about being in prison. You have no control over it. Most situations, however bad it is, you can get up and walk away from it, and you just can't walk away from that, when somebody's locked you in a cell. That's the really frightening thing about it. Just holding yourself together, knowing it's going to be over, but holding yourself together until it's over. That was really scary. I remember one time coming out - I'd been locked up for about 12 hours - and it was raining outside and it was so wonderful to feel the rain on my face. Crying with relief coming out.

*Sarah Benham*

Everyone was just going to prison at that time, and lots of people weren't getting a choice as well. I was glad I went in some ways. I felt like I'd done that now. But as soon as I was there, I was like, what a fucking waste of time this is. I might not have paid my fine, but they're going to get my dole money because I can't sign on. And I'm a bit claustrophobic anyway, and I thought, 'I'll never come back here if I have any choice at all' ... And I just avoided it after that.

*Penny Gulliver*

It was just a massive shock. You know, it's the kind of complete methodical stripping of your personality as soon as you walk through the door you know. Having to take your clothes off straight away. I think that just really gets to you, you know ... Overall I just found it very, very traumatic. And at night, the things that went on at night were always very scary. You'd hear women screaming, not knowing what was happening. And drugs being dispensed. And then I came out and I can remember coming out and my legs just went. I ached for days afterwards and I realized it was because I'd been like this for a week really. Just really tense ...

It was in this atmosphere of the world is on the brink, the end is nigh and all that. And when you feel like those sort of desperate measures make sense. But I suppose as time went on I realised that there was a lot of virtue in trying to avoid going to prison. There were maybe times when you couldn't avoid it in the women's peace movement. But you didn't have to go out and make it happen. So I started to get quite impatient with women who seemed to be in and out of prison all the time. That's partly because they were you know, they were people I loved and didn't want to see them hurting themselves or being hurt. And I think prison does wreck people. You know even short periods in prison. I think it does terrible things to you. And I think it can be a bit illusory that somehow you can make common cause with all these other women who are in prison because your experiences are so different from theirs and there is a huge gulf between you and the rest of the women. I wouldn't, you know, I'm not saying I would never, I wouldn't rule it out again, because I don't think I would rule it out, but I think you have to be very careful about why you're doing it. I mean for me it sort of seemed to coincide with a time of my life where I was suffering a lot, a lot. I mean I was having this very unhappy relationship ... which was very traumatic and stressful and seemed to involve me carrying a lot of guilt for one reason or another and I think to some extent you know, a lot of that on a very kind of deep psychic level I got very confused, so that prison was - I mean this is sort of quite heavy stuff - but it was an acting out of a lot of guilt and distress which I was feeling for completely other reasons ... And I think you know, most of us have at some level quite masochistic feelings which we get from our experiences in different ways and I think prison can do quite frightening things with that.

*Clare Hudson*

## Conclusion

For a lot of women, particularly women who went and saw the way the police behaved and the soldiers and things like that, and saw the way that other women who took more drastic action were treated, I think it led a lot of people into questioning how society is governed and how the choices are made. And about who controls power. It raised lots of questions about power. There's just this huge feeling that it's wrong. We didn't choose it. We didn't make it. And we had to stop it.

*Helen Mary Jones*

You question what people do with power ... Greenham raised so many different issues – questioning authority, questioning power, and all the rest of it.

*Carola Addington*

I'd say I've become more autonomous. I am less fearful of doing what I want to do, if it's not what society would approve of, I think. I understand the consequences of that sort of action more fully than I ever did. But in a way, having braved those consequences, I am more prepared to do what I want to do. I sort of feel like I can weigh that up and decide, yes, I actually need to do that thing ... Instead of saying, 'Oh, I can't do that, it's against the law', I sort of think, that's only one factor, and there are other things that might be more important.

*Katrina Allen*

It's made me brave. I deliberately used to use it sometimes if I felt afraid, particularly in Derby, of doing something. I'd think, come on, you're a Greenham woman. So that aspect of it was important to me. It dragged me up a bit more out of doing as I was told and thinking everyone else knew what to do and not me.

*Barbara Rawson*

It's made me more self-confident about our own ability to get to grips with things. I suppose it's given some strength to the ideas I've always had about anarchism, people's power, people being able to take control of their own lives. I spend ages talking to people down the pub who are forever moaning, and I say it's no good if you sit on your backside and watch that telly, nothing's going to change. You spend years talking like that, and then at Greenham it actually happened, women did take responsibility for their lives and say, 'OK, we're governed by authorities, but we've seen through them.' They are not wise authorities governing us.

They are actually very bad systems, and actually it is up to individuals to take responsibility, to take control and to act. And I found that heartening, because before I felt it was just theorizing.

*Sian Edwards*

As these quotations suggest women at Greenham que(e)ried authority in ways that fundamentally disturbed their previous ways of thinking about themselves and about the world. Their consciousness was transformed as they enacted a multitude of disobediences. As a consequence they felt braver, stronger, empowered. Greenham – 'queer' in the manner of its direct, in-your-face, uncompromising, anti-integrationist challenge to politics-as-normal, 'feminist' in its gendered disruption of the homo-relational, almost men-only world of military and state power – offered a new model of how oppositional politics might be lived.

## Notes

1. According to the 'fraternal social contract' (the founding discourse of the modern state) (Pateman, 1989), only men are political actors, and the public world of politics is a masculine one (Pringle and Watson, 1992: 57).
2. See Harford and Hopkins (1984: 29-30) for the text of the letter and the camp's response.
3. Harford and Hopkins (1984: 46-53). Similar responses to eviction attempts have been enacted by anti-roads protesters in the late 1990s.
4. See Randle (1987) on the 1962 Official Secrets trial.
5. For instance, women at Greenham read Brownmiller (1976) and Enloe (1983), which discuss the sexist socialization processes within the military.
6. There were rumours that at least two Violet Gate women had sexual relationships with soldiers and that one left Greenham and married a soldier.
7. Conversation with Rebecca Johnson, 1990.
8. This is inevitably a brief overview of what could be a major study in its own right. See Harford and Hopkins (1984), Hickman (1986), Johnson (1986) and Young (1990) for further discussion.
9. For a description of the Silos Trial, see Harford and Hopkins (1984: 104-6). The theatrical and lively gathering outside the courtroom is shown in *Carry Greenham Home*.
10. Greenham women uncovered case law which allowed a 'McKenzie friend' to accompany and advise an unrepresented defendant and they regularly made use of this. See Nicky Edwards in Harford and Hopkins (1984: 141-4).
11. It is not unlawful in Britain to call oneself by any name one chooses.
12. Here I speak from personal experience, having served time both in HMP Holloway and HMP Bullwood Hall.

# Chapter 10
# Queering Lives

*Lily of the Arc Lights*
*(by Silver Moon) (to the tune of 'Lily Marlene')*

*Underneath the arc lights*
*By the old Green Gate,*
*I took out my bolt cutters,*
*My hands could hardly wait.*
*I snipped towards her, she snipped to me*
*We both could see the Common free.*
*Oh Lily of the arc lights*
*A-snipping in the rain.*

*Cutting up the silo fence*
*My knees they turned to jelly*
*But standing strongly next to me*
*Was Lily in her wellies.*
*I snipped towards her, she snipped to me*
*We both could see the Common free.*
*Oh Lily of the arc lights*
*Will all this be in vain?*

*Closer to the silo fence*
*My heart it gave a quiver*
*Was it Lily, the fear, the cold, the base*
*Or just a little shiver?*
*I looked towards her, she looked to me*
*We both could see the Common free.*
*Oh Lily of the arc lights*
*A-snipping in the rain.*

*Running up the silos,*
*planting lots of trees*
*Should I have given my heart away*
*Or kept it in deep freeze?*
*Stayed pure, cold and sound ideologically,*
*Or we could be completely silly.*
*Oh Lily of the arc lights*
*Is this true romance or pain?*

*When we got to Newbury nick*
*We shared a little cell,*
*Wrote on walls, sang lots of songs,*
*Drove all the men to hell.*
*I'd snipped towards her, she'd snipped to me*
*We both could see the Common free*
*Oh Lily of the arc lights*
*Will I see you again?*

Greenham was a space out of place, a time out of the ordinary. Queer things happened. It was a time and place where certainties were thrown into question, where gender and sexual identities and practices were destabilized, where new meanings, new identities, new ways of thinking were explored. It was a time and place where lives were turned upside down, disordered, queered. Queering, as I use the term here, refers to these processes of destabilization of regimes of the normal and, in particular, to practices which challenge and transform the gender and sexual normalities of everyday life. In the liminal space of Greenham, women carved time for reflection, imagination and experimentation. Outside the 'realities' of normal life with its expectations and limitations, away from the contexts of families and work, and moving into a community of friendly strangers - women opened themselves to change. And Greenham demanded change. To live at Greenham required openness, flexibility, reflexivity. Boundaries were fluid and in constant motion. Lives were in flux and transition.

## The Queer Feminist Culture of Greenham

In the queer feminist culture which was built at Greenham hetero-normativity was displaced. Heterorelations were decentred by gyn-affective and erotic lesbian relations; heterosexuality was de-normalized, rendered strange and problematic.[1] At Greenham queer was normal. In describing Greenham as a queer feminist culture I am seeking to capture the diversity of the lives which women led at Greenham and of the transformations which they constructed. In previous work I have referred to Greenham as a 'lesbian community'. I no longer think that this adequately expresses the instabilities, differences and dynamic processes of identity construction and practice which were so central to Greenham.[2] The notion of a 'lesbian community' is too static and closed; it suggests a community of women with already firmly established lesbian identities. This was not the case at Greenham.

For much of its history, very large numbers of women who called themselves lesbians, and/or women who engaged in practices commonly called 'lesbian', lived and spent time there. Greenham was a hotbed of lesbian activity, where women fell in love, had sex, rowed and broke up, not necessarily in that order, sometimes slowly, sometimes with great alacrity. Some women came to Greenham already calling themselves lesbians, but many others did not. Some were trying lesbian sex and relationships for the first time, others were old hands. Some women lived through Greenham maintaining relationships with husbands and boyfriends (albeit with difficulty), others ended long-term heterosexual relationships while at Greenham and did not enter new ones. Some had sexual relationships with women while at Greenham and then with men afterwards; one or two even started new relationships with men while at Greenham. Others stayed celibate and uninterested in sex and the categories of sexual identity.

There was no requirement for women to know or state their sexual allegiance and identification at the gate; there were no tests to pass, beyond an openness of mind, an attitude of inqu(ee)ry. Women came to Greenham, amongst many other identities, as 'lesbian feminists', 'lesbian separatists', 'housewives', 'mothers', 'gays', 'bisexuals', 'dykes', with a sense of sexual identity and without. As they lived and worked together at Greenham definitions, boundaries and identities blurred and changed. There was no uniform product of these processes of queering and women engaged in queer transformations to varying degrees, depending on how much time they spent at Greenham and how open they were to change. This wide range of sexual experiences and identity practices is better represented as constituting a queer feminist culture than by a notion of a lesbian community.

## THE GYN-AFFECTIVE AND EROTIC DYNAMICS OF GREENHAM

Some women were drawn to Greenham by friends and lovers who were already involved (such as Bridget Evans, Chapter 3). Others arrived knowing no one, but, looking back, saw themselves attracted by the emotional possibilities which Greenham offered.

> I remember being really shocked when Jane Dennett said that quite a large percentage of the women there were lesbians. That hadn't twigged at all. I'd had a two-year relationship with a girl at school, but I was so closeted. I was completely closeted, to myself as much as to anyone else, and just hadn't made the connection at all. And it was obviously one of reasons I was being so strongly attracted to Greenham - because the place was heaving with dykes.
>
> *Sarah Benham*

Whatever their initial reasons for getting involved, pleasure in the company of other women became a vital part of being there and a reason for continued involvement.

> The women weren't the only reason I was there, but they were certainly a big attraction [laughter]. For the first time in my life I felt I'd found a place where I fitted in and whatever I was was OK, and the same as the others ... There were times when I thought I should leave because I was only there for selfish reasons, and everyone else seemed to be there for quite high ideals. And I thought, 'Oh I'm conning everybody. I'm conning visitors who think I'm wonderful, and actually I'm having an affair.'
>
> *Jinny List*

> I think more reasons for being there emerged. I think the main reason, to protest about Cruise being there, was always there, but I think the other reasons just happened. It was about being very fond of and being very close to women.
>
> *Barbara Rawson*

Women at Greenham formed intense and close relationships with each other, which were very different from friendships which they had experienced with women before.

> I found out what it was like to be really close to women and to be really friends with women, and how good women are together. All that was new to me.
>
> *Barbara Rawson*

> I've made friends who are the most important people in my life ... And I know that it will carry on being like that for ever and ever ... I've had lots of friends in my life but I've never really held on to any of them. I haven't had that quality of friendship with anyone else. They're quite intense friendships.
>
> *Penny Gulliver*

Many women came to realize that they had learnt not to value other women's company and that their social orientations had been constructed as heterorelational.

> I'd never really had friendships with women on their own. When you're married, you have friendships with another couple ... When we first formed the group in Derby it just opened my eyes. I'd never seen anything like it. It was amazing ... It was the way that women could be together and be friends and talk about things and do things together. It was something I hadn't encountered. I'd been brought up to think that anything that you did with women was really secondary, your marriage was the thing and your husband, and the things you did with your husband. If you went and had coffee with another woman that was just a bit of frivolity. It wasn't your real life.
>
> *Leah Thalmann*

> So many women said to me, it's so nice living with women. I never thought it would be. And it was clear that they had these concepts that obviously patriarchy fosters, that women together are just a disaster, that they squabble and fight, and they can't get anything done.
>
> *Katrina Allen*

As a community and a social movement Greenham cohered as much, if not more, through the emotional ties of friendship, love and sexual intimacy as through shared politics and philosophies.[3] Indeed a valuing of gyn-affection, in all its forms, was fundamental to the politics and philosophy of Greenham. There was a common belief, much influenced by Adrienne Rich's classic article, 'Compulsory Heterosexuality and Lesbian Existence' and Lillian Faderman's book *Surpassing the Love of Men* (battered copies of both were widely read at Greenham) that the whole range of forms of expression of love, caring and passion between women were to be celebrated and promoted.[4] This was seen both as part of the feminist political project of transforming the dominant social relations of gender and sexuality and as an everyday, life-sustaining pleasure.

It has been argued by some lesbian theorists that an emphasis on gyn-affection, or what was often called the 'woman-identified-woman' position, has tended to evacuate sex from lesbianism, eradicating the important differences between those who choose to build their lives around a sexual desire for women and those for whom gyn-affection excludes an erotic dimension.[5] For instance, Rich's positing of the existence of a 'lesbian continuum' seems to suggest an inherent (maybe even essential) 'lesbianness', which is not a sexual or erotic category, in all relationships between women. While my notion of Greenham as a queer feminist community animated by gyn-affection has resonances of Rich's formulation, I believe that it is important to maintain a conceptual distinction between gyn-affection in general and lesbian erotic and sexual practices and identities as particular forms of gyn-affection. Moreover, I would emphasise that the gyn-affection of Greenham was consciously chosen and created, in contradistinction to the imputed 'natural' lesbian character of Rich's understanding of relations between women.

That said, an important element of the queerness of Greenham was the way in which it provided a space where the boundaries between friendship and sexual desire were readily and frequently destabilized and traversed, where intimacy and attraction could easily lead to sexual passion. Although it is important to maintain the category of 'lesbian' as one constituted by sexual desire and practice, in the messiness of lived lives the distinctions between forms of love and desire can be harder to make. Women at Greenham tended to be physically affectionate with each other, hugging, kissing and touching their friends far more than was common in British culture. Within this context affection, caring and love could easily cross over into sexual desire.

> We touched each other all the time. You couldn't go anywhere without kissing everyone. It would have been rude. That Greenham thing gets me into trouble a bit now, 'cause it's the difference between flirting or being sexual, and just being lesbians with each other. I do miss that.
>
> *Jinny List*

In general, the women I interviewed, whatever their sexual identity and practices, expressed the view that in daily life at the camp, after the first year or so, differences between lesbians and heterosexual women became less and less relevant. There were tensions between 'queer' and 'respectable' Greenham, but the lines were not always clearly drawn between lesbians and heterosexuals. The real tensions which existed around issues of sexuality tended not to be between women who were living at the camp, because anyone who could not tolerate the queer feminist culture would not stay long. Rather they were between campers and visitors - women from the wider Greenham network who came to do nightwatches, for instance. (This is discussed in more detail in Chapter 7.)

> If someone was a dyke or someone was heterosexual and living at camp, what difference did it make? Unless you fancied them. Do you know what I mean? It didn't come into it at all. It didn't matter if someone was heterosexual because obviously if they lived at camp they weren't wittering on about their boyfriends all the time.
>
> *Rowan Gwedhen*

For Jinny List, it was the fluidity of boundaries and sexual practices at Greenham which dissolved the centrality of identity categories.

> I know that there were women who had relationships with women who were living at Blue Gate and would visit or stay at the camp a while, who then haven't had relationships again with women, but it didn't seem really to matter. When I was first there I don't remember specifically knowing who was a dyke and who wasn't.

But it didn't matter, because everyone was always all over each other anyway – I don't necessarily mean sleeping with each other, but there was a very physical contact between all the women, the straight women as well.

*Jinny List*

Nonetheless, lesbian sexual desire was an important part of life at Greenham. This desire did not only arise out of friendship; it also had its own dynamic of lust and attraction which fuelled passionate affairs and relationships. The atmosphere at Greenham was often experienced as highly sexually charged; and the value placed on pleasure and fun extended to making Greenham's culture a pro-sex one. There were few opportunities for privacy and secrecy, and a keen interest was taken in the unfolding of affairs and relationships, though comments on the sounds of sexual activity in nearby benders were rare.

Sexual relationships at Greenham took a wide variety of forms. Some women formed relationships in which they became clearly identified as a couple, building a bender together, spending their days and nights together. Others were in relationships but maintained separate benders or tents, and sought not to be seen as a couple. Some women were monogamous, others had many concurrent lovers; some relationships lasted months or years, others weeks or days. And there were many one-night stands. At Green Gate for a time, there was an area of the Common which women jokingly called 'monogamy mountain' because it was where women in long-term relationships lived, leaving the area closer to the fire and the hub of Green Gate life for those more open to the maelstrom of camp life.

Co-existing with the relative 'normality' of these monogamous living arrangements were more unusual practices. For instance, at different times at Green Gate, Blue Gate and Yellow Gate groups of maybe six to ten women would make big beds together, under a tarpaulin, in a van, or in the summer under the stars, and sleep together. On occasions some of the women would have sex with each other, on others they would just talk and cuddle. In these circumstances the boundaries between affection and sex, lesbians and heterosexual women, friendship and passion could become blurred. As queer as these collective beds were, events like the Red Gate Wedding in 1984 (a theatrical, parodic party thrown by two women to celebrate the moment of their intense desire for each other) were differently queer.

Blue Gate went en masse to the Red Gate Wedding. There was a big row about it, because some women didn't like it, but it was all a game. It wasn't, let's seriously get married. It was, let's get married because you're just the most amazing piece of flesh I've ever met. It was a lust thing. It was, let's get married, and then see who comes along next week. And there were relationships going on all the time, and very few long-standing relationships.

*Jinny List*

## QUEER NORMALITY, QUEER ACTIVISM

Within the queer feminist culture at the camp women's relationships were the core normality and ordinariness of everyday life. Public displays of affection between women were utterly commonplace and heterosexual relationships were so out of the frame, so off-stage, that when women were confronted by them they were often surprised and shocked.

I got used to women sitting on each other's knees, cuddling each other, lying in bed at night, thinking why don't they shut up? You suffered a lot from that at Blue Gate. There was no way you could not know that lesbians had sex lives, if you lived at Blue Gate. It was the norm.

*Pat Paris*

I'll tell you when I realized what an influence the rampant lesbianism at Greenham had had [laughter]. I'd been staying at the camp, and it was some Easter action, and I went with Rebecca to Burghfield.[6] We were going to deliver leaflets or something, and there was a man and a woman kissing, and I was really shocked [laughter]. And that's when I knew. I thought, god, how shocking, how dreadful [laughter]. But I don't know when all those coachloads of women arrived and found women in hot embrace with each other. There's no way they didn't go back and think about it. Though, what they thought about it is another question.

*Carol Harwood*

I used to have to kick myself because I used to take it that everybody that arrived at camp was a lesbian after I'd been there for about five minutes, and was really shocked when people would say, 'Of course, my boyfriend Rodney ...', and I'd think, god [laughter], it's not a lesbian camp, is it? There were so many lesbians there you did start to forget what was the norm ... After a while I forgot that women could be heterosexual. When I think about it now I can't believe how I felt because it's completely gone again, because you feel completely isolated. There's so much of your life that you censor and you can't do what people take for granted all the time, about how they live their lives and what they can say and how they act and how they're physical with people. And you just spend so much of your time for safety reasons closeted and careful and lying about stuff. I'm out, and I'm out to places that I've worked, not everywhere that I've worked, and everybody in my family has known for a long time. But there's still so much of your life that you lie about and you cover up, and to be somewhere, it was a very odd situation, there you are, in a muddy bender, on the outskirts of the Common, but to be sort of normal, and to get to the point where you're shocked because somebody's heterosexual. Not everybody, not the visitors, but when people come to stay and you half imagine they're lesbians, and then you find out that they're not. That's the only time in my life when I've ever come near to that feeling. And you're getting abuse and things thrown at you, and you can't walk, and you're banned from all the cafes. But with all those other pressures, when you were at the camp, that wasn't one of them. You could actually be completely honest and open about your sexuality.

*Penny Gulliver*

Many women took great pleasure in the experience of this queer normality, revelling in the freedom they felt to express their lesbian desires in public displays of affection which a homophobic world prohibited. Women would kiss their lovers passionately in Newbury pubs and cafés, talk loudly about lesbian sex and make jokes about heterosexuality.

We were young raving dykes and we were holding hands and kissing in the bus stops. We'd found our lesbianism and we'd found a place where we could be lesbians.

*Linda*

Women differed in how they chose to present the gyn-affection and lesbian culture of Greenham to the world and there was a broad general consensus that this diversity of modes of self-presentation was part of the Greenham ethos. From the playful, theatrical 'in your face' queer feminist activism of Blue Gate women (described by Bridget Evans and Jinny List) which the collective energy of Greenham licensed, to quieter forms of action, such as that described by Carol Harwood, heteronormative assumptions were repeatedly challenged.

> The other thing that happened for me was that at the age of 23, realizing that I was definitely a lesbian, I basically had my teenage years over again at that point in my life. The lesbian teenage years that I'd never really had. I'd never been somebody who was very interested in men, and I was really afraid of thinking that I was a lesbian, and therefore I'd really steered away from a lot of frivolous things. And so at Greenham I did a lot of things that I'd never done before or since, things that were quite immature and childish, in some ways, but it was like everybody was into it, so that gave me licence to join in as well. So, we used to take a lot of delight in going into Newbury and ordering beans on toast and then sitting there and ... flaunting our lesbianism at people ... You'd all deliberately go and sit with your arms around each other drinking tea, but sort of acting amazed that anybody was staring at you.
>
> *Bridget Evans*

> We'd do some outrageous things. One day in Jackie's car, there were just four of us and we were driving back to the camp from somewhere, I don't know where, and we happened to overtake this one car, and then we were behind this woman in a wedding car, and we were in this wedding party. And we were yelling out the window, 'Don't do it, don't do it.' And they turned off into this massive house, into the drive, and we went with them, and drove round and round this little fountain, shouting, 'Don't do it, don't do it.' And they were trying to have their wedding pictures taken, and there were these four dykes from Greenham, and they knew where we were from, 'cause of the abuse we were giving them, and they were giving us in return. And there's this woman in tears because we're ruining her wedding day [laughter].
>
> *Jinny List*

You know when the convoy first started doing exercises and Mrs Skull was interviewed and she was hanging out the top window in this low-cut lace nightdress and full make-up in the middle of the night, heaving for the BBC, and going on about their desirable residence and how we ruined the view, which cracked me up, because when you looked from the Skulls' all you could see was this great enormous nuclear base. So we used to do all sorts of things to the Skulls, 'cause they watched us all the time. So women used to sit on chairs on each others' knees and cuddle passionately for hours, right under Mrs Skull's nose. People thought nothing of having a snog at the side of the road, if Mrs Skull was hanging out of the window, 'cause she complained so much about it. Women eventually started doing it to wind her up.

*Pat Paris*

I remember being interviewed on one of the anniversaries of the peace camp, and I was in Wales and it was the peak listening programme, about 8 o'clock in the morning, and he'd rung me on Friday and said, would I come in and talk. The usual thing, token Greenham woman, respectable, three children, white, you know, you name it. So his researcher had been asking me questions all weekend, quite straightforward questions, and I went in on Monday morning, and waited. We shook hands: 'Good morning, Mrs Harwood.' 'No, Carol.' 'Good morning, Carol.' And terribly friendly, and it's going to be live. So he asked me all these questions I was planning on, and then it was the *Daily Mail* he dragged out from under his papers, and he said, finally, 'What do you have to say about these allegations of', I think it was, 'drug-taking, alcoholism and lesbianism at the camp?' I thought, oh fuck. Hands sweating [laughter], and I thought, this is it, girl, you've really got to face up to this one. So I dealt with the alcohol, and I dealt with the drugs, and there was a pregnant silence, and I just looked at him, and I said, 'You tell me what worries you most, the idea of men making war with each other, or the idea of women making love with each other? Which worries you most?' He said, 'Thank you very much, Mrs Harwood. That will be all.' And that was that [laughter].

*Carol Harwood*

Thus women at Greenham, by being lesbians publicly and in large numbers (whether with added production values or not) enacted a politics of presence which made lesbianism exist beyond the privacy of personal relationships and propelled 'lesbian' into the news media and mainstream discourse.

When abuse was directed at Greenham women for being lesbians, and this happened frequently, the usual response was to queer the abuse by greeting it, to defuse and deflate the intended insult by greeting it joyously. Rather than engaging in argument about the equal rights of lesbians to live their lives as they chose, or seeking to explain that while some women at Greenham were lesbians not all were, women collectively accepted the label.

> We got a lot of hassle living on the north side. People shouting. But they'd always get a mouthful back. Like when somebody would go past shouting 'lesbians', and we'd jump up and down and wave our arms in the air, shouting, 'Yes, it's lovely.'
>
> *Jenny Heron*

> There was lots and lots of verbal abuse, people from Newbury and soldiers and stuff, and for some reason, faced with a bunch of thirty lesbians, they scream, 'Lesbians'. And thirty women scream, 'Yes, so what?' To them that's the worse thing they can do. But part of that was a joke too. They were dead right. The fact is they think they're being abusive, and we think, yeah, so?
>
> *Jinny List*

Sometimes, however, the way in which 'lesbian' was used to abuse and discredit women rankled.

> Kirsten's experience with a woman from the *Mail* was classic. This woman had driven her car into the ditch at Blue Gate. Kirsten had gone over and got her out and this woman was limping out in shock, and had helped her over to the fire and sat her down and made her a cup of tea, while everybody else at Blue had pushed her car out of the ditch and driven it round and parked it for her and talked to this woman who was very nice and was really shook up, and in a bit of a state, and as soon as she was fine and OK she went home. And two days later the centre spread

was 'The moment I arrived I was woman-handled by an aggressive lesbian', and people were so fucking mad because they'd spent three hours getting her fucking car out of a ditch and looking after her and waiting on her hand and foot. We laughed about it.

But that actually wasn't as serious as when there were some Scottish women down there at the time, and someone came down from an Edinburgh paper and had printed their names and all about what they were doing and that they were lesbians and stuff. And their families didn't know. And when Lynn went back her stuff was in the back garden. Things like that were much more serious.

*Penny Gulliver*

## Greenham's Queer Feminist Challenges

Both the public perception of Greenham as full of 'burly lesbians' (as the *Sun* put it) and the queer feminist culture of the camp posed challenges to those who got involved, and particularly to those who went to live there. Whether their sexual and emotional relationships were primarily or exclusively with women or men, no one who spent any length of time at Greenham stayed 'straight' in the sense of being firmly identified with sexual and gender 'normality'. Women were queered by their involvement, by association, by the strength of their ties of affection, friendship and love for the women with whom they lived, whether or not they called themselves lesbians, whether they did sex with women or men. In choosing to devote time and energy to creating politics and community with other women, Greenham women were, for a time, stepping outside heterorelations. Being part of Greenham – accepting the identity of 'Greenham woman' – involved taking on the mantle, in much of the world's eyes, of gender and sexual rebel and deviant. Greenham women had to come to terms with this, albeit with varying degrees of internal conflict.

There were a number of ways in which Greenham's queer challenge manifested itself in women's lives. For some, such as Nell Logan, it was a question of rethinking attitudes and beliefs towards lesbians who remained basically 'other' to themselves. For some a more fundamental process of self-examination was set in train. In the context of Greenham's gyn-affection and queer normality, women embarked on projects of self-transformation. As discussed in Chapter 6, great value was placed on openness to change and personal reflexivity, and on the discourse of individual agency which encouraged women to see relationships, sexual identity and sexual practice as arenas in which they could exercise choice and engage in experimentation. Many women described feeling 'freer' and more aware of their own power and autonomy than ever before in their lives. This often posed problems for women in long-standing heterosexual relationships. Many of them were seriously destabilized as women put their energy and time into an arena of activity from which their male partners were excluded. Alongside this, some heterosexual women began to question their sexuality and to experiment with sexual relationships with women. Many women who had had lesbian relationships before Greenham also found their lives significantly changed by the experience. They created identities for themselves and ways of being lesbians with which they felt happy, often for the first time.

Problematic though it was for some women to locate themselves within a lesbian/heterosexual dichotomy, it is worth giving some indication of the overall picture of sexual identities amongst the thirty-five women interviewed. Twenty identified themselves as having been heterosexual at the time they got involved with Greenham, though not all were involved in relationships with men; one woman was both married and in a relationship with a woman; eleven identified themselves as having been lesbians when they got involved with Greenham, though many were not happy with a lesbian identity; three more were in various ways 'doing lesbianism', without thinking of themselves, at the time, as lesbians. At the time of interview, twelve women identified themselves as heterosexual, including one woman who had been a lesbian when she first got involved with Greenham. Twenty-one identified themselves as lesbians and two were self-consciously ambivalent. Such figures conceal as much as they reveal about the complexity of individual women's experiences. The range of ways in which lives were queered through involvement with Greenham can best be understood through women's own stories.

## CHALLENGES TO HETERONORMATIVE ATTITUDES

Ann Armstrong, a nurse, married with grown-up children, and living with her husband in the middle-class town of Weybridge, found herself having to confront her own prejudices and to change her ways of thinking when she started visiting Greenham.

> It was very gradual, but I can remember first coming across lesbians [laughter].
> SASHA: *Had you not come across lesbians before?*
> No, I don't think so ... At first I suppose I thought it was a bit odd, but it soon got to be the norm. It didn't worry me. I suppose at one time there was an awful lot in the press, *Sun* journalism, about lesbians, you'd be saying, they're not like that. You know, this is my friend from Greenham who's got six kids. One tended to overemphasize the normal ones. But it very soon just made no difference at all. Whereas now I suppose, you meet somebody and if you hear somebody is a lesbian, you think, good, she's right on, you know. It seems to have gone completely the other way. I remember my aunt telling me her daughter was, well, I think she's a lesbian mostly, you know, and I was really pleased. I thought, ahh, isn't that nice. A while ago I'd have thought, oh how funny ... I don't know, just lately I've been more and more off men anyway. You see that a lot in women, I think. I seem to have met a lot of women over the years who've had a relationship, had a family, and get to my age, and start to question it all.
>
> *Ann Armstrong*

Like Ann, Nell Logan had her first conscious encounters with lesbianism at Greenham. A life-long Communist activist who was 71 when she first got involved, her response was one of tolerance founded on a belief in the importance of working together against the threat of nuclear war. She explicitly drew on Carol Harwood's challenge to her anti-lesbian radio interviewer.

> It's funny, I must say, I was old-fashioned. I didn't know anything about lesbianism or gays. I didn't know anything at all. And I didn't particularly want to. But I was at Greenham, on the main road, talking to a lot of women visitors, and then some police came up, and started talking and saying, 'It's a lesbian camp, this.' And I said, 'What? What are you talking about?' I said, 'We are anti-war. Good god,' I said, 'anyway, I don't know what it is, and I don't care. I don't care what anyone does, as long as they're all

fighting against what's going on.' He didn't say anything then. I don't care, because, as Carol said, what frightens you more, the idea of women making love to each other, or the idea of men making war with each other?

*Nell Logan*

Leah Thalmann, a married social worker from Derby, also found her experience broadened by daily life at Greenham.

I remember the first time I heard two women talking about planning to have a baby and the methods they might use, and I was amazed. I sat goggle-eyed, listening to it all. When I first went to Greenham I had lots of my assumptions knocked. The first time I saw two women kissing each other, I remember, was the second time I went. I remember thinking they shouldn't. My assumption was to say, 'Ooh, you don't like that sort of thing?' But underneath I think part of me was thinking, 'It's alright.'

*Leah Thalmann*

CHALLENGES TO HETEROSEXUAL RELATIONSHIPS

Women who were in long-term heterosexual relationships when they got involved with Greenham faced a range of challenges, from having to confront being 'queered by association' (as Barbara Rawson describes) to the problem of negotiating time and space for themselves to spend at Greenham, to having to deal with their partners' jealousy.

Den [my husband] told me afterwards, he didn't tell me while I was there, that he had a lot of flack at work. I don't know how they knew I was at Greenham, the power-station men, but Den said that they'd been very, very cruel to him.

SASHA: *What did they say?*

I think I've blocked it all out, but it was something like, 'Well, we know what your wife's like', or making jokes which were obviously about lesbians, dirty women. Oh yes, and I can remember that he got a lot of advice about how to deal with me. So it was very upsetting because he was a quiet man who was a very conforming man, and I found out afterwards that he had had a lot of trouble.

And I had to think to myself that if I had known, would I still have gone? And I think I would have really, because you have to ... Most of the women at Greenham, or a lot of the women, were lesbian. And I am not. But that difference doesn't matter. I am quite happy to be lesbian in that way. Not in a sexual way, but if that's a blanket word that's used for us, that's fine.

*Barbara Rawson*

Eighteen of the women I interviewed were in long-term relationships with men when they got involved with Greenham, all of whom ostensibly shared the anti-nuclear politics of their women partners. However, all eighteen women said that their relationships had been put under strain by their involvement with Greenham, and all but two of the eighteen spoke of their husbands'/partners' difficulty in accepting their commitment to the camp. Only five relationships were still on-going by the time of the interviews. Many male partners expressed more or less open hostility to Greenham in the form of sarcastic remarks, mocking criticisms or 'meaningful silences'; others refused to take responsibility for childcare or domestic tasks so that women could participate to the extent they wished. A few made frequent visits to Greenham in attempts to 'share' it with their partners. A number of women recounted how their husbands'/partners' reactions were due in part to the changes they were undergoing because of their involvement with Greenham, which the men found threatening.

You'd be so full of it [Greenham], and what you'd done. And quite often you've described some stupid thing that you'd done, which really had made you laugh so much, and everyone else, and Ray would say, 'Oh yes, I bet that will get Mrs Thatcher worried.' And you think, well, of course it's silly, but it is important ... My husband always felt jealous because he would have liked to come and spend his nights sitting round a fire, laughing and joking and drinking alcohol. And during the Ten Days [action in 1984] he would come down and bring things. I used to be very embarrassed because I couldn't get rid of him ... I never liked him being there.

SASHA: *Because it was your place?*

Yes, our place.

SASHA: *Has that put a strain on your relationship? Did it at the time?*
Occasionally. I mean I think probably more from my feminism,
which I got from Greenham ... I think I used to be a lot more
amenable than I am now. I used to do as I was told ... When I was
young I definitely let men walk all over me, Ray particularly. He
didn't think so, but I always did everything he wanted, which I
don't do now. Which is to the detriment of our relationship.

*Ann Armstrong*

I had him [male partner] bobbing in and out, upsetting the apple
cart and panicking because I was getting visibly stronger by the day,
and the stronger I got, the more he tried to cut that down and
refused to babysit ... Or he'd discover something really important
to talk about just as you were putting your coat on to go out to a
meeting and he knew perfectly well you'd only got five minutes and
you couldn't actually deal with whether we were going to move in
five minutes. It was that sort of thing. It took me a while to notice
the pattern and then I ignored it. He definitely did try to prevent me
getting involved ... It was the kiss of death to our relationship ...
The public face was that he was incredibly supportive and
incredibly helpful ... I think he was living vicariously through my
experiences ... I had to come back and he would take these
interesting experiences and live off them. But it took me quite a
while to recognize that. It just felt to me like he wouldn't leave me
half an hour just to adjust to being back at the house. I used to
think, if only he would leave me half an hour, I'd probably be
alright about it. But it became more and more oppressive. It built up
to the point where I was dreading coming back.

*Pat Paris*

In Pat's case living at the camp had contradictory effects on her
relationship with her partner. On the one hand, it was producing this
sort of problematic behaviour which was leading her to question the
relationship. On the other hand, she found that being surrounded by a
highly politicized group of lesbians and feminists in some ways made
her more reticent about recognizing and talking about the situation.

By that point I was spending most of my time with very radical
political lesbians and I knew that if I did voice any murmur of

discontent, it would be, well, it's your own responsibility, isn't it? And I think one of the reasons that I didn't actually say anything was because I didn't feel that I would get support for what I was feeling. I'd be told I had to take action. And I obviously hadn't arrived at that point. I knew for a long time that I had to get out and that it was killing me. It was a very slow process of recognizing what was happening. I was angry with myself later because I thought I should have done something earlier. It was a very abusive situation, particularly the last two years, and for some reason I covered it up, and that was my inability to say, this is what's going on ... You do feel it reflects on you. And in a radical lesbian environment that can be very hard. You feel you will be criticized for it. That definitely slowed me down a bit, but I did have some very good friends there, they would put up with watching me suffer and carried on being there.

*Pat Paris*

On the surface of it he thought it was a good thing because his politics were the same as mine and he fully supported doing something. But actually underneath there was a lot of resentment. With hindsight I realized a lot of the things I said and did at Greenham he treated like little girls playing in the woods and having good fun, but nothing really very serious ... He didn't try and stop me going - not specifically. He didn't make a huge fuss about it ... And yet, there was quite a lot of resentment really.

*Leah Thalmann*

Nor was a negative reaction confined to the partners/husbands of women who went to live at Greenham, or who spent significant periods of time as stayers. Someone who only visited Greenham on a handful of occasions describes her partner's response:

He was intellectually committed to feminism and very supportive and a very good socialist and whatever ... He knew that it was politically extremely incorrect to feel threatened by it. But he did. He felt, and he had reason to feel, threatened by my involvement with women.

*Helen Mary Jones*

Women who recounted such behaviour tended to have become conscious of it slowly, accepting for a long time that the declarations of support reflected their partners' 'true' attitudes. Often these women only developed a critical perspective on this behaviour, and an understanding of it as an attempt to exercise control over their involvement, when they mentioned what was happening at home to other women. The feminist analyses proffered by their friends contributed to an increasing awareness of how they were or had been dominated by men in their intimate relationships.

DESTABILIZING HETEROSEXUAL IDENTITIES

In addition to offering new perspectives on many women's relationships with their male partners, Greenham also posed challenges to heterosexual identities. Five of the women I interviewed embarked upon relationships with women while at Greenham or while involved in the Greenham network, which resulted in the ending of their relationships with husbands/partners and the adoption of lesbian identities. Two more began a process of self-questioning at Greenham which later resulted in decisions to finish their relationships with their husbands and to start more or less immediately new relationships with women. The woman who had been married and having a relationship with a woman left her husband and decided that she was a lesbian.

Leah Thalmann, for example, had been unhappy in her marriage for some time, but did not leave her husband and begin a relationship with a woman until after her involvement with Greenham was over.

> Going to Greenham was a sort of catalyst for what was going to have to happen anyway. It sort of set me on that track. And when I went to Greenham I knew nothing about lesbians or anything, and when I first saw them, my assumptions were, mmm, I'm not sure about this. I wished some of the women weren't lesbians. I'd think, oh, she's not a lesbian. And then it would turn out she was. And I'd think, oh what a pity. Oh, is she a lesbian too? It wasn't that I really thought there was anything wrong with lesbians, it was just that I didn't want them all to turn out to be lesbians.
> SASHA: *Why, because that might mean that you had to be too?*
> No, no. I never thought I would be. Oh no, nothing like that could

happen to me. No. Surely not so many women were lesbians? Although I chucked out my assumptions, I really didn't want them all to be lesbians. I wasn't ready to think it was totally alright. But so many of them did turn out to be lesbians. But I didn't think of being one when I was at Greenham. That wasn't going to happen to me. I used to sometimes, latterly especially, when I was at Emerald, I was lonely quite a lot, and I used to think that it would be really nice to have a special woman here, to share a bender with and just talk and be close to. But I didn't think of it in terms of sex, at all. Oh no. Really didn't. Obviously something was going on at Greenham that opened the gates for what happened later, but I wasn't conscious of it at the time ... Just when I started going to Greenham there was all this furore in the local paper about me getting time off work, and Julius [her husband] got this anonymous letter, and it was just an envelope and inside it was a newspaper cutting with a headline saying 'Lesbians Hijack the Peace Movement'.[7] And it was obviously intended to warn him, his wife going to Greenham would be dragged into being a lesbian. He laughed heartily at this, never knowing what the outcome would be.

*Leah Thalmann*

Helen John, who was on the original walk from Cardiff to Greenham and whose motivations for involvement had been strongly maternalist, also underwent a significant transformation in identity through Greenham, entering a relationship with another woman for the first time.

I went there because of the nuclear weapons and so forth and changed my opinion on a whole load of other things and my lifestyle. It was really an incredible time, it was just an enormous change in my life. My whole life stood on end, you know. It was really an incredible experience. And it was absolutely the right thing to do, to acknowledge that side of myself and not run away from it, as I could have done.

*Helen John*

Jenny Heron, who had also had a strongly maternalist orientation when first involved with Greenham and who was a committed environmentalist, had negotiated childcare with her pro-feminist, anti-nuclear husband so that she could live at Greenham for two-and-a-half months at the time when Cruise was arriving. She had never before met lesbians to whom she could relate, but she found the affective and erotic dimensions of Greenham irresistible, as she was swept up by the 'lesbianness' of the camp. Very quickly her reasons for being at Greenham were transformed.

I'd decided to go there on 31 October and be there for the time when Cruise was supposed to come in and stay for a month afterwards. That's what I decided to do. I'd negotiated with Ian that was what I would do, and it was fairly contained so he wouldn't feel that I was never coming back – though I never did really, in spirit. And I felt that was OK.

I was terribly earnest when I went ... I've got an article from the *Chronicle and Echo* [Northampton local newspaper], because Nick Fletcher came up and interviewed me, where I said I came here because I'm determined to say my bit, to say my piece about saving the world. It couldn't have been that gradual that it all changed, because I was only actually there for about two-and-a-half months at that stage. I went there and I was really earnest about that kind of thing, but then I got into the magic and the goddess worship bit earnestly, and I'd only been there two weeks when I started falling in love ... I knew [J.] and [L.], but they were so much into roles. Their style of life wasn't at all eco. When I got to Greenham there were all these women who cared about the environment. You'd see the intimacy going on between certain women and every day you'd notice it was more and more of them. It was marvellous because it was so positive, because everyone was uninhibited. There were no great heartbreaks going on at that time. It was all such positive role models. There haven't been such positive role models anywhere or anytime since. Certainly before that, any time before that, you could meet perhaps a couple or two couples, but there you'd got hundreds of them, and you couldn't resist it really. You'd just got to go along with them. In the end Greenham was about lesbianism. It was about living outside without any constraints of timetables or houses and it was about meeting marvellous women with great imaginations and charisma. It was about learning how to enjoy myself as a woman and get close to other women and have productive relationships with women. More so than anything to do with nukes.

*Jenny Heron*

Pat Paris, whose struggles in her relationship with her male partner was recounted earlier (pp. 295-6), didn't come to question her sexual identity until after she had stopped living at Greenham, and was back at the camp for a short visit.

> When I lived there I never felt pressured to be anything other than I was. It's quite strange really. I was the only heterosexual there, except at weekends. It never occurred to me. It was at Greenham some years later that I finally came out. I spent the night in a tent with a very good friend of mine whom I'd got close to over the last year, and laid awake all night in the tent with this woman, thinking, oooh. And finally when dawn was breaking, I thought, this is just crazy. I've just got to do something about it. I had this wonderful weekend wandering through the woods with this woman, while we didn't actually say anything too specific, and everybody else watching us from a safe distance. And then I got back here on the Sunday. He was quite peculiar, and he said to me, 'You don't want to be with me any more.' And I said, 'Now you come to mention it, no, I don't.' It was great. He handed it to me on a plate. He left the next morning. I think he'd been trying to stave it off for at least two years … And it wasn't until this particular night at Greenham when I literally laid awake all night, realizing that I had this unsatisfactory relationship. And here I was lying next to another woman, and I couldn't sleep because I was lying next to her. And I just thought, you're going to have to face reality here … I didn't want to be involved in that relationship any more, and if I was going to become involved in another one, it would be with a woman. Not necessarily the one I was lying next to. I arrived at this conclusion at 6 o'clock in the morning, and felt much better. I did actually feel incredibly good the day after. I went round and told everyone the next day, the whole world, all my lesbian friends and my straight friends.

Pat saw her own identity transformations as part of a wider pattern.

> It's been extraordinary watching the changes over the years, watching what's happened to people, what they've done. Women that were in that group [Nottingham Women for Peace]. An awful lot have left marriages and come out. When I first went in that

group it was predominately heterosexual, there was a large section of lesbian women, but it was not a lesbian group. And two years later it was a lesbian group. And it was more or less the same women. Some had dropped out, but by and large it was the same women. A lot of them had come out. And a lot of them were probably lesbians already who weren't saying. But quite a lot of women like me actually left heterosexual relationships and come out.

*Pat Paris*

(RE)CONSTRUCTING LESBIAN IDENTITIES

The experience of living in the gyn-affective queer feminist community of Greenham was also transformative for women who were not heterosexual. For example, 20-year-old Jinny List had been, in her own words, 'a closet lesbian' before she got involved with Greenham. She had two relationships with women prior to going to Greenham and had come out to her family, for which her brother had beaten her up.

I'd kind of resigned myself to the fact, quite early on, when I was about fourteen. It was, oh my god, this is so miserable [laughter]. This is going to be so dreadful ... I spent a lot of time hanging around gay bars, which in Nottingham then were mixed. I was quite resigned to it, I suppose, rather than embracing it and feeling, isn't this wonderful and strong.

*Jinny List*

But Greenham changed how she felt about being a lesbian.

It made me feel more lesbian, much more. I was lucky enough to experience some of that good strong positive lesbianness. I'd had glimpses of it before - there were times when I was living with [first girlfriend], say, that were great, and the world couldn't touch us. But it was inside our four walls. And people talk a lot about lesbian strength, and I think I've lived in it and had it keep me warm, without trying to sound too poetic and clichéd. But there is a thing about, you can't describe it, you have to have lived it, and you have to feel it, and you have to know what it means when you wake up in the morning. God, there must be something when you'll go to bed in a big bed and there's six women there, and you wake up and you're all snuggled up. Something's happening there ... I could have gone through a lot more years thinking that most lesbians were pretty much like [first girlfriend] and worked for the civil service and had a pretty suit. It could have taken me much longer to discover the range and the power and the beauty and all that kind of stuff.

I learnt a lot quickly at Greenham, with the space to explore things, which I probably would have got to anyway, but slower. Because when you've got twenty hours at a stretch to do nothing but make a fire, and there's no television, there's no newspapers, you talk. You find out. I believe in women more. We live in a homophobic society that told me for so long that women and lesbians were bad news, whether that included me or not. Something had to show me that that wasn't right. And Greenham did that. I don't care how much you're politically right on, or politically correct and you read the right books, if you're an isolated lesbian, how much do you believe about women's strength? If it's there, in your face, you learn, pretty damn quick.

*Jinny List*

Sarah Benham's story has many parallels with Jinny's. She had had a two-year relationship with another girl while at school and had tried very hard to resist a lesbian identity, but later came to understand her desire to be at Greenham as being, in large part, about seeking a way to be happy as a lesbian.

I came across all her letters the other day and it was full of this stuff, we're not really gay, we're just very special friends to each other. We were completely closeted. And then that time that Jane said, I'd say that about 80 per cent of the women here are lesbians I was just very shocked by it. It hadn't occurred to me. I think Greenham was about ... realizing I was a lesbian. And it was about being involved in the peace movement, and it was about leaving home.

*Sarah Benham*

Studying for her A Levels as the only girl at Eton (the boys' public school), she spent more and more time at Greenham - weekends, half-terms and the Easter holidays. She finally decided to leave home, though because her family home was so close to Greenham, she initially went to live at the mixed peace camp at Faslane in Scotland.

> I wrote my parents a letter one day: 'I'm leaving home and, by the way, I'm a lesbian.' I came out, but I thought that getting involved at that time with Greenham was more to do with getting involved with the peace movement, and now I realize that it's more to do with being a lesbian. It was the Easter holidays, and I absolutely hated being at Eton, and I said to my parents that I hated it, and they talked me into staying, and said, 'It's only two years, get your A levels out of the way and then you can leave.' I was there at the beginning of the Easter holidays and I had an ordinary haircut, and when I was there I had all my hair cut off, I had about a quarter-inch of hair. And I thought, there's no way I'm going back to Eton with this haircut.
>
> *Sarah Benham*

Bridget Evans, who had followed her first girlfriend from Liverpool to Greenham (Chapter 3, pp. 64-5), experienced the gyn-affection of Greenham rather differently from Jenny, but for her, too, Greenham offered a place in which she could work out her feelings about relationships with women. Her story also illustrates the difference in the culture between Green Gate, where Jenny lived, and Blue Gate, where Bridget was. When she discovered that her girlfriend wanted to finish their relationship, she was devastated:

> I was really, really upset. But as it turned out I actually got a lot of support from other lesbians at Greenham. So by the end of the first weekend I ended up sitting crying at the campfire, a total heap, because it was really the end. We didn't finalize things that weekend, but that was the end. And I was able to tell people really pretty quickly, and I was immediately aware that there were a lot of other lesbians there. And I was still in the process of coming out. Up until then I'd accepted that I was heterosexual and telling everyone that I was a lesbian wasn't easy. And one of the distressing things was that having a relationship with [girlfriend] was making all that much easier for me. And then being a single lesbian, you don't have the same support or you don't have any immediate reason for being a lesbian really, because you don't

have a relationship ... And of course with all those pressures about am I really a lesbian? And in some ways I think the lesbian community is quite bad about that – there's this real thing that in order to be a lesbian you have to be actively in a relationship or you're nothing, you don't count. But one of the things I liked about Greenham was that you could choose your own level of activity around lesbianism. And basically I was very hurt after I split up with [girlfriend]. And I really was quite wary about getting emotionally involved with anyone else and what Greenham allowed me was actually a very comfortable level to be a lesbian. In other words, there was lots of physical affection without that being like dead sexual one-to-one. There was an awful lot of people sitting around cuddling people, and there was lots of conversation about lesbianism and I really felt that people accepted me as a lesbian without me having to demonstrate it. And it was actually quite a young group of lesbians at Blue Gate then. I was about 23 at that time and I was actually one of the older women there. There were a lot of 19- and 20-year-olds, and there were a lot of women who'd just decided they were lesbians as well, and then there were some older women as well, and some of them were heterosexual, and some didn't really define themselves as anything, but were comfortable with everyone else being a lesbian ...

And we were continually drunk. There were all these women all the time bringing down all these bottles of booze. And I mean morning, noon and night we would just open them up and drink them up, and then we'd be drunk and we'd be stoned, and Jesus, the level of debauchery was dreadful. And I think for me the other thing was that it was sort of group debauchery, so it was like lesbianism, and there was a real feeling of lesbianism, but it wasn't like one-to-one private sexual relationships, that actually happened a real minority of the time. And so things like we all used to sleep with each other in these great big benders, and we'd be like half a dozen to ten of us all piled in there at night, and we'd just like laugh and giggle and tell stories.

*Bridget Evans*

Even women who were already part of lesbian communities and/or who were comfortable with their lesbian identity described how Greenham supported and empowered them, offering as it did a place where they were able to be open about their desire for women. Barbara Shulman was an American, a lesbian who came to Greenham having already been involved in the women's peace movement in the United States. Penny Gulliver had come out while at drama school, and had been living in a women-only squat before moving to Greenham.

It made me feel great about being a lesbian. Subsequent to Greenham I came out to my mother, and it made me feel really connected to my mother ... Seeing women of her age at all these events made me feel that it was within the realm of possibility for her to be there, and it gave me the courage in a way to want to bring her into my life.

*Barbara Shulman*

I think the most important thing for me was that I was actually surrounded by a lot of lesbians. That was really nice and really important. Because you could be open about it was better fun. We didn't talk about being a lesbian, we talked about things to do with the fact that you *were* a lesbian. And that was really nice because when people find out that you're a lesbian they want to talk about it all the time. If you come out to people, they want to know, they ask all sorts of questions. It was moving on from that level of talking about it, being able to talk about things which are on a much deeper level, or things that are much more subtle about being a lesbian, which other lesbians know, but you don't talk about. You recognize a lot more. Suddenly people say something and you say, yeah, that's right, and you find that you've got a lot more in common than you thought, and things are much more complicated about being a lesbian than actually it just being difficult. The subtleties of being a lesbian, the things that you learn to do so that you're not recognized, or so that you don't get into trouble, and things that you don't even realize that you do. You suddenly twig, yes I do that and I have done that since I came out, and you realize what a strange state you have to live your life in.

*Penny Gulliver*

## Ambivalences, Exceptions and Open Endings ...

In order to recognize the complexity of women's experiences of Greenham and the multiplicity of ways that women have interpreted the meanings of their involvement, it is vital to hear the dissenting voices, the stories that do not quite fit the accounts I've developed thus far. Women expressed a range of ambivalences and exceptions to *my* narrative of the queering of lives.

For instance, besides the many women who saw Greenham as having provided the space in which to make important changes in their lives, there were others who stayed in their existing heterosexual relationships, often with some ambivalence and sometimes regrets about the choices they were making and what they might have been missing. But the fact that they saw themselves as making choices was evidence of a reflexivity about heterosexuality which they had developed by being involved with Greenham.

> I didn't feel excluded. What I missed out on in a sense was what women who were in a lesbian relationship had, the fun of being with somebody else, of doing things together. You obviously can't, if you're involved with somebody who isn't there, whether it's a man or woman, you miss out on that sharing and egging each other on and giving each other love and support.
>
> *Carola Addington*

Several of the women I interviewed clearly expressed a sense of ongoing openness about their sexual identities.

> When I got involved I was beginning to question my sexuality, and that is something I continue to do. I'm no clearer now ten years later than I was then, about what I am, if one has to give oneself labels. And I was involved in a series of what I suppose you'd describe, if this was the eighteenth century, as passionate friendships with women, that I didn't view in a romantic sexual light then ... Greenham didn't make me question my own sexuality, but it did make me more comfortable with the ambiguities, with not having to have clear answers.
>
> *Helen Mary Jones*

I think the big experience for me was coming into contact with women who were lesbians, and who were very strong in that way ... I'd met many before, but I met many many more because of Greenham ... I can't understand my own position really, because I've often felt I just stand in the middle. I could easily be on this side or that side, and that's why I now feel wary about categories of any kind ... Although I knew that I wasn't anti-men as such, I was anti-men in certain contexts. I got quite prickly and annoyed if some bloke came up to the fire, even if it was daylight, and I'd be quite relieved when he'd go. At first I thought it was because I was picking up the vibes of other women who did object very strongly and couldn't stand the sight of men coming up and felt very invaded. But later on, when I'd be sitting there with other women who were heterosexual, then I knew it was coming from me. I know it was me that felt like that. Hearing more about Aboriginal ways of life, they'd have women-only events and time, and that's quite proper. I felt it was our space. Even though I was in a happy relationship with a man. But I always felt I could have been in a happy relationship with a woman. It just depends sometime who you meet and who you get on with.

*Carmel Cadden*

There were a small number of women for whom Greenham did not appear to have set in train radical changes in attitudes, identity or sexual practice. Those least affected tended to be those who spent least time there; some identified themselves as lesbians, others as heterosexual. Sian Edwards, for instance, an active member of Plaid Cymru (the Welsh nationalist party), strongly supported Greenham within her local branch in Cardiff and was involved in Cardiff Women for Peace. She took part in local women's peace actions (such as those against the Royal Ordnance Factory) and visited Greenham for a few days at a time several times a year. But she never had any desire to live there and, despite being a lesbian, did not feel drawn to the queer feminist community of the camp. Her sexual politics remained very different from those which held sway at Greenham.

I'd been a lesbian since forever. I've never had bad experiences like some women I know. I've always thought absolutely naturally that that's what I am. Ever since I was eleven or twelve I realized that. It was never like a big deal. And I've always taken the line of, it's my private business, my sexual life, and therefore been condemned by other lesbians for not parading it. It was nice if women were able to be happy at Greenham and whatever, but I didn't much feel like joining in, in any way. I thought it was good, but it doesn't make any great difference to my life.

*Sian Edwards*

Sisters Christine King, Susan Lamb, Lesley Brinkworth and Lynne Fortt, who lived in Porth, South Wales and who regularly spent short periods of time at Greenham, faced considerable hostility from their local community. They were often spat at in the street and were referred to locally as 'the incestuous lesbians'; through all of this they maintained the position that sexuality was 'irrelevant', their own or anyone else's.

The missiles were in the base, we were talking about global destruction. Sexuality is not relevant. I think it was used as an issue to undermine what was going on there. There were lesbians and heterosexual women there, but that was not the issue.

*Lynne Fortt*

Finally, of those many women who told their stories of life transformation at and through Greenham with great joy and who expressed pleasure with the new identities they created for themselves, many were also ready to admit to the problems that the queering of their lives brought and to recognize that there is no ultimate point of self-transformation, no point where problems cease.

But it has its costs. I'm not in contact with my family, which isn't a bed of roses. Becoming a lesbian is not the answer to every problem in the world, and probably opens up more problems than it ever solved. But it's a different way of life, and for me a more fulfilling way of life, so the cost has had its benefits as well. But I don't know any woman who hasn't paid some price. And some women paid very heavy prices, had their children removed.

*Helen John*

Without Greenham I wouldn't be where I am today. I wouldn't have come out as a lesbian at seventeen if I hadn't been to Greenham, and if I wasn't a lesbian I wouldn't be me. I'd be floundering away trying to make it work in relationships with men, I should imagine. Instead of floundering away trying to make it work in relationships with women!

*Sarah Benham*

## Notes

1.  I take the concepts of 'gyn-affection' (affection between women) and 'hetero-relations' from Raymond: 'in a heterorelational society ... most of women's personal, social, political, professional, and economic relations are defined by the ideology that woman is for man' (Raymond 1986: 11).
2.  In *Disarming Patriarchy* I referred to Greenham as a 'lesbian community' (1995: 56).
3.  I have argued elsewhere (Roseneil, 1998) that social movement researchers have vastly underestimated the importance of the emotional and affective dynamics of movements.
4.  Rich (1980) and Fadermann (1981).
5.  See, for instance, Ferguson (1982). It should be noted that Raymond does underline the significance of the differences between lesbian identities and lives, and those of female friends and communities.
6.  At Easter 1983 CND organized a 'human chain' demonstration linking the Atomic Weapons Establishment at Aldermaston, the Royal Ordnance Factory at Burghfield and Greenham Common.
7.  Leah worked for Derbyshire County Council and was granted unpaid leave to spend time at Greenham. In September 1984 the Council offered unpaid leave to all its women employees in order to allow them to spend time at Greenham for the Ten Million Women Action.

# Chapter 11
# A Queer New World?

## Three Unanticipated Moments

*I*

*The final two decades of the twentieth century have seen a radical re-configuration of the world order. In 1983 the global gaze was on Reagan's missiles; in 1998 it rested instead on Clinton's penis (and cigar). The needs of the Cold War have given way to the need for a cold shower. Greenham's queer feminism poked fun at the sexual symbolisms of nuclear militarism, ridiculing yet simultaneously taking deadly seriously the big boys' toys, their 'missile envy', and their preparations for nuclear 'spasm attacks'.[1] Little did we anticipate that one day, in the post-Cold War world, the phallic politics of the White House would so literally be exposed.*

*II*

*Equally unexpected – in September 1997, after years of vitriolic and often violent hostility to the women of Greenham – was the sight of hundreds of Newbury residents, including the local MP and the leader of the District Council, converging on Greenham with bolt-cutters to join Greenham women in cutting down the fence.[2] After the base was closed in 1992 the Ministry of Defence sold the 800 acres occupied by the base to the Greenham Common Trust and Newbury District Council, to return the land to common use as the largest area of heathland in Berkshire.[3] The buildings which had once housed military personnel and weaponry are now leased out as a gym, a cafe and light industrial units, manufacturing bubble bath and assembling computers; the silos are being used as a mushroom farm; and an extensive programme of environmental restoration is underway to repair the damage of military occupation.[4] The dream of returning Greenham Common to the people has been realized.*

*III*

*Perhaps even more surprising was the mass outpouring of public grief in the same month following the death of Diana, Princess of Wales. In the week of mourning, ordinary people across Britain expressed their sense of loss by bringing hundreds of thousands of personal symbols of their feelings to Kensington Palace. They decorated the grass, the fences and the trees with flowers, children's toys, photographs, handwritten messages and poems, and, as night fell, burned incense and lit candles and lanterns. The scene was extraordinary – magical and deeply moving. The only precedent for such a creative, emotional collective action in recent British history was Embrace the Base at Greenham in 1982. This 'emotionalisation' and 'feminisation' of public life was much commented upon in the weeks that followed, as people demanded that Diana's legacy to the world be the elimination of landmines. In 1982 Greenham's emotional responses to issues of military policy were considered fringe lunacy. In 1997 Diana's emotional response to issues of military policy was unquestionable. The landscape of politics in the postmodern world is shifting.*

## A Place in History

The end of the 1980s saw a rapprochement between the United States and the Soviet Union, with President Gorbachev forging the path towards the removal of Cruise, Pershing and SS-20 nuclear weapons from Europe by 1991.[5] The largely non-violent revolutions which took place across Eastern Europe in 1989, culminating in the fall of the Berlin Wall, dissolved the Communist bloc. In the early 1990s the US, the former Soviet Union and Britain all made drastic cuts in military spending and further multilateral agreements were reached to reduce nuclear weapons. This end to the Cold War has not brought peace to the world. Ordinary men across former Yugoslavia have killed, maimed and raped tens of thousands in ethnic conflicts. The Gulf War of 1991 killed thousands of Iraqis and left many more suffering the long-term effects of depleted uranium and chemical weapons.[6] But the world no longer stands poised on the brink of nuclear annihilation as it did when Greenham began. The intensity and immediacy of fear of nuclear war have ebbed, although the risk still remains.

I don't think you can live at that level of intense fear all the time. You have to get on with your everyday life. But I don't feel fundamentally any safer, the same system underpins what produced Cruise missiles. The INF Treaty is only a scratch. It hardly touched the whole military industrial complex.

*Sarah Benham*

It's on my mind a lot less now. I suppose with the superpowers a lot of the heat's been taken out of it. And it seemed when I was at Greenham, and before I went, it seemed like at any moment it could all happen and it would be the end of the world, and it was all very sharp focus. And now it seems like I don't think it will, somehow.

*Jenny Heron*

I don't think I feel safer ... It's not just nuclear weapons ... the nuclear power industry as well is just very, very unsafe and unstable so I'll feel like that as long as there is nuclear material around and that now is going to be forever because there's the waste. And I feel like at any point in time there could be an accident at any nuclear power station that could basically destroy us all. And I think so long as there are nuclear weapons anywhere in the world, then somebody could decide to use them and while there's conflict in the world somebody could decide to use them.

*Vee Wright*

At the moment, yeah, it's safer. But the structures, the whole structures of threat, it's all still there. And if you had those sort of personalities, or those types of personalities in that position again ... I'm excited by what's happening in Eastern Europe, seeing the dismantling of the blockades ... The Warsaw Pact is crumbling before our eyes. But the problem is that NATO isn't. And we need that people power this side of the bloc ... No end of the world parties. But we're not at the end of the road.

*Helen Mary Jones*

Conscious of the complexities of global change and of the difficulties in analysing the range of social, political and economic factors which contributed to the demise of the Eastern bloc and the ultimate removal of Cruise missiles from Greenham, women were hesitant about claiming a straightforward victory. Many identified the importance of one individual, President Gorbachev, to the process, but, schooled in the experiences of collective action, they also attributed a significant role to social movements, to 'people power' in the West and the East, particularly the peace movement, and not least to themselves.[7] Greenham, they believed, put Cruise on the agenda, made people all over the world aware of the issues and ultimately forced the West to take disarmament seriously.

> I guess the argument that the peace movement has used, and that Greenham has used, all along, that none of us can afford the economic pressures of keeping up the military escalation is right ... And the Soviet Union couldn't afford it either. So they were in a position where they had to de-escalate. But I think it must have helped Gorbachev to know that there was a strong pressure from people in the West, on their governments. And it's true because for a long time the States was always the one who was not co-operating, or not coming across with anything, and the Soviet Union was always, well, we're willing to de-escalate if you'll do something. But in the end they were getting a lot of pressure from peace groups, a lot of criticism, saying, 'Well who is the warmonger anyway? You always said you were interested in multilateral disarmament, now you get the opportunity, you're the one that destroys it.' So I think the peace movement had a lot of effect that way. And I think we had more effect than we realized. Because they're never going to come out and say, actually it's down to you [laughter], good luck to you, when they're 80 years old and on their deathbed ... I think we've had an enormous effect. I think Greenham particularly touched a chord across the world. I think everybody had heard about it.
>
> *Carmel Cadden*

> I think it's true to say that the changing international climate, that the very successful, very sophisticated pressures of the peace movement in general, the women's peace movement in particular, have been able to bring to bear on both sides of the Iron Curtain, and we mustn't forget that we weren't on our own here, have made a difference to international power relations.
>
> *Helen Mary Jones*

I'm sure it's created the environment in which Gorbachev's reforms in the USSR have been, instead of blocked by the West, have had to be taken up by the West, because if they'd been seen to block them in the way that they would have blocked them ten years ago, I think it would have been an unacceptable package to the voters … I think it's created the sort of receptiveness to that sort of change on a political level. I think if you talked to most people they'd actually rather not have those things, rather than have them. But you couldn't get that into a political context, with the people who are actually wheeling and dealing, until you showed them that there was a very, very strong peace movement. And I think Greenham was part of that. I don't think it was separate. I think it drew a lot of its strength from the rank and file of the peace movement.

*Katrina Allen*

I think Cruise missiles would have just slipped in and nothing would have been done [without Greenham]. I think movements of people just take such a long time to have any effect. I think it's all cumulative, and I do think it's made a difference. I mean when we first started they wouldn't even, everybody thought Cruise missiles, nuclear weapons, were a good thing. They wouldn't even talk about multilateral disarmament. I mean now disarmament is obviously a good thing. I think the climate's changed considerably.

*Ann Armstrong*

I think it was successful, the whole education and consciousness-raising about nuclear issues, all of that was terribly important. Not just women, men as well, have become more involved in the anti-nuclear movement and made them think of new ways of getting involved and things that can be done. We've had an agreement on Cruise. I refuse to let that be taken away from us, however much people say it's only 3 per cent of nuclear weapons or whatever. I still think that to start to have weapons negotiated away is incredible … A part of it had to do with the difficulties Reagan and Gorbachev had themselves. But much more than that was just the voice of people being heard. You've got something like Greenham, a constant running sore to the authorities and in Sicily too. Yes, of course, I think it plays a part in it. I think we shouldn't sell ourselves short about that and we should keep saying it over and over again.

*Sian Edwards*

I think it's very important because people wouldn't have known about it. For the first five years of the 1980s it was a constant focal point for anti-nuclear and for peace work. And I just don't think that people would have known about Cruise, and what was happening, and what was going on, and all that, had that not happened. It's been lost now. People have talked about the 1980s and Greenham isn't mentioned. And that's just the tip of history forever. All the big social changes and things that have happened, women have been a central part of it and it's completely lost. And it's still happening now like that.

*Penny Gulliver*

As well as claiming a role for Greenham in the political changes of the end of the 1980s, many women drew attention to the transformative impact of Greenham on the lives of individual women, including themselves. They often believed, in keeping with the values of Greenham, that this was of a greater significance than geopolitical restructuring.

I think it was a real focus for the world, and I think because of that focus it energized a lot of women, it got them politicized over more than just the peace movement. It was a starting-point. I think it actually has had an impact if you're talking about masculine international politics. I think the women's peace movement especially, and the peace movement generally, are part of the move towards disarmament. You can't prove it's had a direct impact, but I think it has been very important. I think success can best be judged in terms of the women, individual women, and what they got out of it, a real base, a real starting-point.

*Sarah Benham*

I think only each woman can say what it's done for her. I think it's safest to think of it in those terms. You can't possibly say that because we were there they're dismantling Greenham. You can suspect that we were part of it. I think it's just how it's changed every woman, that's spread right across the world really. Every woman who's gone has taken it with her, inside her. And I know that if the crunch comes, I can live in a bender from scratch. I feel really strong.

*Leah Thalmann*

I always felt that every time any woman took part in any action, whether it was just standing on a vigil or sitting in the middle of the road, no matter what it was, that something within her was changed forever by having been part of that action and that that was the success. The internal changes that happened to that woman and how she took those out and used that knowledge in other ways ... I mean I think it had political success as well, but I actually think the real success was in the internal process that went on for each individual woman.

*Simone Wilkinson*

Carol Harwood emphasized the range of impacts of Greenham, at both the global and the personal levels:

There's the one's that everybody knows about - like Cruise missiles are being sent back, and I don't think that would ever have happened, I really don't. That's a product of the women's peace camp at Greenham. But I think at a much larger level, it has made a huge difference to women's lives. I think the best thing it has done is that it has made women discontented. They know that they don't have to put up with the sort of shit that they get at home. One of the things that I feel personally is that it brought the possibility of a lesbian lifestyle to the surface for women ... from all backgrounds. It's put 'lesbian' back into the vocabulary. They might have been burly, and they might have been muddy, and they might have been grubby, but ... people didn't say they're a gang of well-meaning housewives. They said that they're a gang of dykes, and on balance they were right. I think that's been very important. And the idea that women can take control of their own lives, and take control of other people's lives, and can say to politicians, we're not going to have this sort of shit. We don't like these things, take them back. And like lambs in the end, they take them back. And everybody wants a slice of the action. A few years ago nobody would want to claim the responsibility for having Cruise missiles sent back. But now they do. Even people like Reagan, claiming responsibility for peace in the world.

And then of course you have Gorbachev, and that whole movement all over the world. But I do think that Greenham influenced that. It said that peace was a possibility. Alright it was a dream, but too many women believed in it for it to be dismissed. And too many women made it become a reality for it to be dismissed.

*Carol Harwood*

Like Carol several women also identified Greenham's role in the creation of a visible lesbian culture in Britain.

When I was growing up male homosexuals were visible. You had a stereotype in every television comedy. You had Oscar Wilde. When I was growing up I got hold of gay male culture because there wasn't a lesbian culture. The word 'lesbian' never came up. I started out calling myself 'gay', a word which I now abhor. But it's very recently the term 'gay and lesbian' has been used ... There were no visible lesbians ... It's not about feeling that now there's been Greenham, young dykes won't feel so isolated. But I think that Greenham helped towards the whole lesbian culture that has built up. And it's a fact that there is now a lesbian culture.

*Rowan Gwedhen*

There must be thousands of dykes in this country who would never have been if it hadn't been for Greenham, because it was a safe place to explore that.

*Pat Paris*

Other women stressed the part played by Greenham in establishing the legitimacy and need for women-only political and social actions, the struggle for which was hard fought.

I think it was a success in giving women a space, the ultimate women-only space if you like, that most men you know, on the

political left finally had to admit that it was right for Greenham to
be a women-only space.
SASHA: *Do you think they did?*
With a very bad grace often. But I think they had to accept that.

*Helen Mary Jones*

Greenham cannot be seen outside the wider history of the women's
movement. Through its activation of tens of thousands of women who
had previously been largely untouched by feminism, it widened and
strengthened feminist politics in Britain. Alongside and after Greenham, women became involved in well-women centres (Jenny Heron),
Women's Aid (Pat Paris), feminist counselling (Jinny List), anti-
harassment campaigns (Barbara Schulman), campaigns against child
sexual abuse (Liz Galst, Jinny List), radical midwifery (Ann Armstrong
and Penny Gulliver), women's centres (Jinny List, Pat Paris), Women
for a Nuclear Free and Independent Pacific (Carmel Cadden), lesbian
custody groups (Pat Paris) and campaigns against Clause 28 (Jinny
List). Greenham women have taken women's studies courses (and
taught them); set up businesses in non-traditional trades (gardening,
carpentry, cabinetmaking, painting and decorating); and in their daily
lives have contributed to the creation of feminist, lesbian and queer
communities all over Britain. It is no coincidence that the two most
daring and effective actions of the campaign against Clause 28 in the
late 1980s were the work of Greenham women - invading the BBC Six
O'Clock News studio, and abseiling into the House of Lords.

Greenham has done a lot in releasing women's energies and
drawing in other women who might never have thought of any
aspect of any of the women's movement ... A lot of women who
went to Greenham ... went there because of their children and if
that was what had brought them in, fair enough ... they learnt at
Greenham to think about violence against women and rape and
abuse and stuff like that.

*Sian Edwards*

**Unfinished Stories**

Leaving Greenham - disengaging from the passionate intensity of life
at the camp and returning to the world of work, houses and normal

life – was almost universally difficult, particularly for those women who had made Greenham their home for a long time. Everyone was changed in significant ways by the experience and many found that they could not or would not slot back into their former lives.

I had like post-natal Greenham. I was really depressed for about six months afterwards.

*Trina*

The loss of Greenham has been massive for me. It just so radically altered my life. I didn't have a clue what to do after Greenham ... It's only just now, literally now, I'm starting to make a post-Greenham life, and that's seven years on ... How do you fit back into society when you've been an outlaw? How do you fit back into it? Greenham is so different and so unique from anything else. Once you've been doing that, how can you, what do you do then? How can you live after that? If one lived there, because as I said I think people who lived there did because that was your ideal way of living, which notch do you step down to? What do you do when you've been an outlaw? ... And it's hard getting back into a place after that. After you've had that much self-freedom.

*Rowan Gwedhen*

I realized after I'd been at Greenham for a month that I just couldn't go back to being a social worker. There were specific aspects of the work I did that I just couldn't stomach anymore, like having to work with the police and having to take people to psychiatric hospitals and section them. I felt that I'd always worked as well as I could within the system, but I came to see that I was still part of it and colluding with it. And I just didn't want to do that anymore. It was quite a difficult decision.

*Leah Thalmann*

While the camp disbanded long before this book was written, and most of the women had already ceased their involvement with Greenham several years before I interviewed them, I am resisting the temptation to end the book with nicely closed stories. I could follow the women into their post-Greenham lives – Margery Lewis in her ongoing activism against the Royal Ordnance Factory in Cardiff; Helen John in her new life as a lesbian and as a founder member of the Menwith Hill Women's Camp in Yorkshire, protesting against US spy technology; Simone Wilkinson in her work as an acupuncturist; Penni Bestic in hers in disability services; the Porth Women in their progress through higher education and their involvement in the welfare rights and anti-poverty movement; Liz Galst's career as a writer; Rowan Gwedhen's work as a cabinetmaker; and Bridget Evans's job as a social worker. Such endings have the appeal of narrative tradition and tidiness but to do justice to the twists and turns of women's lives, to the textures of their experiences after Greenham would require another research project and another book.

## Queer Feminisms for the Future

Instead, I want to close by opening up the question of the legacies of Greenham's queer feminisms for the future.

Greenham developed its own peculiar set of common values and ethics and its distinctive mode of doing politics within the particularities of its historical and geographical situation – in Britain at the height of the Cold War. It was never the intention of those involved that Greenham should become a universal, unchanging blueprint for how to build a community, a movement, a politics. Greenham was experimental, exceptional and liminal, located physically outside ordinary life and many of its routines, structures and norms. Greenham was the radical, anarchic edge of feminism. Yet rather than disqualifying Greenham from having anything to offer more everyday times and places, Greenham's uncommon-ness should perhaps be what is carried into other spaces.

There are times when it is necessary to play by the rules, to play feminism straight, but there are many more times than realized when we should be playing it queer; when we should veer off the path of respectability, integration and adaptation; when we should find ways of overturning convention and tradition, of disrupting expectations and confounding categories. There are times when we must demand access to arenas of male power, but there are others when we should side-step the homorelational world and instead carve new spaces for ourselves. There are times when we need to appeal to reason and rationality in our politics, but there are perhaps many others when we should allow ourselves to express the emotional and affective dimensions of our political desires. There are times for serious hard work and many others when we should unleash our capacities for creativity, humour and fun, when we should admit to and celebrate the pleasure-seeking, erotic and sexual dynamics in our politics and communities.

Greenham was not a manifesto, a political programme or a coherent ideology. It had no grand plan or systematic theory and never claimed to speak the 'truth'. It did not and cannot resolve all the conflicts and problems of contemporary feminism, but then it never sought to do so. Rather it was an attitude and a spirit, created in the coming together of thousands of women who valued both equality and communality, difference and individuality. It drew its strength from a reflexive openness to change. It wanted women neither to behave like men nor to behave like women as either is currently constructed. Greenham moved beyond the same/different fixation of modern feminism. It employed a symbolic, strategic essentialism which mobilized women on the basis of their lived experiences of gender, while questioning, destabilizing and transforming gender and sexual identities. It queered lives and, just a little, queered the world.

## Notes

1. 'Take the Toys away from the Boys' was a popular slogan in the women's peace movement. The phrase 'missile envy' is Caldicott's (1984). Cohn (1987a,b; 1993) discusses the gender discourses of nuclear militarism.
2. See *The Times*, the *Express* and the *Yorkshire Post*, 14 September 1997.
3. Source: Job specification and background information for Greenham Common Project Officer, Newbury District Council (1996).
4. The silos remain under MoD control until 2001, under the terms of the INF Treaty. The concrete runway and ten 'frying pans' - aprons - are being dug up and, in an interestingly symbolic development, the concrete is being sold off as aggregate for the Newbury bypass, the scene of an anti-roads camp which has drawn heavily on the model of Greenham in its non-violent, persistent defiance of eviction. The proceeds from the sale of the aggregate are being used to tackle the diesel and petrol contamination which has seeped into the ground from storage tanks. The land around the runways has been declared an SSSI (site of special scientific interest). (Source: Telephone conversation with Dianne Tilbury, the officer responsible for the sale of the base, Aldershot, 1996).

5.   The Intermediate Nuclear Forces Treaty was signed in 1987; by 1991 all the missiles had been removed from Greenham.

6.   Severe birth defects have been reported in Iraq and amongst Allied military personnel (*Guardian Weekend*, 21 December 1998: 2-4).

7.   For a more detailed discussion of the role of peace movements, and of Greenham in particular, in ending the Cold War, see Roseneil (1995), Einhorn (1991), Kaldor (1991), Shaw (1991).

# References

Adam, B. (1987) *The Rise of a Gay and Lesbian Movement*. Boston: G.K. Hall.

Adams, C. (1990) *The Sexual Politics of Meat*. Cambridge: Polity Press.

Ainsley, R. (1995) *What Is She Like? Lesbian Identities from the 1950s to the 1990s*. London: Cassell.

Alderson, L. (1983) 'Greenham Common and all that', in Onlywomen Press (ed.), *Breaching the Peace*. London: Onlywomen Press.

Amos, V. and P. Parmar (1984) 'Challenging imperial feminism', *Feminist Review*, no.17: 3–19.

Anderson, B. (1991) *Imagined Communities: Reflections on the Origin and Spread of Nationalism*. London: Verso.

Angelides, S. (1994) 'The queer intervention', *Melbourne Journal of Politics*, 22: 66–88.

Bacchi, C.L. (1990) *Same Difference: Feminism and Sexual Difference*. Sydney: Allen and Unwin.

Bauman, Z. (1989) *Modernity and the Holocaust*. Cambridge: Polity.

Bauman, Z. (1993) *Postmodern Ethics*. Oxford: Blackwell.

Bauman, Z. (1995) *Life in Fragments: Essays in Postmodern Morality*. Oxford: Blackwell.

Beck, U., A. Giddens and S. Lash (1994) *Reflexive Modernization*. Cambridge: Polity.

Benhabib, S. (1995) 'Feminism and postmodernism', in S. Benhabib, J. Butler, D. Cornell and N. Fraser, *Feminist Contentions: A Philosophical Exchange*. New York: Routledge.

Black, N. (1984) 'The Mothers' International: The Women's Co-operative Guild and feminist pacifism', *Women's Studies International Forum*, 7(6): 467–76.

Bock, G. and S. James (eds) (1992) *Beyond Equality and Difference: Citizenship, Feminist Politics and Female Subjectivity*. London: Routledge.

Bookchin, M. (1971) *Post-Scarcity Anarchism*. Wildwood House.

Bowden, P. (1997) *Caring: Gender Sensitive Ethics*. London: Routledge.

Braverman, S. (1996) *Queer Fictions of the Past*. Cambridge: Cambridge University Press.

Brown, W. (1984) *Black Women and the Peace Movement*. London: Falling Wall Press.

Brownmiller, S. (1976) *Against Our Will: Men, Women and Rape*. Harmondsworth: Penguin.

Bunch, C. (1987) *Passionate Politics: Feminist Theory in Action*. New York: St. Martins Press.

Bussey, G. and Tims, M. (1965) *Women's International League for Peace and Freedom*. London: Allen & Unwin.

Butler, J. and J.W. Scott (eds) (1992) *Feminists Theorize the Political*. New York: Routledge.

Caldicott, H. (1984) *Missile Envy: The Arms Race and Nuclear War*. New York: William Morrow.

Center for Constitutional Rights (1984) *Greenham Women Against Cruise Missiles*. New York: Center for Consitutional Rights.

CND (1983) 'Report of Research', unpublished paper.

Cohn, C. (1987a) 'Nuclear language and how we learned to pat the bomb', *Bulletin of Atomic Scientists*, **43**(9): 17-24.

Cohn, C. (1987b) 'Sex and death in the rational world of defense intellectuals', *Signs*, **12**(4): 687-712.

Cook, A. and G. Kirk (1983) *Greenham Women Everywhere: Dreams, Ideas and Actions from the Women's Peace Movement*. London: Pluto Press.

Cotgrove, S. and A. Duff (1980) 'Environmentalism, middle class radicalism and politics', *Sociological Review*, **28**(2): 333-51.

Cotgrove, S. (1982) *Catastrophe or Cornucopia*. Chichester: Wiley.

Coulter, J., S. Miller and M. Walker (eds) (1984) *State of Siege: Miners' Strike 1984 - Politics and Policing in the Coal Fields*. London: Canary Press.

Cox, J. (1981) *Overkill*. Harmondsworth: Penguin.

Crawford, V.L., J.A. Rouse and B. Woods (eds) (1993) *Women in the Civil Rights Movement*. Bloomington: Indiana University Press.

dalla Costa, M. and S. James (1972) *The Power of Women and the Subversion of the Community*, Bristol: Falling Wall Press.

Daly, M. (1979) *Gyn/Ecology: The Meta-ethics of Radical Feminism*. London: Women's Press.

Delphy, C. and D. Leonard (1992) *Familiar Exploitation: A New Analysis of Marriage in Contemporary Western Societies*. Cambridge: Polity.

Early, F.H. (1986) 'The historic roots of the women's peace movement in North America', *Canadian Woman Studies*, **7**(4): 43-53.

Eckersley, R. (1992) *Environmentalism and Political Theory*. London: UCL Press.

Edwards, N. (1986) *Mud*. London: Women's Press.

Eglin, J. (1987) 'Women and peace: from the suffragists to the Greenham women', in R. Taylor and N. Young (eds), *Campaigns for Peace: British Peace Movements in the Twentieth Century*. Manchester: Manchester University Press.

Ehrenreich, B. and D. English (1976) *Witches, Midwives and Nurses*. London: Readers and Writers Press.

Einhorn, B. (1991) ' "New enemy images for old": the "boys' debate" around Timothy Garton Ash's "We The People" ', in M. Kaldor (ed.), *Europe from Below: An East-West Dialogue*. London: Verso.

Einhorn, B. (1993) *Cinderella Goes to Market: Citizenship, Gender and Women's Movements in East Central Europe*. London: Verso.

Emberley, J. and D. Landry (1989) 'Coverage of Greenham and Greenham as "coverage" ', *Feminist Studies*, **15**(3): 485-98.

Enloe, C. (1983) *Does Khaki Become You? The Militarisation of Women's Lives*. London: Pandora.

Epstein, S. (1996) 'A queer encounter: sociology and the study of sexuality', in S. Seidman (ed.), *Queer Theory/Sociology*. Oxford: Blackwell.

Erlich, C. (n.d) 'Socialism, anarchism and feminism', in *Quiet Rumours: An Anarcha-Feminist Anthology*. London: Dark Star.

Evans, S. (1979) *Personal Politics: The Roots of Women's Liberation in the Civil Rights Movement and the New Left*. New York: Vintage Books.

Fadermann, L. (1981) *Surpassing the Love of Men: Romantic Friendships and Love Between Women from the Renaissance to the Present*. London: Women's Press.

Feminism and NonViolence Collective (1983) *Piecing it Together: Feminism and NonViolence*. Devon: Feminism and NonViolence Collective.

Ferguson, A.., J. Zita and K. Addelson 'On "Compulsory heterosexuality and lesbian existence": defining the issues', *Signs*, **7**(1): 158-99.

Finch, S. (1986) 'Socialist feminists and Greenham', *Feminist Review*, **23**: 93-100.

Foster, C. (1989) *Women for All Seasons: The Story of the Women's International League for Peace and Freedom*. Athens: University of Georgia Press.

Frazer, E., J. Hornsby and S. Lovibond (eds) (1992) *Ethics: A Feminist Reader*. Oxford: Blackwell.

Freeman, J. (1975) *The Politics of Women's Liberation*. New York: Longman.

Freeman, J. (1984) 'The tyranny of structurelessness', in *Untying the Knot: Feminism, Anarchism and Organisation*. London: Dark Star Press and Rebel Press.

Friedan, B. (1963) *The Feminine Mystique*. Harmondsworth: Penguin.

Fuss, D. (1989) *Essentially Speaking: Feminism, Nature and Difference*. New York: Routledge.

Gerth, H.H and C. Wright Mills (eds) (1970) *From Max Weber*. London: Routledge and Kegan Paul.

Giddens, A. (1991) *Modernity and Self-Identity: Self and Society in the Late Modern Age*. Cambridge: Polity.

Gilligan, C. (1982) *In a Different Voice: Essays on Psychological Theory and Women's Development*. Cambridge, MA: Harvard University Press.

Goldman, E. (1977) 'The failure of the Russian Revolution', in G. Woodcock (ed.), *The Anarchist Reader*. Glasgow: Fontana.

Green, S.F. (1997) *Urban Amazons: Lesbian Feminism and Beyond in the Gender, Sexuality and Identity Battles of London*. Basingstoke: Macmillan.

Center for Constitutional Rights (1984) *Greenham Women Against Cruise Missiles* (Legal Education Pamphlet), New York.

Griffin, S. (1978) *Women and Nature*. New York: Harper & Row.

Griffin, S. (1989) 'Ideologies of madness', in D. Russell (ed.), *Exposing Nuclear Phallacies*. New York: Pergamon Press.

Harford, B. and S. Hopkins (1984) *Greenham Common: Women at the Wire*. London: Women's Press.

Harris, A. and King, Y. (1989) (eds) *Rocking the Ship of State: Towards a Feminist Peace Politics*. Boulder, CO: Westview Press.

Hastings, E. H. and P. K. Hastings (1984) (eds) *Index to International Public Opinion 1982-1983*. Westport, CT: Greenwood Press.

Heelas, P., S. Lash and P. Morris (eds) (1996) *Detraditionalization*. Oxford: Blackwell.

Held, V. (1993) *Feminist Morality: Transforming Culture, Society and Politics*. Chicago: University of Chicago Press.

Hester, M. (1992) *Lewd Women and Wicked Witches*. London: Routledge.

Hickman, J. (1986) 'Greenham women against Cruise missiles and others versus Ronald Reagan and others', in J. Dewar *et al.* (eds), *Nuclear Weapons, the Peace Movement and the Law*. London: Macmillan.

Hill Collins, P. (1990) *Black Feminist Thought: Knowledge, Consciousness and the Politics of Empowerment*. New York: Routledge.

Ingram, G.B., A. Bouthillette and Y. Retter (eds) (1997) *Queers in Space*. Seattle: Bay Press.

Jaggar, A. (1988) *Feminist Politics and Human Nature*. Totowa, NJ: Rowan & Littlefield.

Jamieson, L. (1998) *Intimacy: Personal Relationships in Modern Societies*. Cambridge: Polity.

Jeffreys, S. (1994) *The Lesbian Heresy*. London: Women's Press.

Johnson, R. (1986) 'Alice Through the Fence: Greenham women and the law', in J. Dewar, A. Paliwala, S. Picciotto and M. Rueke (eds), *Nuclear Weapons: The Peace Movement and the Law*. London: Macmillan.

Johnson, R. (1989) ' Greenham women: the control of protest', in C. Dunhill (ed.), *Boys in Blue*. London: Virago.

Jones, L. (1983) 'On common ground: the women's peace camp at Greenham Common', in L. Jones (ed.), *Keeping the Peace*. London: Virago.

Jones, L. (1987) 'Perceptions of "peace women" at Greenham Common 1981-1985', in S. MacDonald, P. Holden and S. Ardener (eds), *Images of Women in Peace and War: Cross Cultural and Historical Perspectives*. Basingstoke: Macmillan.

Junor, B. (1996) *Greenham Common Women's Peace Camp: A History*. London: Working Press.

Kaldor, M. (1991) *Europe from Below: An East-West Dialogue*. London: Verso.

Kaldor, M., G. Holden and R. Falk (eds) (1989) *The New Detente*. London: Verso.

Kidron, B. and A. Richardson (1983) *Carry Greenham Home*. (Film distributed by Four Corners.)

King, Y. (1983) 'All is connectedness: scenes from the women's Pentagon Action USA', in L. Jones (ed.), *Keeping the Peace*. London: Virago.

Kitzinger, J. (1984) 'The Social Construction of Gender: A Case Study of the Women's Peace Movement', B.A dissertation, New Hall, University of Cambridge.

Kirk, G. (1989a) 'Our Greenham Common: feminism and nonviolence', in A. Harris and Y. King (eds), *Rocking the Ship of State: Towards a Feminist Peace Politics*. Boulder, CO: Westview Press.

Kirk, G. (1989b) 'Our Greenham Common: not just a place but a movement', in A. Harris and Y. King (eds), *Rocking the Ship of State: Towards a Feminist Peace Politics*. Boulder, CO: Westview Press.

Knelman, F. (1985) *Reagan, God and the Bomb: From Myth to Policy in the Nuclear Arms Race*. Toronto: McClelland & Stewart.

Liddington, J. (1983) 'The Women's Peace Crusade', in D. Thompson (ed.), *Over Our Dead Bodies*. London: Virago.

Liddington, J. (1989) *The Long Road to Greenham: Feminism and Anti-Militarism in Britain Since 1820*. London: Virago.

Liddington, J. and J. Norris (1978) *One Hand Tied Behind Us: The Rise of the Women's Suffrage Movement*. London: Virago.

Linton, R. (1989) 'Seneca Women's Peace Camp: shapes of things to come', in A. Harris and Y. King (eds), *Rocking the Ship of State: Towards a Feminist Peace Politics*. Boulder, CO: Westview Press.

Linton, R. and Whitham, M. (1982) 'With mourning, rage, empowerment and defiance', *Socialist Review*, **12**(3-4): 11-36.

Lloyd, C. (1985) 'A national riot police: Britain's "third force"?', in B. Fine and R. Millar (eds), *Policing the Miners' Strike*. London: Lawrence and Wishart.

Lloyd, G. (1984) *The Man of Reason: 'Male' and 'Female' in Western Philosophy*. Minneapolis: University of Minnesota Press.

Lovenduski, J. and V. Randall (1993) *Contemporary Feminist Politics*. Oxford: Oxford University Press.

McAllister, P. (ed.) (1982) *Reweaving the Web of Life: Feminism and Nonviolence*. Philadelphia: New Society Publishers.

McDonagh, C. (1985) 'The women's peace movement in Britain', *Frontiers*, **8**(2): 53-8.

Marshall, P. (1993) *Demanding the Impossible: A History of Anarchism*. London: Fontana.

Martin, B. (1996) *Femininity Played Straight: The Significance of Being Lesbian*. New York: Routledge.

Merck, M. (1993) *Perversions: Deviant Readings*. London: Virago.

Miles, A. (1989) 'Introduction', in A. Miles and G. Finn, *Feminism: From Pressure to Politics*. Montreal: Black Rose Books.

Oakley, A. (1974) *The Sociology of Housework*. Oxford: Martin Robertson.

Oldfield, S. (1989) *Women against the Iron Fist: Alternatives to Militarism 1900-1989*. Oxford: Blackwell.

Onlywomen Press (ed.) (1983) *Breaching the Peace*. London: Onlywomen Press.

Pateman, C. (1989) 'Feminist critiques of the public/private dichotomy', in *The Disorder of Women*. Cambridge: Polity.

Phelan, S. (ed.) (1997) *Playing with Fire: Queer Politics, Queer Theories*. New York: Routledge.

Plant, S. (1992) *The Most Radical Gesture: The Situationist International in a Postmodern Age*. London: Routledge.

Plummer, K. (1998) 'Afterword: the past, present, and futures of the sociology of same-sex relations', in P. Nardi and B.E. Schneider (eds), *Social Perspectives in Lesbian and Gay Studies*. London: Routledge.

Pringle, R. and S. Watson (1992) ' "Women's interests" and the post-structuralist state', in M. Barrett and A. Phillips (eds), *Destabilizing Theory: Contemporary Feminist Debates*. Cambridge: Polity.

Randle, M. (1987) 'Non-violent direct action in the 1950s and 1960s', in R. Taylor and N. Young (eds), *Campaigns for Peace: British Peace Movements in the Twentieth Century*. Manchester: Manchester University Press.

Raymond, J. (1986) *A Passion for Friends: Towards a Philosophy of Female Affection*. London: Women's Press.

Rich, A. (1980) 'Compulsory heterosexuality and lesbian existence', *Signs* **5**(4): 631-60.

Richardson, D. (1997) 'From lesbian nation to queer nation: sexual politics and social change', paper presented to the British Sociological Association Annual Conference, University of York, 8-11 April.

Riley, D. (1988) *Am I That Name? Feminism and the Category of 'Women' in History*. London: Macmillan.

Roach Pierson, R. (1987) (ed.) *Women and Peace: Theoretical, Historical and Practical Perspectives*. Beckenham: Croom Helm.

Roseneil, S. (1993) 'Greenham revisited: researching myself and my sisters', in D. Hobbs and T. May (eds), *Interpreting the Field*. Oxford: Oxford University Press.

Roseneil, S. (1994) 'Feminist Political Action: The Case of the Greenham Common Women's Peace Camp', unpublished PhD thesis, London School of Economics and Political Science.

Roseneil, S. (1995) *Disarming Patriarchy: Feminism and Political Action at Greenham*. Buckingham: Open University Press.

Roseneil, S. (1998) 'Queering the sociology of social movements: towards a new agenda for social movements research', paper presented at the World Congress of Sociology, Montreal, July 1998.

Roseneil, S. (1999) 'Postmodern feminist politics: the art of the (im)possible? *European Journal of Women's Studies*, **6**(2): 161-82.

Rothenbuhler, E.W. (1988) 'The liminal fight: mass strikes as ritual and interpretation', in J. Alexander (ed.), *Durkheimian Sociology: Cultural Studies*. Cambridge: Cambridge University Press.

Rowbotham, S. (1989) *The Past Is Before Us: Feminism in Action Since the 1960s*. Harmondsworth: Penguin.

Ruddick, S. (1990) *Maternal Thinking: Towards a Politics of Peace*. London: Women's Press.

Schott, L. (1985) 'The women's Peace Party and the moral basis for women's pacifism', Frontiers, **8**(2): 18-24.

Scott, J. (1990) 'Deconstructing equality-versus-difference: or, the uses of poststructuralist theory for feminism', in M. Hirsch and E. Fox Keller (eds), *Conflicts in Feminism*. New York: Routledge.

Scraton, P. (1985) 'From Saltley Gates to Orgreave: a history of the policing of recent industrial disputes', in B. Fine and R. Millar (eds), *Policing the Miners' Strike*. London: Lawrence and Wishart.

Sedgwick, E.K. (1994) *Tendencies*. London: Routledge.

Segal, L. (1987) *Is the Future Female? Troubled Thoughts on Contemporary Feminism*. London: Virago.

Seidman, S. (ed.) (1996) *Queer Theory/Sociology*. Oxford: Blackwell.

Seidman, S. (1997) *Difference Troubles: Queering Social Theory and Sexual Politics*. Cambridge: Cambridge University Press.

Sevenhuijsen, S. (1998) *Citizenship and the Ethics of Care*. London: Routledge.

Shaw, M. (1991) *Post Military Society*. Cambridge: Polity.

Smart, C. (1993) 'Proscription, prescription and the desire for certainty: feminist theory in the field of law', *Law, Politics and Society*, **13**: 37-54.

Snitow, A. (1985a) 'Holding the line at Greenham', *Mother Jones*, February/March: 30-47.

Snitow, A. (1985b) 'Pictures for 10 million women', *Frontiers*, **8**(2): 45-9.

*Social Text* (1997), December, No. 53.

Spender, D. (1984) *There's Always Been A Women's Movement This Century*. London: Routledge.

Spivak, G. (1987) *In Other Worlds: Essays in Cultural Politics*. New York: Methuen.

Spretnak, C. (1982) (ed.) *The Politics of Women's Spirituality: Essays on the Rise of Spiritual Power within the Feminist Movement*. Garden City, NY: Anchor/Doubleday.

Stein, A. and K. Plummer (1996) '"I can't even think straight": "queer" theory and the missing sexual revolution in sociology', in S. Seidman (ed.), *Queer Theory/Sociology*. Oxford: Blackwell.

Swerdlow, A. (1989) 'Pure milk, not poison: Women Strike for Peace and the test ban treaty of 1963', in A. Harris and Y. King (eds), *Rocking the Ship of State: Toward a Feminist Peace Politics*. Boulder, CO: Westview Press.

Swerdlow, A. (1993) *Women Strike for Peace*. Chicago: University of Chicago Press.

Taylor, R. (1988) *Against the Bomb: The British Peace Movement 1958-1965*. Oxford: Clarendon Press.

Taylor, R. and C. Pritchard (1980) *The Protest Makers: The British Nuclear Disarmament Movement of 1958-65, Twenty Years On*. Oxford: Pergamon Press.

Taylor, R. and N. Young (1987) (eds) *Campaigns for Peace: British Peace Movements in the Twentieth Century*. Manchester: Manchester University Press.

Tiryakian, E. (1988) 'From Durkheim to Managua: revolutions as religious revivals', in J. Alexander (ed.), *Durkheimian Sociology: Cultural Studies*. Cambridge: Cambridge University Press.

Tong, R. (1993) *Feminine and Feminist Ethics*. Belmont: Wadsworth.

Tronto, J. (1993) *Moral Boundaries: Essays on Ethics*. Boston: Harvard University Press.

Tronto, J.C. (1995) 'Care as a basis for radical political judgements', *Hypatia: A Journal of Feminist Philosophy*. **10**(2): 141-9.

Turner, V. (1977) *The Ritual Process: Structure and Anti-Structure*. Ithaca, NY: Cornell University Press.

Vaneigem, R. (1983) *The Revolution of Everyday Life*. n.p., Left Bank Books and Rebel Press.

Vellacott, J. (1993) 'A place for pacifism and transnationalism in feminist theory: the early work of the Women's International League for Peace and Freedom', *Women's History Review*, **2**(1): 23-56.

Walby, S. (1997) *Gender Transformations*. London: Routledge.

Wallsgrove, R. (1983) 'Greenham Common: so why am I still ambivalent?', *Trouble and Strife*, **1**: 4-6.

Warner, M. (1991) 'Fear of a queer planet', *Social Text*, **9**(14): 3-17.

Weed, E. and N. Schor (1997) *Feminism Meets Queer Theory*. Bloomington: Indiana University Press.

Weeks, J. (1995) *Invented Moralities: Sexual Values in an Age of Uncertainty*. Cambridge: Polity.

Wilkinson, S. and C. Kitzinger (1994) 'Dire straights? Contemporary rehabilitations of heterosexuality', in G. Griffin, M. Hester, S. Rai and S. Roseneil (eds), *Stirring It: Challenges for Feminism*. London: Taylor and Francis.

Williams, J. (1987) *Eyes on the Prize*. New York: Viking Penguin.

Williamson, J. (1992) 'Nuclear family? No thanks', in E. Frazer, J. Hornsby and S. Lovibond (eds), *Ethics: A Feminist Reader*. Oxford: Blackwell.

Wiltsher, A. (1985) *Most Dangerous Women: Feminist Peace Campaigners of the Great War*. London: Pandora.

Woodcock, G. (1962) *Anarchism*. Harmondsworth: Penguin.

Woodcock, G. (1977) (ed.) *The Anarchist Reader*. Glasgow: Fontana.

Woolf, V. (1977) *Three Guineas*. Harmondsworth: Penguin.

York, J. *et al.* (1979) 'We are the feminists that women have warned us about', reprinted in S. Gunew (ed.), *A Reader in Feminist Knowledge*. London: Routledge (1991).

Young, A. (1990) *Femininity in Dissent*. London: Routledge.

Young, I. M. (1990) 'Throwing like a girl: a phenomenology of feminine body comportment, motility and spatiality', in *Throwing Like a Girl and Other Essays in Feminist Philosophy and Social Theory*. Bloomington: Indiana University Press.

# Index